The Great Family Knitting Book

Nancy Vale

Mills & Boon Limited,
LONDON, SYDNEY, TORONTO

Contents

First published in Great Britain 1980 by
Mills & Boon Limited, 17-19 Foley Street,
London W1A 1DR.

Printed in Great Britain by Fletcher &
Sons Ltd. Norwich and bound by Richard
Clay & Co. Bungay, Suffolk.

Design and Layout
Mushroom Production · London

Line illustrations
Katrina Dallamore

Children's Wear

Garments for All Ages

Ladies' Wear

Men's Wear

Jackets

Glossary

Introduction

This comprehensive knitting book is intended to provide readers with a large variety of patterns across every age range, and I hope it will become a constant knitting companion and source of reference. In compiling the book I am drawing not only on knitting experience, but also my practical experience as mother, nursery nurse and director of a hand-knitting business. From the hundreds of patterns I have designed over the years, I have selected not only my own personal favourites but those I feel will be the most valuable basic garments in everyone's wardrobe.

A hand-knitted garment can be a work of art. It can be as delicate and intricate as fine lace or as rich and colourful as a painting. It can be made in one of the wealth of yarns now available to hand knitters. These include pure wool such as Shetland wool, lamb's-wool, bouclés; a multitude of man-made fibres of many weights and finishes; and the luxury yarns such as mohair, angora, alpaca and cashmere.

Knitting can be extremely satisfying: watching the pattern develop and the garment taking shape and then seeing the completed garment being worn. Another important feature is its mobility. It can be taken almost anywhere at any time: travelling, talking, reading or watching television. It is also very relaxing to do and is a highly popular pastime the world over.

Colour plays an extremely important part in design and knitting, reflecting the ever changing moods of fashion. Any garment can look totally different in varying colours and a basic pattern can be adjusted to suit most needs just by altering the colour of the yarn used. A Jacquard pattern is often unrecognizable in a different blend of colours: replace a dark shade with a light one or a bright colour with a subdued tone and so on — it works wonders! Another way of ringing the changes is to replace either a plain or patterned garment with stripes, using a blend of whichever colours you prefer. Irregular stripes are probably the most striking and effective, and the odd narrow stripe in mohair or lurex can also add a beautiful touch. Alternatively you can put a band of stripes or Fair Isle just above body and sleeve welts and on the yoke. Simple embroidery on the finished garment in a constrasting colour also looks most attractive. Another very effective way of altering a basic pattern is by using different yarns. This is very successful as long as the yarn substituted is exactly the SAME WEIGHT as the original. It is absolutely essential in any case of substitution to KNIT UP A TENSION SQUARE (see page 10), adjusting needles, if necessary, to get tension right against pattern. If you like, you can use two strands of a finer yarn or a strand each of two different yarns as long as this tension rule is followed. With the array of different yarns now available to hand knitters, this kind of substitution can be very exciting.

Suggested substitutions for different weights of yarn

4-ply
Crêpe finishes, bouclé, cotton, lurex or

metallic yarn, angora, alpaca, cashmere of like weight.

Double-knit

Crêpe finishes, bouclé, cotton, mohair, mohair/acrylic or wool mixtures, brushed yarns, alpaca, cashmere, looped or nobbly finishes, — again, of like weight, or a strand of each of two fine yarns.

Mohair

Brushed yarns, bouclé, and most fancy yarns of double-knit weight.

The third way to alter a basic pattern is to change the shape of a garment to follow variations in fashion. Most changes can be relatively simple. A short and fitted sweater can be turned into a longer, loose style simply by using a size larger needles and by making the side seam several centimetres longer. Necklines, be they 'V' neck, round (crew neck), turtle, polo, square, straight (boat neck) or collared, can be altered. For adults, 'V', round, or square necks should be approximately 13 cm (5 in) across (measuring from side to side at shoulder level), although extra width and depth can always be allowed for round necks which look very attractive lower. Square necks, and 'V' necks in particular should always fit neatly and closely to back and sides of the neck or they are liable to lose their shape with wear. The front depth for round and square necks is usually about 6.5 cm (2½ in) while 'V' necks average about 1.3 cm (½ in) shorter than the armhole (shaping for a 'V' neck usually starts level with the armhole or just above it, with a rib finish of about 1.3 cm - 2 cm (½-¾ in)). Collars can easily be added to round or 'V' necks or can be omitted and replaced by a few rows of garter stitch, moss stitch or rib. A round neck can be turned into a turtle or polo neck merely by making the neckband as long as the wearer wishes, i.e. about 1.5 cm

(3 in) for a turtle neck and about 20.5 cm (8 in) for a polo neck. Just as easily, a polo or turtle neck pattern can be shortened by the same lengths if a round neck is required.

An ordinary classic cardigan can easily be made into the style of a jacket by replacing body and sleeve welts with a few rows of garter or moss stitch, worked on same size needles as those used for the main body of the garment so both body and sleeve hang straight. Side seam lengths can be adjusted to suit.

Sleeves can be altered in various ways and are indeed a very prominent fashion feature. They can obviously be made short or long (requires no alteration to the top of the sleeve). Otherwise, they can be raglan styled, fitted, dropped, saddle shouldered and so on — the first three styles being by far the most common. The drop sleeve requires no armhole shaping on the body of the garment and no sleeve top at all. All stitches are cast off as soon as the sleeve is the right length underarm. The fitted sleeve needs to be shaped at the armhole and the raglan slopes back from underarm to neck (for instructions on shaping various sleeves see Glossary page 237). Sleeves can also be omitted to make a sleeveless garment, an armhole band then being made by picking up stitches all round armhole and working about eight rows in rib, moss stitch or garter stitch. Alternatively, a band the length of the armhole can be knitted and sewn on afterwards. Pockets are another prominent fashion feature and are relatively easy to omit from or add to a basic pattern. There are two main types of pockets, the simplest being patch pockets which can be made to any dimension in the pattern of the garment and sewn on anywhere afterwards. Otherwise, inset pockets are knitted into the garment, and these again can be straight, curved, or on the slant (instructions for both types are included in the Glossary page 236).

I have divided the book into garment groups. Babies' wear, children's wear, garments suitable for adults and children and sized through all age groups, ladies' wear, men's wear and lastly jackets and heavy outdoor wear. Accessories, i.e. hats, scarves, gloves, shawls and socks, are included in each of the sections.

I have used the general term 'multicoloured' for several garments throughout the book to describe patterns which have the Fair Isle or Jacquard look.

General Notes

Two very important tips when knitting garments

Whenever possible as you knit, slip the first stitch and knit into the back of the last stitch on EVERY row. This gives neat tidy edges and regular little notches along edges which makes sewing up easy and neat by just flatsewing or oversewing the notches together. It also makes it easier to align piece to piece. Where edges show, i.e. frontbands, it makes all the difference to the appearance of the garment. NEVER JOIN YARN IN THE MIDDLE OF A ROW. If you feel the yarn will run out before you finish the next row, leave the excess hanging at the beginning of the row for sewing up and start a new ball. Not only does ANY sort of join show to a certain extent, but with wear, and certainly with washing, there is a risk of the join coming undone due either to stress or perhaps slight shrinkage. If this happens, a hole will suddenly appear in the garment.

Tension

It is ABSOLUTELY ESSENTIAL that you knit an appropriate tension square before embarking on any garment. I have not given a specific tension against each pattern as it is easier to knit a square in two or three weights of yarn on different needle sizes in stocking stitch (the easiest stitch over which to test tension) to test general tension. If your tension is correct you will have no problems with any of the patterns in this book.

Work a 5 cm (2 in) square in:
a) 4-ply yarn on 3.25-mm (No. 10) needles. The correct tension should be 14 sts and 8 rows.
b) Double-knitting yarn on 4-mm (No. 8) needles. The correct tension should be 10 sts and 14 rows.
c) Double double-knitting yarn on 5.5-mm (No. 5) needles. The correct tension should be 8½ sts and 10½ rows.

If your measurement is larger than that specified your tension is too loose, so try a smaller needle. If your knitted sample measurement is smaller, your tension is too tight, so try a larger needle. Then correspondingly change your needle sizes throughout the pattern. There are, of course, exceptions (e.g. where bouclé yarn is used or when two yarns are knitted together) and in these cases tensions are clearly specified on the pattern.

Sizes

Often I refer to 'small', 'medium' and 'large'. This is because it is difficult to guarantee an ABSOLUTE dimension. Small, medium and large represent the following sizes:
Ladies' small — 81.5 - 86.5 cm (32 - 34 in), medium — 86.5 - 91.5 cm (34 - 36 in) and large — 91.5 - 96.5 cm (36 - 38 in). Outsize — 96.5 - 102 cm (38 - 40 in).
Men's small — 91.5 - 96.5 cm (36 - 38 in), medium — 96.5 - 102 cm (38 - 40 in), large 102 - 107 cm (40 - 42 in) and extra large — 107 - 112 cm (42 - 44 in).

Choice of yarn

Particular brands of yarn have not been specified in this book because there is no reason why knitters should not use their own favourite brands, or one of those most easily available — sometimes the choice of a very special colour will dictate the brand. The brand used, in fact, should make no difference as long as an equivalent weight is used and the tension rule followed. It is always advisable to use a branded yarn to ensure correct yardage and a fast dye.

Each type of yarn has its attributes — and its shortcomings.

ORDINARY FLAT WOOL Knits up beautifully, is very easy to work with and is excellent for keeping shape and giving elasticity to welts and so on. Is very hard wearing and washes admirably. It makes little difference if there is a small percentage of another yarn.

ACRYLICS These are popular mainly because they are machine washable. They are strong and hard-wearing — ideal for children's clothes and babies' wear. They do not on the whole have the same elasticity nor keep shape as well as wool.

MOHAIR This has a feel of sheer luxury, lightness and warmth. Reasonably good for keeping body shape but does not give very good elasticity to welts.

BOUCLÉ This can be knitted quickly and easily, needing no pattern stitch because of the very attractive surface given by the yarn itself. Like mohair it is reasonably good for keeping body shape, but is not good for welts.

COTTON Very popular in warmer climates for its cool qualities but it has very little elasticity and does not keep its shape well. Lurex and fancy yarns vary considerably and it is always advisable to follow instructions on wrappers.

Washing
Washing instructions are usually printed on yarn wrappers and with so many different types of yarn now available I would strongly advise

careful reading of these instructions. In general, however, I have found that ordinary wool washes beautifully and will give years and years of wear if treated well. I always hand wash woollen garments in WARM water. DO NOT RUB — and NEVER LEAVE TO SOAK, as this causes matting. Rinse very thoroughly and then after removing excess water by squeezing between two towels (DO NOT TWIST), fold the garment carefully into shape and dry flat slowly in a warm place. Alternatively, after rinsing and folding, give it a very short spin — just enough to take the weight of water out of the garment (this is very important) and then hand smooth back into shape. The garment can then be hung out to dry or dried in a tumble dryer on low heat. I always use this second method myself — line drying in good weather, tumble drying in winter — and my woollens remain beautifully soft and keep perfect shape.

Most other yarns can be treated in much the same way, except of course that acrylics can be machine washed in WARM water. Bouclé or most rough yarns can be spun a little more as they do not crease. In fact, I treat mohair garments in exactly the same way as wool and have found that they keep their shape and remain soft. However, many people prefer to dry-clean mohair.

Making up
Whenever possible garments should be sewn up in the yarn they are knitted in — and in the case of Fair Isles, Jacquards, or stripes, each colour should be sewn up in that same colour. No problems are caused if the garment is made in wool, wool mixtures, acrylics, mohair or cotton. In the case of bouclé or rough surface yarns which cannot either be threaded through a needle or easily be sewn with, use an ordinary wool or acrylic yarn in matching colour. With lurex choose a matching cotton, and with fancy yarns

whichever flat yarn is nearest in texture and colour.

Make sure sewing up is neat. This is as important as the knitting of a garment — good finishing makes all the difference.

There are various methods of sewing up. I always advise flatstitch or overstitch for they do not leave a chunky seam inside the garment, as in the case of backstitch. If you have slipped the first stitch of every row and knitted into the back of the last stitch, just sew from notch to corresponding notch of the pieces you are aligning and your seam will lie flat and hardly be seen. Never make seams taut by pulling the sewing yarn too tightly and do remember to sew several times over the stitch at the end of a row, or when finishing a length of sewing yarn, to prevent seams opening.

Pressing

The entire finish of a flatstitch woollen garment is improved with pressing. It is usually best to join up the shoulder seams and neatly sew sleeves into armholes, if there are sleeves, and then press garment still open with a warm iron and damp cloth. Give it a final press when it has been completely sewn up. Never press bobbly or textured stitches. Mohair, in my opinion, never needs pressing. I find it perfectly adequate to smooth and fold with the hands.

As far as acrylics are concerned, do be very careful about pressing as this can knock all life out of the garment and it will go limp and lifeless. I never press acrylics, just smooth the garment into shape and fold very carefully.

Abbreviations

alt	**alternate**
beg	**begin(ning)**
c	**cable**
cont	**continue**
dec	**decrease**
inc	**increase**
k	**knit**
m1	**make one**
mb	**make bobble**
p	**purl**
psso	**pass slip stitch over**
rep	**repeat**
sl	**slip**
st	**stitch**
st st	**stocking stitch**
tbl	**through back of loop**
tog	**together**
wlfwd	**wool forward**
won	**wool over needle**
wrn	**wool round needle**

In case you find, as I do, the English and metric knitting needle sizes all rather confusing, I am including a chart. This also includes American sizing.

English size	Metric	American
000	9.00	15
00	8.50	13
0	8.00	12
1	7.50	11
2	7.00	10½
3	6.50	10
4	6.00	9
5	5.50	8
6	5.00	7
7	4.50	6
8	4.00	5
9	3.50	4
10	3.25	3
11	3.00	2
12	2.50	1
13	2.25	0
14	2.00	00

Babies' Wear

You will notice that for the double weight garments in this section I use 3-ply yarn double instead of double weight yarn. This is for two reasons: a strand of white with another colour gives such a delightful 'soft' effect, and it is also most economical as it enables you to use up any 3-ply yarns left over from the 3-ply garments.

I have stated total number of grams used in these baby patterns as the number of grams per ball varies so much from manufacturer to manufacturer.

Feather stitch dress

Measurements To fit 48[51]cm (19[20]in) chest. Length 33 cm (13 in).
Materials 70 gms of 3-ply baby yarn, plus 3 buttons.
Needles One pair each 2.5-mm, 3-mm, 3.25-mm, 3.5-mm and 4-mm (Nos. 12, 11, 10, 9 and 8) needles.
Tension 20 rows and 15 sts to a 5 cm (2 in) square on 3-mm needles in st st.
Abbreviations See page 12.

Back
Using 4-mm needles cast on 106 sts and work 6 rows in garter st.
Cont in pattern as follows:
1ST ROW (Right side of work) k.
2ND ROW p.
3RD ROW k1 *(p2 tog) twice, k1 (wlfwd, k1) 4 times, (p2 tog) twice. Rep from * to last st, k1.
4TH ROW p.
5TH ROW k.
6TH ROW k1 *(k2 tog) twice, p1 (wrn, p1) 4 times, (k2 tog) twice. Rep from *

to last st, k1.
These 6 rows form the pattern. Rep from 1st to 6th row inclusive 5 more times (6 patterns in all).** Change to 3.5-mm needles and work 2 more patterns, then change to 3.25-mm needles and cont until work measures 25.5 cm (10 in) ending with a 6th pattern row (this changing of needle size gives the flare effect down the skirt). Change to 3-mm needles and shape armholes. Cast off 6 sts at the beg of the next 2 rows [the 3rd pattern row will now start: k2 (wlfwd, k1) twice, and the 6th pattern row will now start: p2 (wrn, p1) twice]. Cont in pattern until 2 whole patterns have been worked from the start of the armhole shaping. Leave sts on a spare needle.

Front
Work as for back.

Sleeves

With 3-mm needles cast on 40 sts and work 5 rows in garter st.

NEXT ROW k7, inc in every st to last 6 sts, k6 (67 sts). Now work 2 complete patterns (12 rows). Cast off 6 sts at the beg of the next 2 rows and then work 10 more rows in pattern as on back and front (2 patterns in all). Leave sts on a spare needle.

Yoke

Using 3-mm needles k across 55 sts of first sleeve, 94 sts of front, 55 sts of second sleeve and 94 sts of back (298 sts). With wrong side facing work 1st row of yoke as follows:

1ST ROW k1 *k2 tog. Rep from * to last st, k1 (150 sts)

2ND ROW (k2 tog, k3) to end of row (120 sts). K 11 rows.

NEXT ROW k1 *wlfwd, k2 tog, wlfwd, k3 tog. Rep from * to last 4 sts, wlfwd, k2 tog, wlfwd, k2 tog. K 9 rows.

NEXT ROW k1 *wlfwd, k3 tog. Rep from * to last 2 sts, k2. Change to 2.5-mm needles and k 5 rows. With right side facing work 4 rows in st st.

NEXT ROW (To make holes for picot edge) *k2 tog, wlfwd. Rep from * to end. Work 3 more rows in st st. Cast off.

Making up

Overstitch or flat stitch all seams leaving back left raglan seam open to the base of yoke. Fold neck at picot hemline and slip stitch down on to wrong side. Crochet or blanket stitch 3 buttonholes evenly down left side. Attach 3 buttons on right side. Do not press this garment as pressing with an iron flattens the charm of the stitch. Just hand fold and press. Take the dress and put your hands inside the skirt gently pressing out the side seams so the full flare of the skirt is seen. Then fold the sides of the skirt in, fold the garment in half between shoulder and hem, all the time gently smoothing with your hands. Folding in this way acts as sufficient pressing and shaping.

Christening dress

All details as for feather stitch dress except that 130 gms of 3-ply yarn will be needed. Also pair of 4.5-mm (No. 7) needles.

Back and front

Using 4.5-mm needles cast on 106 sts and work 6 rows in garter st. Cont in pattern exactly as for dress working on 4.5-mm needles until work measures 18 cm (7 in) from beg, finishing at end of a pattern (6th row). Work 6 more patterns on 4-mm needles and now cont exactly as for dress from **. The only difference in the patterns is the length.

Feather stitch matinée coat, bonnet and bootees

Abbreviations See page 12.

Note If you prefer an angel top put buttonholes on the left front instead of the right front and put it on the baby so it buttons up at the back.

Measurements To fit the average baby from birth to six months.

Materials 80 gms of 3-ply baby yarn (including bootees on page 16), 6 buttons.

Needles A pair of 3.25-mm (No. 10) and 3-mm (No. 11) needles.

Tension 20 rows and 15 sts to a 5 cm (2 in) square on 3-mm needles in st st.

Back
Using 3.25-mm needles cast on 93 sts and work 6 rows in garter st (every row k). Change to 3-mm needles and cont in pattern as follows:
1ST ROW (Right side facing) k.
2ND ROW p.
3RD ROW k1 *(p2 tog) twice, k1, (wlfwd, k1) 4 times, (p2 tog) twice. Rep from * to last st, k1.
4TH ROW p.
5TH ROW k.
6TH ROW k1 *(k2 tog) twice, p1, (wrn, p1) 4 times, (k2 tog) twice. Rep from * to last st, k1.

These 6 rows form the pattern. Cont in pattern st until work measures 15 cm (6 in) ending with a 6th pattern row.
Shape armholes Cast off 6 sts at the beg of the next 2 rows and then cont in pattern until the work measures 19 cm (7½ in) ending with a 5th pattern row and dec 1 st at each end of last row (79 sts). Leave these sts on a spare needle.
Note After casting off the 6 sts for the armhole the shaping pattern rows will start:
3RD ROW k2, (wlfwd, k1) twice.
6TH ROW p2, (wrn, p1) twice.

Sleeves
With 3.25-mm needles cast on 67 sts and work 6 rows in garter st. Change to 3-mm needles and cont in pattern as for back until work measures 13.5 cm (5¼ in) ending with a 6th pattern row.
SHAPE TOP Cast off 6 sts at the beg of next 2 rows, then cont in pattern as on back until the work measures 16 cm (6¼ in) ending with a 5th pattern row and dec 1 st at each end of last row (53 sts). Leave sts on a spare needle.

Right front
With 3.25-mm needles cast on 46 sts and work 6 rows in garter st. Change to

3-mm needles and cont in pattern with garter st edge as follows:

1ST ROW k.

2ND ROW p to last 6 sts, k6.

3RD ROW k6 *(p2 tog) twice, k1, (wlfwd, k1) 4 times, (p2 tog) twice. Rep from * to last st, k1.

4TH ROW p to last 6 sts, k6.

5TH ROW k.

6TH ROW k1 *(k2 tog) twice, p1, (wrn, p1) 4 times, (k2 tog) twice. Rep from * to last 6 sts, k6. Rep these 6 pattern rows 5 more times. On the next row make a buttonhole in the garter st edge as follows: k3, wlfwd, k2 tog, k1. Buttonholes should then be made on this band on the first row of every alt pattern (every 12th row) continuing right up yoke. Cont until work measures 15 cm (6 in). Cast of 6 sts at the beg of the next armhole row. Cont pattern until work measures 19 cm (7½ in) ending with a 5th pattern row, and dec 1 st at armhole edge of the last row. Leave these sts on a spare needle.

Left front

Work as for right front reversing all shapings and omitting buttonholes.

Yoke

Using 3-mm needles and with right side of work facing pick up all sts on needle as follows: right front, 1st sleeve, back, 2nd sleeve, left front. Work as follows:

1ST ROW (Wrong side facing) k6 *(k2 tog) twice, k5, (k2 tog) twice. Rep from *. (AT THE SAME TIME k tog the last st of one piece and the first st of the next piece) to the last 6 sts, k6.

2ND ROW k3, wlfwd, k2 tog, k1 (buttonhole should be due here) k2 *(k2 tog) 3 times, k3. Rep from * to last 6 sts, k6. K 11 rows.

NEXT ROW k3, wlfwd, k2 tog, k1 (buttonhole) *wlfwd, k2 tog, wlfwd, k3 tog. Rep from * to last 6 sts, k6. K 11 rows.

NEXT ROW Make buttonhole as above. *wlfwd, k2 tog. Rep from * to last 6 sts, k6. K 3 rows. Cast off.

Making up

Backstitch or overstitch all seams. Make crochet chain cords with little button ends to thread through holes at neck and also through first pattern row at wrists. Sew on buttons.

Do not press this garment (see instructions for dress, page 14).

Bonnet

With 3.25-mm needles cast on 80 sts and work 4 rows in garter st. Change to 3-mm needles and work in pattern as for back of matinée coat until work measures 10 cm (4 in) ending with a 6th pattern row.

NEXT ROW (Right side facing) k1, *k2 tog, k4. Rep from * to last st, k1. K 5 rows.

NEXT ROW k1, *k2 tog, k3. Rep from * to last st, k1. K 5 rows.

NEXT ROW k1, *k2 tog, k2. Rep from * to last st, k1. K 5 rows.

NEXT ROW k1, *k2 tog, k1. Rep from * to last st, k1. K 5 rows.

NEXT ROW k1, and then k2 tog all along row to last st, k1. (15 sts). Break off yarn, thread through remaining loops of sts and fasten off. Join back seam down length of garter st.

Lower band

With 3-mm needles pick up and k 49 sts evenly round lower edge of bonnet. K 3 rows and then make row of holes by k1, wlfwd, k2 tog all along row. K 3 rows. Cast off. Make a cord as on the matinée coat and thread through holes at neck edge making the cord long enough to tie comfortably under the baby's chin.

Pressing See page 14.

Bootees

With 3.25-mm needles cast on 41 sts and work 4 rows in garter st. Then rep the 6 pattern rows of feather st 3 times and then the 1st and 2nd rows once again.

NEXT ROW k1 *wlfwd, k2 tog. Rep from * to end (row of holes).

NEXT ROW k. DIVIDE FOR INSTEP

NEXT ROW k26, turn.

NEXT ROW k11, turn. Work 18 rows of

garter st on these 11 sts. Break yarn. Rejoin yarn at beg of instep and k up 11 sts from side of instep. K across instep sts, k up 11 sts from 2nd side of instep, k to end (63 sts). Work 13 rows garter st.
SHAPE TOE: 1ST ROW k2, k2 tog, k22, sl 1, k1, psso, k7, k2 tog, k to last 4 sts, sl 1, k1, psso, k2.
2ND ROW k.
3RD ROW k2, k2 tog, k21, sl 1, k1, psso, k5, k2 tog, k to last 4 sts, sl 1, k1, psso, k1. Cast off.

Join leg and foot seams. Make cords to thread through holes at ankles.

Feather stitch jumpsuit

Measurements To fit the average baby from birth to 6 months.
Materials 60 gms of 3-ply baby yarn, 4 buttons.
Needles A pair of 2.5-mm (No. 12), 3-mm (No. 11) and 2.25-mm (No. 13) needles
Tension 20 rows and 15 sts to a 5 cm (2 in) square on 3-mm needles in st st.
Abbreviations See page 12.

Right Leg
Using 2.5-mm needles cast on 81 sts and work 5 rows in k1, p1 rib. Then make a row of holes for the cord: *rib 2, wrn, k2 tog. Rep from * to last st, k1. Work 4 more rows in rib. Change to 3-mm needles and cont in st st until work measures 16.5 cm (6½ in) from beg.
Shape leg Cast off 2 sts at beg of the next 2 rows and then k2 tog at each end of the next and every following 3rd row until 55 sts remain. Cont without further dec until work measures 12.5 cm (5 in) from start of the leg shaping, finishing with a k row.
NEXT ROW p2 *p2 tog, p3. Rep from * to last 3 sts, p2 tog, k1 (44 sts). Change to 2.25-mm needles and work 4 rows in single rib. Change back to 3-mm needles and work foot as follows:

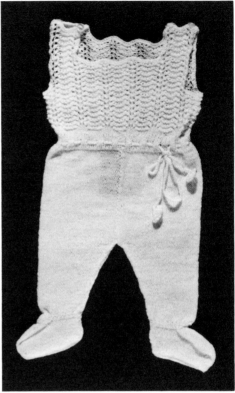

1ST ROW k29, turn.
2ND ROW p14, turn. Cont in st st on these 14 sts for 6.5 cm (2½ in) ending with a p row. Break off yarn. With the right side facing, rejoin yarn picking up and knitting 15 sts up side of instep, 14 sts from instep, 15 sts down side of instep, k15. Commencing with a p row work 9 rows in st st.
Shape sole 1ST ROW k1, sl1, k1, psso, k27, sl1, k1, psso, k10, k2 tog, k27, k2 tog, k1.
2ND AND ALT ROWS p.
3RD ROW k1, sl1, k1, psso, k26, sl1, k1, psso, k8, k2 tog, k26, k2 tog, k1. Cont dec in this manner until 8 rows have been worked. Cast off.
Left leg Work as for right leg, reversing all shapings. Join front and back seams with flatstitch or overstitch.

Jumpsuit top
Back With right side facing, using 3-mm needles, pick up and k 80 sts from cast

on sts across back of legging. P1 row.
Commence pattern:
1ST ROW (Right side facing) k.
2ND ROW p.
3RD ROW k1 *(p2 tog) twice, k1 (wlfwd, k1) 4 times, (p2 tog) twice. Rep from * to last st, k1.
4TH ROW p.
5TH ROW k.
6TH ROW k1 *(k2 tog) twice, p1 (wrn, p1) 4 times, (k2 tog) twice. Rep from * to last st, k1. Rep these 6 rows of pattern 3 more times.
Shape armholes Cast off 6 sts at the beg of the next 2 rows. Cont in pattern without further dec until 5 more patterns have been worked.
Note After casting off 6 sts at the armhole, 3rd pattern row will start: k2 (wlfwd, k1) twice — and 6th pattern row: p2 (wrn, p1) twice.
Shape neck Pattern 15, cast off 38 sts, pattern 15. Cont on these last 15 sts for 6 rows (1 pattern). Cast off. Work the other side of the neck in the same way.

Front Work as for the top back but working only 3 patterns instead of 5 after the armhole shaping.

Shape neck Pattern 15, cast off 38, pattern 15. Cont on these last 15 sts until 3 patterns have been worked from neck. Cast off. Work the other side of the neck in the same way.

Making up
Join remaining seams with flatstitch or overstitch and then work a row of double crochet round armholes, across shoulders and round the neck. Make two loop buttonholes on each front strap. Attach buttons to back strap. Make a crochet chain cord with little button ends to thread through the row of holes at the waist.
Pressing See page 14.

Feather stitch pram-set with mittens for boys and girls

Measurements To fit babies from 3 to 6 months, [6 to 12 months].
Materials 240 gms of 3-ply baby yarn. Yarn must be used double throughout. Use either a single colour for a solid shade, or 2 colours and twisted together for the 'flecked' effect. 3 buttons.
Needles A pair of 3.25-mm (No. 10) and 4-mm (No. 8) needles. For the larger sizes use 3.5-mm (No. 9) and 4.5-mm (No. 7) needles.
Tension 1st size: 12 sts and 16 rows to a 5 cm (2 in) square on 4-mm needles. 2nd size: 11 sts and 14 rows to a 5 cm (2 in) square on 4.5-mm needles. Both in plain st st.
Abbreviations See page 12.

Coat
Back With 4-[4.5]mm needles cast on 93 sts and work 4 rows in garter st (every row k). Cont in pattern as follows:
1ST ROW (right side facing) k.
2ND ROW p.
3RD ROW k1 *(p2 tog) twice, k1, (wlfwd, k1) 4 times, (p2 tog) twice. Rep from * to last st, k1.
4TH ROW p.
5TH ROW k.
6TH ROW k1 *(k2 tog) twice, p1, (wrn, p1) 4 times, (k2 tog) twice. Rep from * to last st, k1. These 6 rows form the pattern. Rep these 6 pattern rows until work measures 16.5[19]cm (6½[7½]in) ending with a 6th pattern row.
NEXT ROW (k2 tog, k1) 7 times, (k2 tog) 24 times, (k1, k2 tog) 8 times (54 sts).
NEXT ROW p. **Make row of holes for cord as follows:
NEXT ROW *k1, wlfwd, k2 tog. Rep from * to end of row. Now cont in st st starting with a p row until work

measures 19[21.5]cm (7½[8½]in) ending with the right side facing**.

Shape raglan as follows

1ST AND 2ND ROWS Cast off 3 sts, work to end.
3RD ROW k1, k2 tog tbl, k to the last 3 sts, k2 tog, k1.
4TH ROW k2, p to the last 2 sts, k2.
5TH ROW k.
6TH ROW k2, p to the last 2 sts, k2. Rep the 3rd to the 6th row until 40 sts remain, ending with a 3rd row.
NEXT ROW k2, p to the last 2 sts, k2.
NEXT ROW k1, k2 tog tbl, k to last 3 sts, k2 tog, k1. Rep the last 2 rows until 18 sts remain, ending with right side facing. Leave these sts on a spare needle.

Left front

With 4-[4.5-]mm needles cast on 41 sts and work 4 rows in garter st. Then work in the pattern as for back until work measures 16.5[19]cm (6½[7½]in), ending with a 6th pattern row and increasing 1 st at end of last row (42 sts).
NEXT ROW k1, (k1, k2 tog) 4 times, k1, (k2 tog) 7 times, k1, (k2 tog, k1) 4 times, k1 (27 sts).
NEXT ROW p. Work as for back from ** to **.

Shape raglan as follows

1ST ROW cast off 3 sts, k to end.
2ND ROW p to last 2 sts, k2.
3RD ROW k1, k2 tog tbl, k to end.
4TH ROW p to last 2 sts, k2.
5TH ROW k. Rep 2nd to 5th rows until 20 sts remain, ending with a 3rd row.
NEXT ROW p to last 2 sts, k2.
NEXT ROW k1, k2 tog tbl, k to end. Rep last 2 rows until 15 sts remain, ending with right side facing.

Shape neck as follows

NEXT ROW k1, k2 tog tbl, k to last 3 sts. Turn and leave these 3 sts on a safety pin. Now dec 1 st at the neck edge on evey row AT THE SAME TIME continuing to dec 1 st at the raglan edge as before, until 3 sts remain, ending with right side facing. K1, k2 tog tbl. P back. K2 tog and fasten off.

Right front

Work as for the left front reversing all shapings and remembering that k2 tog will be worked instead of k2 tog tbl at the raglan shapings.

Sleeves

With 3.25-[3.5-]mm needles cast on 27 sts and work 4 cm (1½ in) in garter st.
NEXT ROW k4 (m1, k9) twice, m1, k5 (30 sts). Change to 4-[4.5-]mm needles and work in st st starting with a k row and shaping the sleeve by increasing 1 st at each end of the 3rd and every following 7th row until there are 40 sts. Work without shaping until the sleeve measures 16.5[19]cm (6½[7½]in) ending with the right side facing.

Shape raglan top as follows 1ST AND 2ND ROWS Cast off 3 sts, work to end.
3RD ROW k1, k2 tog tbl, k to the last 3 sts, k2 tog, k1.
4TH ROW k2, p to the last 2 sts, k2.
5TH ROW k.
6TH ROW k2, p to the last 2 sts, k2. Rep from the 3rd to the 6th row until 26 sts remain, ending with a 3rd row.
NEXT ROW k2, p to the last 2 sts, k2.
NEXT ROW k1, k2 tog tbl, k to last 3 sts, k2 tog, k1. Rep the last 2 rows until 6 sts remain, ending with the right side facing.
NEXT ROW k1, k2 tog tbl, k2 tog, k1 (4 sts).
NEXT ROW p2 tog twice (2 sts). Leave these 2 sts on a safety pin.

Neckband

With right side facing and using 3.25-mm needles, start at the right front neck and pick up sts as follows: k3 sts from safety pin, 8 sts up right side of neck, k2 sts from sleeve, k18 sts from back of neck, k2 sts from 2nd sleeve. K up 8 sts down left side of neck, then 3 sts from safety pin (44 sts). Work 6 rows in garter st. Cast off using 4-mm needles.

Button border

With 3.25-mm needles cast on 6 sts and work in garter st until the border fits up the front to top of neckband (very slightly stretched). Cast off.

Buttonhole border

Work as for the button border working 3 buttonholes. Work the first buttonhole at the start of the raglan shaping, the last one just below the top of the neckband, and the other evenly spaced between the two. To get them evenly spaced mark their positions with pins on the button border already done, then work the buttonholes to correspond. To make the buttonholes (right side facing) k2, wlfwd, k2 tog, k2. Make a chain cord to thread through holes at waist and tie at front. Join seams using overstitch or flatstitch, remembering that you can sew the buttonhole border to whichever side you wish (for a boy or a girl). Attach buttons to correspond with buttonholes.

Pressing See page 14.

The mittens

Using 3.25-[3.5-]mm needles, cast on 28 sts and work in garter st for 4 cm (1½ in) increasing once at each end of the last row (30 sts).

NEXT ROW sl1, *wlfwd, k2 tog. Rep from * to last st, k1. Change to 4-(4-5-)mm needles, and commencing with a p row, work 15 rows in st st.

Shape top 1ST ROW sl1, *k2, k2 tog. Rep from * to last st, k1.

2ND, 4TH AND 6TH ROWS sl1, p to the last st, k1.

3RD ROW sl1, *k1, k2 tog. Rep from * to last st, k1.

5TH ROW sl1, *k2 tog. Rep from * to last st, k1. Break off yarn and run it through the remaining sts, draw up and fasten off. Stitch seam. Make two cords about 35.5 cm (14 in) long and thread through holes at wrist. Place the back of the mittens to the back of the pram coat sleeves. Sew 14 of the 28 cast on sts at the back of the mitten to 15 of the 30 sts on the last row of garter st on the back of the sleeve. The mitten can then be folded back if the baby does not need it, or put over the hand when necessary.

Bonnet

With 3.25-mm needles cast on 80 sts and work 4 rows in garter st. Change to 4-mm needles, then work in pattern as for back until work measures 10[11.5]cm (4[4½]in), ending after a 6th pattern row.

Shape crown as follows 1ST ROW (Right side facing) k1, *k2 tog, k4. Rep from * to last st, k1. K 5 rows.

NEXT ROW k1, *k2 tog, k3. Rep from * to the last st, k1. K 5 rows.

NEXT ROW k1, *k2 tog, k2. Rep from * to the last st, k1. K 5 rows.

NEXT ROW k1, *k2 tog, k1. Rep from * to the last st, k1. K 3 rows.

NEXT ROW k1, *k2 tog. Rep from * to the last st (15 sts). Break wool, thread through remaining loops and fasten off. Join back seam of crown only.

Lower band With 3.25-mm needles pick up and k 49 sts evenly along back lower edge of bonnet. K 3 rows, then make a row of holes thus:

NEXT ROW *k1, wlfwd, k2 tog. Rep from * to end. K 3 more rows and cast off. Make a chain cord and thread through these holes. Make a cord long enough to tie comfortably under the baby's chin.

Boy's cap

Using 4-[4.5-]mm needles cast on 81[85]sts and work 14 rows in garter st. Change to 3.25-[3.5-]mm needles and work as follows:

1ST ROW sl1, k2, *k2 tog, k9. Rep from * to last 3[5] sts, k2 tog, k1[3] (73[77] sts). Work in single rib for 10 rows. Change to 4-[4.5-]mm needles and, starting with a k row, work in st st for another 4.5[5]cm (1¾[2]in), decreasing once at the end of the last row for the smaller size only (72[77]sts).

Shape crown 1ST ROW *k2 tog, k10[9]. Rep from * to end of row.

2ND AND EVERY ALT ROW sl1, k to end of row.

3RD ROW *k2 tog, k9[8]. Rep from * to end of row. Cont in this manner, working 1 st less between the decs in the next and every alt row until 18[14] sts remain.

NEXT ROW sl1, k to end of row.

NEXT ROW *k3 tog [k2 tog]. Rep from * to

end of row (6[7] sts). Break off yarn, thread it through remaining sts, draw up and fasten off.

Earflaps (optional)
Using 4-[4.5-]mm needles cast on 2 sts.
1ST ROW Inc once in each st.
2ND, 4TH AND 6TH ROWS sl 1, k to end.
3RD ROW sl 1, (inc once in next st) twice, k1.
5TH ROW sl 1, inc once in next st, k1, inc once in next st, k2.
7TH ROW sl 1, inc once in next st, k to last 3 sts, inc once in next st, k2.
8TH ROW sl 1, k to end of row. Rep the 7th and 8th rows 1[2] times, (12[14]sts). Work 10 rows in garter st without shaping. Cast off.

Making up
With right side facing and starting at cast on edge, stitch seam for 4 cm (1½ in). Turn the work inside out and stitch rest of seam. Turn back brim. Sew cast off edge of earflaps to edge of brim 4.5[5]cm (1¾[2]in) in from the back seam. Make crochet or twisted cords about 30.5 cm (12 in) in length and sew to earflaps. Sew a tassel on to the end of each cord, or make little crochet button ends.

Leggings
Right leg With 3.25-mm needles cast on 61 sts and work in single rib thus:
1ST ROW sl 1, (k1, p1) to end of row.
2ND ROW sl 1, (p1,k1) to end of row. Rep these 2 rows once more, then make a row of holes as follows: sl 1, k1 *wlfwd, k2 tog. Rep from * to last st, k1.
NEXT ROW As 2nd row. Rep 1st and 2nd rows 3 more times. Change to 4-[4.5-]mm needles and work in st st until work measures 21.5[23]cm (8½[9]in) from the start, ending with a p row. Place a marker at each end of this last row.
Shape leg as follows Cast off 2 sts at the beg of the next 2 rows and then dec 1 st at both ends of next and every following 3rd row until 39 sts remain. Cont without shaping until work measures

12.5[14]cm (5[5½]in) from marked point, finishing with a p row. Divide for foot as follows:
NEXT ROW k31, turn.
NEXT ROW k1, p16, k1 (18 sts). Work 16 rows in st st. Break off yarn. Rejoin yarn to inside edge of 13 sts left and, with right side facing, k up 14 sts along side of foot. Work across 18 sts on needles as follows: k8, k2 tog, k8, k up 14 sts along other side of foot and then across remaining 8 sts (66 sts). K 11 rows then shape foot as follows:
1ST ROW k3, k2 tog, k1, k2 tog, k25, k2 tog, k1, k2 tog, k to end.
2ND AND ALT ROWS k.
3RD ROW k2, k2 tog, k1, k2 tog, k23, k2 tog, k1, k2 tog, k to end.
5TH ROW k1, k2 tog, k1, k2 tog, k21, k2 tog, k1, k2 tog, k to end. Cast off.

Left leg
Work as for right leg until work measures 12.5[14]cm (5[5½]in) from marked points. Divide for foot as follows:
NEXT ROW k26, turn.
NEXT ROW k1, p16, k1, turn. Work 16 rows st st on these 18 sts. Break off yarn. Rejoin to inside edge of 8 sts left and with right side facing, k up 14 sts along side of foot. Work across 18 sts on needle as follows: k8, k2 tog, k8, k up 14 sts along other side of foot, and finally k across 13 sts (66 sts). K 11 rows and then shape foot as follows:
1ST ROW k28, k2 tog, k1, k2 tog, k25, k2 tog, k1, k2 tog, k3.
2ND AND ALT ROWS k.
3RD ROW k27, k2 tog, k1, k2 tog, k23, k2 tog, k1, k2 tog, k2.
4TH ROW k26, k2 tog, k1, k2 tog, k21, k2 tog, k1, k2 tog, k1. Cast off. Join all seams using overstitch or flatstitch. Make a crochet chain or twist cord about 91 cm (36 in) in length and thread this cord through row of holes at waist.
Pressing See page 12.

Feather stitch cardigan

Measurements To fit the average baby of 4 to 8 months.

Materials 80 gms of 3-ply baby yarn. YARN MUST BE USED DOUBLE THROUGHOUT. Again, this can be done using two colours for the 'flecked' effect. 6 buttons.

Needles a pair of 3.25-mm (No. 10) and 4.5-mm (No. 7) needles.

Tension 11 sts and 14 rows to 5 cm (2 in) square on 4.5-mm needles in st st.

Abbreviations See page 12.

Back

With 3.25-mm needles and using yarn double, cast on 54 sts and work in single rib for 12 rows. Change to 4.5-mm needles and pattern as for back of Matinée Coat, page 15. Work 3 patterns (18 rows) and then work in st st until work measures 12.5 cm (5 in).

Shape raglan Cast off 3 sts at the beg of the next 2 rows.

NEXT ROW k1, k2 tog tbl, k to the last 3 sts, k2 tog, k1.

NEXT ROW k1, p to the last st, k1. Rep these last 2 rows until 16 sts remain. Cast off.

Left front

Using 3.25-mm needles cast on 34 sts and work in single rib for 12 rows. Change to 4.5-mm needles and pattern including rib band as follows:

1ST ROW k27, rib 7.

2ND ROW rib 7, p27.

3RD ROW k1, *(p2 tog) twice, k1, (wlfwd, k1) 4 times, (p2 tog) twice. Rep from * once more, rib 7.

4TH ROW rib 7, p27.

5TH ROW k27, rib 7.

6TH ROW rib 7, *(k2 tog) twice, p1 (wrn, p1) 4 times, (k2 tog) twice. Rep from * once more, k1. Rep these 6 rows twice more.

NEXT ROW k to last 7 sts, k7.

NEXT ROW rib 7, p to end.

NEXT ROW k14, (p2 tog) twice, k1, (wlfwd, k1) 4 times, (p2 tog) twice, rib 7.

NEXT ROW rib 7, p to end.

NEXT ROW k to last 7 sts, rib 7.

NEXT ROW rib 7, (k2 tog) twice, p1 (wrn, p1) 4 times, (k2 tog) twice, p to end. Rep these last 6 rows once more. Work now measures 12.5 cm (5 in).

Shape armhole Cast off 3 sts, k to last 7 sts, rib 7.

NEXT ROW rib 7, p to end.

NEXT ROW k1, k2 tog tbl, k8, pattern 13, rib 7. Cont in this way keeping 13 sts of pattern inside the rib band and dec 1 st

at the armhole edge on every alt row until 22 sts remain, finishing at the armhole edge.

NEXT ROW k1, k2 tog tbl, k to 7 rib sts, turn (slipping the 7 rib sts on to a safety pin).

Neck shaping NEXT ROW cast off 3 sts, p to end.

NEXT ROW k1, k2 tog tbl, k to last 2 sts, k2 tog tbl.

NEXT ROW p. Rep the last 2 rows until 3 sts remain.

NEXT ROW k1, k2 tog tbl.

NEXT ROW p2. Cast off.

Right front

Work as for the left front reversing all shapings and making a simple wlfwd, k2 tog buttonhole in the rib band on the 5th and then every following 12th row up the front band. The 13 st pattern on this front comes at the beg of k rows and raglan shaping will come at the end of k rows (right side) and should be k2 tog, k1 (not tbl).

Sleeves Using 3.25-mm needles cast on 32 sts and work in single rib for 4 cm (1½ in), increasing 9 sts evenly along the last rib row (41 sts). Change to 4.5-mm needles and work 2 complete patterns as on back. Now work the rest of the sleeve in st st, without shaping until work measures 14 cm (5½ in).

Shape raglan Cast off 3 sts at the beg of the next 2 rows.

NEXT ROW sl 1, k2 tog tbl, k to last 3 sts, k2 tog, k1.

NEXT ROW sl 1, p to last st, k1. Rep these last 2 rows until 5 sts remain. Cast off.

Neckband

Using 3.25-mm needles and with right side facing pick up and rib 7 sts from right frontband, 10 sts up side of front, 4 sts across first sleeve, 16 sts across back, 4 sts across second sleeve, 10 sts down left front and 7 sts from left frontband (58 sts). Work 6 rows in single rib making a buttonhole on the 3rd row. Cast off ribwise.

Making up

Join all seams using overstitch or flatstitch and set the sleeves into the armholes. Sew on buttons.

Pressing See page 14.

Shawl with feather stitch border

Measurements About 91 cm (36 in) square.

Materials 400 gms 3-ply baby yarn USED DOUBLE.

Needles A pair of 5.5-mm (No. 5) needles.

Tension See page 10.

Abbreviations See page 12.

USE YARN DOUBLE THROUGHOUT

Using No. 5.5-mm needles cast on 168 sts and work 10 rows in garter st.

Now change to working in feather st with garter st border:

**1ST ROW k.

2ND ROW k6, p to last 6 sts, k6.

3RD ROW k6, *(p2 tog) twice, k1, (wlfwd, k1) 4 times, (p2 tog) twice. Rep from * to last 6 sts, k6.

4TH ROW k6, p to last 6 sts, k6.

5TH ROW k.

6TH ROW k6, *(k2 tog) twice, p1 (wrn, p1) 4 times, (k2 tog) twice. Rep from * to last 6 sts, k6.

Work 11 more complete patterns in this way.**

Cont as follows:

1ST ROW k6, pattern 26, k to last 32 sts, pattern 26, k6.

2ND ROW k6, pattern 26, p to last 32 sts, pattern 26, k6. Continue in this way until work measures about 76 cm (30 in) ending with the last row of a pattern.

Now work from ** to ** again. Work 10 rows in garter st. Cast off.

Making up

If you have used wool lightly press THE ST ST CENTRE ONLY. Feather st does not

need pressing and is considerably more attractive unpressed. Just hand smooth as you fold the shawl.
OPTIONAL If edges seem a little untidy a crochet edge all round the shawl may help.

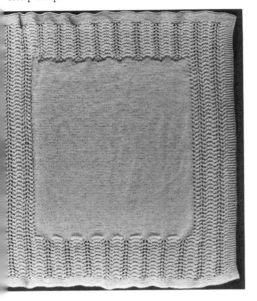

Sleeping bag

Materials Double-knitting yarn used double. 500 gms of double-knitting yarn (20 × 25 gm balls). 4 buttons.
Needles One pair each of 7.5-mm and 3.5-mm (Nos. 1 and 9).
Tension See page 10.
Abbreviations See page 12.

Back
Using 7.5-mm needles and double yarn cast on 42 sts and work 3 rows in garter st.
NEXT ROW k3, *k2 tog, wrn, k5. Rep from * to last 4 sts, k4.
Work 2 rows in garter st.
NEXT ROW k6, *wlfwd, k2 tog tbl, k3. Rep from * to last 6 sts, k6.
NEXT ROW k6, p to last 6 sts, k6.
Rep these 2 rows twice more, then the last row twice more.
NEXT ROW k6, *p2, k2. Rep from * to last 8 sts, p2, k6.
NEXT ROW k8, *p2, k2. Rep from * to last 6 sts, k6.
NEXT ROW k6, *k2, p2. Rep from * to last 8 sts, k8.
NEXT ROW k8, *k2, p2. Rep from * to last 6 sts, k6.
Rep first 2 rows again.
K 4 rows.
NEXT ROW k6, *wlfwd, k2 tog, k1. Rep from * to last 6 sts, k6.
NEXT ROW p.
Rep these 2 rows twice more.
Work 4 rows in garter st.
NEXT ROW ** sl 1, *k2 tog, wrn, k3. Rep from * to last st, k1 tbl.
NEXT ROW p.
Rep these 2 rows 3 times more, then p 2 rows.
NEXT ROW sl 1, *p2, k2. Rep from * to last st, k1 tbl.
NEXT ROW as above.
NEXT ROW sl 1, *k2, p2. Rep from * to last st, k1 tbl.

NEXT ROW as above.
Rep first 2 rows again.
K 3 rows.
NEXT PATTERN (wrong side facing) 1ST ROW
sl 1, *p1, k1 tbl. Rep from * to last st,
k1 tbl.
2ND ROW p.
Rep these 2 rows twice more.
P 3 rows.
NEXT PATTERN 1ST ROW sl 1, *wlfwd, k2
tog, k1. Rep from * to last 2 sts, k1,
k1 tbl.
2ND ROW p.
Rep these 2 rows twice more.
Work 4 rows in st st.
Work 8 rows in moss st.
Work 4 rows in garter st.
NEXT PATTERN 1ST ROW sl 1, *k4, p4. Rep
from * to last st, k1 tbl. Rep this row 3
times more.
2ND ROW sl 1, *p4, k4. Rep from * to last
st, k1 tbl. Rep this row 3 times more.
Work the first 4 rows once more.
Work 4 rows in garter st.
Rep from ** until work measures
53.5 cm (21 in) from cast on edge.
Cast off 13 sts at beg of next 2 rows, slip
remaining sts on to a spare needle.

Front

Using 7.5-mm needles and double yarn
cast on 42 sts and work 6 rows in
garter st.
Work from ** as on back until work
measures 35.5 cm (14 in) from cast
on edge.

NEXT ROW Continuing in pattern k18, cast
on 6 sts, keeping these 6 sts in garter st
for rest of front. Work in pattern until
front measures 18 cm (7 in) from beg of
the front opening, ending at front edge.
Slip first 8 sts on to a spare needle. Cont
in pattern, decreasing 1 st at neck edge
on every alt row until 13 sts remain.
Work any rows needed to bring front to
same length as back. Cast off. Rejoin yarn
to other group of sts and work to
correspond with first side, working 6 sts
in garter st at front edge throughout.
Work 4 buttonholes on this band.

Sleeves

Using 3.5-mm needles and yarn double
cast on 30 sts and work 6.5 cm (2½ in)
in single rib.
Change to 7.5-mm needles and work 12
rows in st st and 4 rows garter st. Work
these 16 rows again. Work 3 rows in st
st. Cast off.

Neckband

Join shoulder seams. With right side
facing, double yarn and 7.5-mm needles,
pick up sts evenly around neck (not
tight). Work 8 rows in garter st working 7
buttonholes evenly on 5th row. Cast off
loosely.

Hood

Using 7.5-mm needles and double yarn
cast on 50 sts and work 10 rows in
garter st.
Cont in garter st and dec 1 st at each end
of every row until 10 sts remain. Work 2
rows without decreasing.
Cont in garter st, inc 1 st at each end of
row by picking up dec edge at each end
of every row until 50 sts are on needle.
NEXT ROW Cast on 10 sts, k to end of row,
cast on 10 sts. Work 8 rows in garter st.
Cast off loosely.
Sew cast on 10 sts to 10 garter st rows at
hood front edge.
Sew buttons around hood edge to
correspond with buttonholes on neck
edge.

Making up

Sew sleeves into place WITHOUT GATHERING
SEAM. Sew sleeve and side seams. Fold
bottom back edge over and sew buttons
on front to correspond with buttonholes.
Sew cast on sts at front opening into
place, and again sew buttons on in
correct place.

Pram cover

Materials 12 × 25gm balls double-knitting
yarn.
Needles, Tension and Abbreviations as

for sleeping bag.

Using 7.5-mm needles cast on 70 sts and work 8 rows in garter st.

Now work from ** on sleeping bag keeping a border of 5 sts in garter st at each end ALWAYS REMEMBERING TO SLIP THE FIRST STITCH AND KNIT INTO BACK OF LAST STITCH TO GIVE A NEAT TIDY EDGE TO THE COVER.

Continue, repeating the 4 patterns until cover measures 71 cm (28 in) from start. Work 8 rows in garter st. Cast off.

Flared dress

Measurements To fit 48[51]cm (19[20]in) chest.

Length 33 cm (13 in)

Materials 80 gms of 3-ply baby yarn, 3 buttons.

Needles One pair each of 3.25-mm, 3-mm and 2.5-mm (Nos. 10, 11 and 12) needles.

Tension 20 rows and 15 sts to a 5 cm (2 in) square on 3-mm needles in st st.

Abbreviations See page 12.

Back

Using 3.25-mm needles cast on 183 sts and k 7 rows.

Commence pattern:

1ST ROW (right side) *k12, p1, won, sl 1, k1, psso, k1, k2 tog, wrn, p1. Rep from * to last 12 sts, k12.

2ND ROW *p12, k1, p5, k1. Rep from * to last 12 sts, p12.

3RD ROW *k12, p2, won, sl 1, k2 tog, psso, wrn, p2. Rep from * to last 12 sts, k12.

4TH ROW *p12, k2, p3, k2. Rep from * to last 12 sts, p12.

5TH ROW *k12, p2 tog, won, k3, wrn, p2 tog. Rep from * to last 12 sts, k12.

6TH ROW As 2nd row.

These 6 rows form the pattern and from now on the sts of the lace panel will be referred to as pattern 7.

Rep these 6 rows once more.

NEXT ROW *sl 1, k1, psso, k8, k2 tog, pattern 7. Rep from * to last 12 sts, sl 1, k1, psso, k8, k2 tog (163 sts).

NEXT ROW *p10, pattern 7. Rep from * to last 10 sts, p10.

NEXT ROW *k10, pattern 7. Rep from * to last 10 sts, k10.

NEXT ROW *p10, pattern 7. Rep from * to last 10 sts, p10.

Rep the last 2 rows 5 times more.

NEXT ROW *sl 1, k1, psso, k6, k2 tog, pattern 7. Rep from * to last 10 sts, sl 1, k1, psso, k6, k2 tog (143 sts).

NEXT ROW *p8, pattern 7. Rep from * to last 8 sts, p8.

NEXT ROW *k8, pattern 7. Rep from * to last 8 sts, k8.

NEXT ROW *p8, pattern 7. Rep from * to last 8 sts, p8.

Rep the last 2 rows 5 times more.

NEXT ROW *sl 1, k1, psso, k4, k2 tog, pattern 7. Rep from * to last 8 sts, sl 1, k1 psso, k4, k2 tog (123 sts).

NEXT ROW *p6, pattern 7. Rep from * to last 6 sts, p6.

NEXT ROW *k6, pattern 7. Rep from * to last 6 sts, k6.

NEXT ROW *p6, pattern 7. Rep from * to last 6 sts, p6.

Rep the last 2 rows 5 times more.

NEXT ROW *sl 1, k1, psso, k2, k2 tog, pattern 7. Rep from * to last 6 sts, sl 1, k1, psso, k2, k2 tog (103 sts).
NEXT ROW *p4, pattern 7. Rep from * to last 4 sts, p4.
NEXT ROW *k4, pattern 7. Rep from * to last 4 sts, k4.
NEXT ROW *p4, pattern 7. Rep from * to last 4 sts, p4.
Rep last 2 rows 5 times more.
NEXT ROW *sl 1, k1, psso, k2 tog, pattern 7. Rep from * to last 4 sts, sl 1, k1, psso, k2 tog (83 sts).
NEXT ROW *p2, pattern 7. Rep from * to last 2 sts, p2.
NEXT ROW *k2, pattern 7. Rep from * to last 2 sts, k2.
NEXT ROW *p2, pattern 7. Rep from * to last 2 sts, p2.
Cont in this main pattern until another 2 patterns are completed ending with a wrong side row.
Change to 3-mm needles and **Shape armhole** as follows (still continuing main pattern).
Cast of 5 sts at the beg of the next 2 rows then dec 1 st at each end of the next and every following alt row until 65 sts remain.**
Cont without further shaping until work measures 4 cm (1½ in) from start of armhole shaping ending with a wrong side row.
Divide for neck opening Pattern 30 sts, k5. Turn, leaving remaining sts on a spare needle.
NEXT ROW k5, pattern to end.
BUTTONHOLE ROW Pattern to last 5 sts, k2, wlfwd, k2 tog, k1.
NEXT ROW k5, pattern to end.
NEXT ROW Pattern to last 5 sts, k5. Rep the last 2 rows until work measures 9 cm (3½ in) from start of armhole shaping ending at armhole edge and AT THE SAME TIME continue to make buttonholes 2.5 cm (1 in) apart.
Shape shoulder Cast off 6 sts at beg of next and following alt row and then 7 sts on the next alt row. Work 1 row. Leave remaining 16 sts on spare needle.
Rejoin wool at neck edge to other set of

sts. Cast on 5 sts. K across these 5 sts and pattern to end.
NEXT ROW Pattern to last 5 sts, k5.
Complete this side to match first side reversing all shapings and omitting buttonholes.

Front
Work as for back to ** (65 sts). Cont without further shaping until work measures 4.5 cm (1¾ in) from start of armhole shaping ending with a wrong side row.
Shape neck Pattern 26. Turn, leaving remaining 39 sts on a spare needle. Dec 1 st at neck edge on next 7 rows. Cont without further shaping until work measures same as back to shoulder, ending at armhole edge.
Shape shoulder Cast off 6 sts at beg of next and following alt row.
Work 1 row. Cast off remaining 7 sts.
Slip centre 13 sts on a spare needle.
Rejoin wool to remaining sts, pattern to end. Complete to match first side of neck.

Sleeves
Using 2.5-mm needles cast on 44 sts and k 6 rows.
NEXT ROW k1, *work twice into next st, k1. Rep from * to last st, k1 (65 sts).
Change to 3-mm needles and work in pattern as follows:
1ST ROW *k2, p1, won, sl 1, k1, psso, k1, k2 tog, wrn, p1. Rep from * to last 2 sts, k2.
2ND ROW *p2, k1, p5, k1. Rep from * to last 2 sts, p2.
3RD ROW *k2, p2, won, sl 1, k2 tog, psso, wrn, p2. Rep from * to last 2 sts, k2.
4TH ROW *p2, k2, p3, k2. Rep from * to last 2 sts, p2.
5TH ROW *k2, p2 tog, won, k3, wrn, p2 tog. Rep from * to last 2 sts, k2.
6TH ROW As 2nd row.
These 6 rows form the pattern. Cont in pattern until work measures 4 cm (1½ in) from the start, ending with a p row (wrong side).
Shape top Cast off 5 sts at the beg of the next 2 rows. Dec 1 st at each end of next and every following alt row until 43 sts

remain, then 1 st at each end of every row until 17 sts remain. Cast off.

Neckband

Using overstitch join shoulder seams. With right side of work facing and using 2.5-mm needles, k across the 16 sts on the left side of back neck, pick up and k 16 sts down left side of front neck, k across 13 sts on centre front, pick up and k 16 sts up right side of front neck and k across the 16 sts on right side of back neck (77 sts). K 7 rows, working a buttonhole 2.5 cm (1 in) from the previous one.

Making up

Using overstitch, join side and sleeve seams and set in sleeves. Catch down underlap on back neck. Sew on buttons. Using 3 strands of wool together work a crochet chain 91.5 cm (36 in) long and thread through holes in lace panels around the waist, bringing ends out at the centre front to tie, and make little button ends to the chain.

Classic matinée coat

Measurements To fit baby of up to 6 months.
Materials 70 gms of 3-ply baby yarn.
Needles One pair of 3-mm (No. 11) needles.
Tension 20 rows and 15 sts to a 5 cm (2 in) square on 3-mm needles in st st.
Abbreviations See page 12.

Body

This garment is worked in one piece to armhole. Cast on 144 sts. Starting with a p row work 3 rows in st st.
NEXT ROW (picot edge) sl 1, *wlfwd, k2 tog. Rep from * to last st, k1 tbl. Cont in st st until coat measures 15 cm (6 in) from row of holes (picot edge).
Divide sts for armhole k34, k2 tog. Turn, leave remaining sts on a spare needle.

Cont in st st decreasing 1 st at armhole edge on every row until there are 21 sts on the needle and then every other row until 8 sts remain, ending with a p row. Leave these sts on a safety pin. Join yarn to remaining sts, k2 tog, k68, k2 tog. Turn again leaving remaining sts on a spare needle. Cont in st st decreasing 1 st at each end of every row until there are 42 sts, then dec at each end of every alt row until there are 16 sts, ending with a p row. Leave sts on safety pin. Join yarn to remaining sts and work left side to correspond with right side, reversing all shapings.

Right sleeve

Cast on 42 sts and work 6 rows in st st. Now work the row of holes as for body. Work 8 rows in st st.
NEXT ROW Inc evenly along row to 60 sts. Cont in st st until sleeve measures 15 cm (6 in) from row of holes ending with a p row. Cont in st st and dec 1 st at each end of next and every alt row until there are 18 sts on needle, ending with a k row.

Left sleeve

Work as for right sleeve to the 18 sts, ending with a p row.
NEXT ROW k10, turn, p to last st, k1 tbl. Leave sts on safety pin.

Neckband

With right side of work facing k up 8 sts from right front, 18 sts from right sleeve, 16 sts from back, 18 sts from left sleeve, 8 sts from left front (68 sts). P 1 row.
NEXT ROW (row of holes for cord) sl 1, *wlfwd, k2 tog. Rep from * to last st, k1 tbl. Work 2 rows in st st starting with a p row. Make another row of holes as above for picot edge. Work 2 more rows in st st. Cast off.

Front borders

With right side of work facing pick up and k 66 sts along each front of coat.

Work 3 rows in st st, starting with a p row. Work a row of holes for picot edge followed by 3 more rows of st st. Cast off.

Making up
Carefully sew all seams. Fold over all hems at row of holes to form picot edges and stitch. Make a crochet chain cord to thread through neck and put a bobble or tassel on each end.

'A' line dress

Measurements To fit 48[51]cm (19[20]in) chest. Length 33 cm (13 in).
Materials 75 gms of 3-ply baby yarn, 2 buttons.
Needles One pair of 3-mm (No. 11) needles, one pair of 2.25-mm (No. 13) needles.
Tension 20 rows and 15 sts to a 5 cm (2 in) square on 3-mm needles in st st.
Abbreviations See page 12.

Front
With 3-mm needles cast on 112 sts and work 4 rows in st st.
NEXT ROW Make holes for picot edge: k1, *wlfwd, k2 tog. Rep from * to last st, k1 tbl.
Commencing with a p row work 5 more rows in st st. Now start pattern:
1ST ROW k3, *wlfwd, k2 tog tbl, k6. Rep from * to last 5 sts, wlfwd, k2 tog tbl, k2, k1 tbl.
2ND AND EVERY ALT ROW sl 1, p to last st, k1 tbl.
3RD ROW k3, *k2 tog tbl, wlfwd, k6. Rep from * to last 5 sts, k2 tog tbl, wlfwd, k2, k1 tbl.
5TH ROW TO 10TH ROW Rep rows 1 to 4 once, and then 1 and 2 again.
11TH ROW k3, *k2 tog, wlfwd. Rep from * to last 3 sts, k2, k1 tbl.
12TH ROW As 2nd. Rep these 12 rows once more. Now work rows 1 to 4 (the main pattern) until the front measures 16.5 cm (6½ in) from row of holes making the picot edge, ending on a 4th pattern row.

leave these on a stitch-holder or safety pin for neck. Work to end of row and work this side to match first side reversing all shapings.

Back

Work as for front to end of armhole shaping and to where neck shaping starts and cont straight until work measures same as front to shoulders. Cast off 9 sts at beg of next 4 rows and leave remaining sts on a holder for neckband.

Sleeves

Cast on 40 sts and work 4 rows in st st. NEXT ROW make picot edge: k1, *wlfwd, k2 tog. Rep from * to last st, k1 tbl. Commencing with a p row work 4 more rows in st st. P 1 more row increasing sts evenly along row to 46 sts. Work 6 rows in st st.

Shape top Cast off 3 sts at the beg of next 2 rows then dec 1 st at both ends of next and following alt row until 28 sts remain. Now dec 1 st at each end of every row until 14 sts remain. Cast off.

Neckband

Join right shoulder seam and using 2.25-mm needles pick up and k 74 sts round neck. Starting with a p row work 3 rows in st st. NEXT ROW (picot edge) k1, *wlfwd, k2 tog. Rep from * to last st, k1 tbl. NEXT ROW p. K 1 more row and cast off.

Making up

Using overstitch, join up side and sleeve seams and insert sleeves into armholes. Sew up left shoulder seam for 2.5 cm (1 in) from armhole edge. Turn all picot edges under at the row of holes and stitch carefully into position. Work a single row of double crochet round left shoulder opening (do it in blanket stitch if you cannot crochet). Make 2 loops for buttonholes and attach 2 buttons to correspond.

1ST DECREASE ROW sl 1, k2 tog, *wlfwd, k2 tog tbl, k4, k2 tog. Rep from * to last 5 sts, wlfwd, k2 tog tbl, k2 tog, k1 tbl. Cont to work in pattern with sts as now set having 1 st less between lace panels. Cont for 24 rows (6 patterns).

2ND DECREASE ROW k2 tog, *wlfwd, k2 tog tbl, k3, k2 tog. Rep from * to last 4 sts, wlfwd, k2 tog tbl, k2 tog. Work in pattern with sts as set (82 sts) until work measures 25.5 cm (10 in) ending with a 4th pattern row.

Shape armholes (and 3rd decrease row). Cast off 6 sts *wlfwd, k2 tog tbl, k2, k2 tog. Rep from * to last 7 sts, k4, k2 tog tbl, k1 tbl.

2ND ARMHOLE ROW cast off 6 sts, p to last st, k1 tbl (59 sts). Cont without further shaping until work measures 6 cm (2½ in) from beg of armhole shaping, ending with a p row.

Shape neck Pattern 24 sts, turn and work on these sts for left side. Dec 1 st at neck edge on next 3 rows and then on every alt row 3 times. Work without shaping until armhole measures 10 cm (4 in) on the straight ending at armhole edge.

Shape shoulders Cast off 9 sts at the beg of the next row. Work 1 row. Cast off. Return to sts left, work across 11 sts and

RIGHT: CHILD'S STRIPED CARDIGAN

Vest

Measurements To fit 46[50]cm
(18[19½]in) chest.
Materials 55 gms 3-ply yarn.
Needles One pair 3.25-mm (No. 10)
needles.
Tension See page 10.
Abbreviations See page 12.

Front

Using 3.25-mm needles cast on 76 sts
and work for 4 cm (1½ in) in double rib
(k2, p2). Change to st st and work
without shaping until work measures
18 cm (7 in).
NEXT ROW sl 1, k to last st, k1 tbl.
NEXT ROW sl 1, k7, p to last 8 sts, k7, k1
tbl. Rep these last 2 rows until work
measures 24 cm (9½ in) from start keeping the garter st border which makes a
neat little cap sleeve.
To shape neck Work across 24 sts, turn.
Work straight on this side only, continuing garter st band, until work measures
28 cm (11 in). Cast off. Rejoin yarn to remaining sts. Slip the next 28 sts on to a
safety pin to pick up for the neck and
work other side to match first side.

Back

Work exactly as for front, the only difference being that shapng for neck should
start 2.5 cm (1 in) higher than on the
front.

Neckband

Join left shoulder seam. Then with right
side facing and starting at right shoulder
pick up and k 15 sts down right side of
shoulder, 28 sts from front, 15 sts up left
shoulder, 5 sts from side of back, 28 sts
from back and 5 sts up other side of back
(96 sts). Work 1 row in p then make a
row of holes for the cord as follows: sl 1,

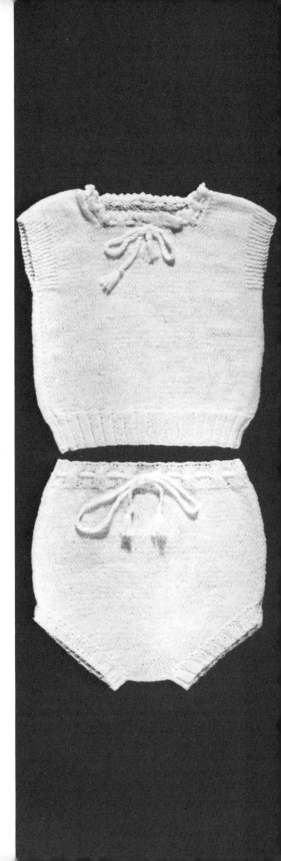

*wlfwd, k2 tog, k1. Rep from * to last 2 sts, k1, k1 tbl. P 1 row, k 1 row, p 1 row, then make another row of holes as before (omitting the k1 after the wlfwd, k2 tog). Work 2 more rows in st st. Cast off.

Making up

Join all seams using neat overstitch. Fold neck edge over at top row of holes to make picot edge and stitch down. Make a chain cord to thread through lower row of holes and attach a tiny bobble or tassel at each end of this cord.

Panties

Measurements Length from waist to crutch 23 cm (9 in). Width round 56 cm (22 in).

Materials Just over 50 gms 3-ply yarn Other details as for vest.

Beginning at the top of waistband cast on 64 sts and work 4 rows in double rib (k2, p2). On next row make holes for elastic or a cord as follows: *k2, wrn, p2 tog. Rep from * to end of row. Work 5 more rows in double rib.

On next row inc 12 sts evenly along row (76 sts).

Now work in st st until work measures 15 cm (6 in) from beg.

NEXT ROW k1, k2 tog, k to last 3 sts, sl 1, k1, psso, k1 tbl.

NEXT ROW k1, p2 tog, p to last 3 sts, p2 tog, k1 tbl.

Rep these 2 rows until 12 sts remain. Work 4 rows without shaping. Cont in st st increasing 1 st at each end of every row until there are 76 sts on needle.

Then work to correspond with the front remembering to dec 12 sts before rib.

Leg bands

With right side of work facing, pick up and k 72 sts along edge of leg. Work 5 rows in double rib (k2, p2). Cast off loosely in rib (best done by holding a needle 2 sizes larger in right hand when casting off).

Making up

Stitch side seams. Thread elastic through holes in rib, or make a crochet cord with a tassel on each end.

Hooded pram-set with mittens

Suitable for boy or girl.

Materials As for feather stitch pram-set YARN MUST BE USED DOUBLE. A strand of yellow and a strand of white look lovely.

Measurements To fit the average baby up to 9 months.

Needles One pair each of 4.5-mm and 3.5-mm (Nos. 7 and 9) needles.

Tension See page 10.

Abbreviations See page 12.

Back

Using 4.5-mm needles cast on 81 sts.

1ST ROW sl 1, *p1, k1. Rep from * to end of row.

2ND ROW sl 1, k1, *p1, k1. Rep from * to last st, k1.

3RD ROW as 2nd row.

4TH ROW as 1st row.

Rep 1st row again.

6TH ROW sl 1, p to last st, k1 tbl.

Cont in pattern as follows (pattern is only to shape coat):

1ST ROW sl 1, sl 1, k1, psso, k24, sl 1, k1, psso, k23, k2 tog, k24, k2 tog, k1.

Commencing with a p row, work 5 rows in st st without shaping, and work 5 rows like this also after 7th, 13th, 19th, 25th and 31st rows.

7TH ROW sl 1, sl 1, k1, psso, k23, sl 1, k1, psso, k21, k2 tog, k23, k2 tog, k1 tbl.

13TH ROW sl 1, sl 1, k1, psso, k22, sl 1, k1, psso, k19, k2 tog, k22, k2 tog, k1 tbl.

19TH ROW sl 1, sl 1, k1, psso, k21, sl 1, k1, psso, k17, k2 tog, k21, k2 tog, k1 tbl.

25TH ROW sl 1, sl 1, k1, psso, k20, sl 1, k1, psso, k15, k2 tog, k20, k2 tog, k1 tbl.

31ST ROW sl 1, sl 1, k1, psso, k19, sl 1, k1, psso, k13, k2 tog, k19, k2 tog, k1 tbl.

37TH ROW sl 1, sl 1, k1, psso, k18, sl 1, k1, psso, k11, k2 tog, k18, k2 tog, k1 tbl (53 sts).

Commencing with a p row work 7 rows in st st without shaping.

Shape for armholes Cast off 2 sts at the beg of the next 2 rows.

1ST ROW sl 1, sl 1, k1, psso, k to last 3 sts, k2 tog, k1 tbl.

2ND ROW sl 1, p to last st, k1 tbl.

3RD ROW sl 1, k to end.

4TH ROW sl 1, p to last st, k1.

Rep 1st and 2nd rows 16 times. Cast off remaining 15 sts.

Left front

Using 4.5-mm needles cast on 47 sts.

1ST ROW sl 1, *p1, k1. Rep from * to end of row.

2ND ROW sl 1, k1, *p1, k1. Rep from * to last st, k1.

3RD ROW as 2nd row.

4TH ROW as 1st row. Rep 1st row once more.

6TH ROW sl 1, (k1, p1) 6 times, k1, p to last 2 sts, inc in next st purlwise, k1 tbl (48 sts).

Proceed as follows:

1ST ROW sl 1, sl 1, k1, psso, k24, sl 1, k1, psso, k5, (k1, p1) 6 times, k2.

2ND ROW sl 1, (p1, k1) 6 times, p to last st, k1 tbl.

3RD ROW sl 1, k to last 14 sts, (p1, k1) 7 times.

4TH ROW sl 1, (k1, p1) 6 times, k1, p to last st, k1 tbl.

5TH ROW sl 1, k to last 14 sts, (k1, p1) 6 times, k2.

6TH ROW sl 1, (p1, k1) 6 times, p to last st, k1 tbl.

7TH ROW sl 1, sl 1, k1, psso, k22, k2 tog, k5, (p1, k1) 7 times.

Keeping the continuity of the st st and double moss st border throughout, work 5 rows without shaping and do the same after 13th, 19th, 25th and 31st rows.

13TH ROW sl 1, sl 1, k1, psso, k21, sl 1, k1, psso, k4, (k1, p1) 6 times, k2.

19TH ROW sl 1, sl 1, k1, psso, k19, k2 tog, k4, (p1, k1) 7 times.

25TH ROW sl 1, sl 1, k1, psso, k18, sl 1, k1, psso, k3, (k1, p1) 6 times, k2.

31ST ROW sl 1, sl 1, k1, psso, k16, k2 tog, k3, (p1, k1) 7 times.

37TH ROW sl 1, sl 1, k1, psso, k15, sl 1, k1, psso, k2, (k1, p1) 6 times, k2 (34 sts).

Work 7 rows without shaping.

Shape for armhole Cast off 2 sts, k to last 14 sts, (k1, p1) 6 times, k2.

2ND ROW sl 1, (p1, k1) 6 times, p to last st, k1 tbl.

3RD ROW sl 1, sl 1, k1, psso, k to last 14 sts, (p1, k1) 7 times.

4TH ROW sl 1, (k1, p1) 6 times, k1, p to last st, k1 tbl.

5TH ROW sl 1, k to last 14 sts, (k1, p1) 6 times, k2.

6TH ROW sl 1, (p1, k1) 6 times, p to last st, k1 tbl.

Keeping the continuity of the st st and the double moss st border throughout dec once at the armhole edge as before on next and every alt row until 22 sts remain.

NEXT ROW sl 1, (k1, p1) 6 times, k1, p to last st, k1 tbl.

Shape neck 1ST ROW sl 1, sl 1, k1, psso, k5, slip the remaining 14 sts on to a holder and leave for neckband.

2ND ROW sl 1, p5, k1 tbl.

3RD ROW sl 1, sl 1, k1, psso, k2, k2 tog.

4TH ROW sl 1, p3, k1 tbl.

5TH ROW sl 1, sl 1, k1, psso, k2.

6TH ROW sl 1, p2, k1 tbl.

7TH ROW (k2 tog) twice.

8TH ROW k2 tog. Break wool and fasten off.

Right front

Using 4.5-mm needles cast on 47 sts.

1ST ROW sl 1, *p1, k1. Rep from * to end of row.

2ND ROW sl 1, k1, *p1, k1. Rep from * to last st, k1.

3RD ROW as 2nd row.

4TH ROW as 1st row.

5TH ROW as 1st row.

6TH ROW inc once in first st, p to last 14

sts, (k1, p1) 6 times, k2.
Proceed as follows
1ST ROW sl 1, (k1, p1) 6 times, k6, k2 tog, k24, k2 tog, k1.
2ND ROW sl 1, p to last 14 sts, (p1, k1) 7 times.
3RD ROW sl 1, (p1, k1) 6 times, p1, k to end of row.
4TH ROW sl 1, p to last 14 sts, (k1, p1) 6 times, k2.
5TH ROW sl 1, (k1, p1) 6 times, k to end of row.
6TH ROW sl 1, p to last 14 sts, (p1, k1) 7 times.
7TH ROW sl 1, (p1, k1) 6 times, p1, k5, sl 1, k1, psso, k22, k2 tog, k1.
Keeping the continuity of the double moss st border and st st throughout, work 5 rows without shaping, also after the 13th, 25th and 31st rows.
13TH ROW sl 1, (k1, p1) 6 times, k5, k2 tog, k21, k2 tog, k1.
19TH ROW sl 1, (p1, k1) 6 times, p1, k4, sl 1, k1, psso, k19, k2 tog, k1.
20TH ROW sl 1, p to last 14 sts, (k1, p1) 6 times, k1.
21ST ROW sl 1, k1, p1, wrn, p2 tog, (k1, p1) 3 times, wrn, p2 tog, k to end of row. Work 3 rows without shaping.
25TH ROW sl 1, (k1, p1) 6 times, k4, k2 tog, k18, k2 tog, k1.
31ST ROW sl 1, (p1, k1) 6 times, p1, k3, sl 1, k1, psso, k16, k2 tog, k1.
37TH ROW sl 1, k1, p1, wrn, p2 tog, (k1, p1) 3 times, wrn, p2 tog, k3, k2 tog, k15, k2 tog, k1 (34 sts).
Work 8 rows without shaping.
Shape armhole 1ST ROW Cast off 2 sts, purlwise, p to last 14 sts, (p1, k1) 7 times.
2ND ROW sl 1, (p1, k1) 6 times, p1, k to last 3 sts, k2 tog, k1.
3RD ROW sl 1, p to the last 14 sts, (k1, p1) 6 times, k2.
4TH ROW sl 1, (k1, p1) 6 times, k to end of row.
5TH ROW sl 1, p to last 14 sts, (p1, k1) 7 times.
Rep the 2nd and 3rd rows once more.
8TH ROW sl 1, k1, p1, wrn, p2 tog, (k1, p1) 3 times, wrn, p2 tog, k to last 3 sts,

k2 tog, k1. Rep 5th row once more.
Keeping the continuity of the double moss st border and st st throughout, dec once at the armhole edge as before in the next and every alt row until 22 sts remain.
NEXT ROW sl 1, p to last 14 sts, (k1, p1) 6 times, k2.
Shape neck 1ST ROW sl the first 14 sts on to a safety pin and leave for the neckband. Join in a second ball of wool to the remaining 8 sts and k5, k2 tog, k1.
2ND ROW sl 1, p5, k1.
3RD ROW k2 tog, k2, k2 tog, k1.
4TH ROW sl 1, p3, k1.
5TH ROW sl 1, k1, k2 tog, k1.
6TH ROW sl 1, p2, k1.
7TH ROW (k2 tog) twice.
8TH ROW k2 tog. Fasten off.

Mittens (attached)
Using 3.5-mm needles cast on 28 sts.
1ST ROW sl 1, k2 *p2, k2, Rep from * to last st, k1.
2ND ROW sl 1, *p2, k2. Rep from * to last 3 sts, p2, k1.
Rep the 1st and 2nd rows 6 times increasing once at each end of the last row (30 sts).
NEXT ROW sl 1, *wlfwd, k2 tog. Rep from * to last st, k1.
Change to 4.5-mm needles and starting with a p row work 13 rows in st st.
Shape top 1ST ROW sl 1, *k2, k2 tog. Rep from * to last st, k1.
2ND, 4TH AND 6TH ROWS sl 1, p to last st, k1.
3RD ROW sl 1, *k1, k2 tog. Rep from * to last st, k1.
5TH ROW sl 1, *k2 tog. Rep from * to last st, k1. Break off wool. Run through remaining sts, draw up and fasten off.
Sew up seams and with 3 strands of wool make 2 cords 35.5 cm (14 in) long to thread through holes at wrists.

Right sleeve
Using 3.5-mm needles cast on 28 sts.
1ST ROW sl 1, k2, *p2, k2. Rep from * to last st, k1.
2ND ROW sl 1, *p2, k2. Rep from * to last 3 sts, p2, k1.

Rep the 1st and 2nd rows 5 times.
Change to 4.5-mm needles and proceed as follows:

1ST ROW sl 1, k to end of row.
2ND ROW sl 1, p to last st, k1.
Rep rows 1 and 2 once more.
Cont in st st increasing once at each end of the next and every following 4th row until there are 38 sts on the needle. Cont without shaping until the work measures 14 cm (5½ in) from the beg ending on the wrong side of work.

Shape for the top Cast off 2 sts at the beg of the next 2 rows. Proceed as follows:

1ST ROW sl 1, sl 1, k1, psso, k to last 3 sts, k2 tog, k1.
2ND ROW sl 1, p to the last st, k1.
3RD ROW sl 1, k to end of row.
4TH ROW sl 1, p to the last st, k1.
Rep from the 1st to the 4th rows inclusive twice.
Rep the 1st and 2nd rows 8 times then the 1st row once (10 sts)**
NEXT ROW sl 1, p to the last st, k1.
Proceed as follows:

1ST ROW cast off 5 sts, k1, k2 tog, k1.
2ND ROW sl 1, p2, k1.
3RD ROW sl 1, k2 tog, k1.
4TH ROW sl 1, p1, k1.
5TH ROW k2 tog, k1.
6TH ROW k2 tog. Break off wool and fasten off.

Left sleeve
Work exactly as given for the right sleeve to **.
Proceed as follows:

1ST ROW cast off 5 sts purlwise, p3, k1.
2ND ROW sl 1, sl 1, k1, psso, k2.
3RD ROW sl 1, p2, k1.
4TH ROW sl 1, sl 1, k1, psso, k1.
5TH ROW sl 1, p1, k1.
6TH ROW sl 1, sl 1, k1, psso.
7TH ROW k2 tog. Break off wool and fasten off.
Using an overstitch join up seams.

Neckband
Using 3.5-mm needles, with the right side of work facing and starting at the right front border, sl 1, k1, p1, wrn, p2 tog, (k1, p1) 3 times, wrn, p2 tog, k1, pick up and k 5 sts evenly along the right side of the neck, 10 sts evenly across the sleeve top, 15 sts evenly from the 15 cast off sts at the back of the neck, 10 sts evenly across the other sleeve top, 6 sts evenly down the left side of the neck and work across the sts of the left front border, (k1, p1) 6 times, k2 (74 sts).

1ST ROW sl 1, (p1, k1) 6 times, p1 (p2, k2) 11 times, p2, (p1, k1) 7 times.
2ND ROW sl 1, (p1, k1) 6 times, p1, (k2, p2) 11 times, k2, (p1, k1) 7 times.
3RD ROW sl 1, (k1, p1) 6 times, k1, (p2, k2) 11 times, p2, (k1, p1) 6 times, k2.
Cast off loosely in pattern.

The hood
Using 3.5-mm needles cast on 68 sts.
1ST ROW sl 1, k2, *p2, k2. Rep from * to last st, k1.
2ND ROW sl 1, *p2, k2. Rep from * to last 3 sts, p2, k1.
Rep the 1st and 2nd rows 3 times increasing once at the end of last row.
Change to 4.5-mm needles and proceed as follows:

1ST ROW sl 1, *p1, k1. Rep from * to end of row.
2ND ROW sl 1, k1, *p1, k1. Rep from * to last st, k1.
3RD ROW sl 1, *k1, p1. Rep from * to last 4 sts, k1, p2 tog, turn.
4TH ROW sl 1, *p1, k1. Rep from * to last 4 sts, p1, k2 tog, turn.
5TH ROW sl 1, *p1, k1. Rep from * to last 5 sts, p1, k2 tog, turn.
6TH ROW sl 1, *p1, k1. Rep from * to last 5 sts, k1, p2 tog, turn.
7TH ROW sl 1, *p1, k1. Rep from * to last 6 sts, k1, p2 tog, turn.
8TH ROW sl 1, *p1, k1. Rep from * to last 6 sts, p1, k2 tog, turn.
Keeping the continuity of the pattern throughout cont in this manner decreasing once in every row until 17 sts remain in the centre (the last row should be worked on the wrong side). Proceed as follows:

1ST ROW sl 1, (p1, k1) 8 times, pick up the loop between the last st worked and the next st and p this loop tog with the next st on the left hand needle (thus avoiding a hole), turn.

2ND ROW sl 1, (p1, k1) 8 times, p1, pick up the loop between the last st worked and the next st and k tog with the next st (thus avoiding a hole), turn.

3RD ROW sl 1, (p1, k1) 9 times, pick up a loop between sts and p tog with next st, turn.

4TH ROW sl 1, (p1, k1) 9 times, p1, pick up loop between sts and k tog with next st, turn.

Cont in this manner working 1 st more in every row, always picking up a loop between the last 2 sts to be worked until all sts are worked on to 1 needle (43 sts). Cast off in pattern.

Making up
Placing the right side of the hood to the right side of the work and commencing 14 sts in from the right front, sew the cast off edge of the hood in position to the neckband of the coat. Attach mittens as for feather stitch pram-set (page 18).

Double-knit matinée coat

Measurements To fit chest 48.5[53.5]cm (19[21]in). Length 24[28]cm (9½[11]in).
Materials 80 gms 3-ply baby yarn used DOUBLE or double-knitting yarn.
3 buttons.
Needles One pair 4-mm (No. 8) needles.
Tension See page 10.
Abbreviations See page 12.

Sleeves
Using 4-mm needles cast on 24[27] sts and k 12[16] rows.
NEXT ROW k2[4] (inc in next st, k1, inc in next st, k2) 4 times, inc in next st, k to end (33[36] sts).
NEXT ROW k1, p to last st, k1.
Cont in st st increasing 1 st at both ends of 3rd and every following 8th row until there are 41[44] sts. Cont on these sts

until work measures 12.5[14.5] cm (5[5¾]in) from cast on edge finishing with a p row.
Shape raglan 1ST ROW cast off 3 sts, k to end.
2ND ROW cast off 3 sts, p to last st, k1 tbl.
3RD ROW k1, k2 tog tbl, k to last 3 sts, k2 tog, k1 tbl.
4TH ROW k1, p to last st, k1 tbl.
Rep 3rd and 4th rows 4[5] times then 3rd row once (23[24] sts). Slip these sts on to a safety pin and leave to one side.

Back and fronts
Knitted in one piece up to the division for armhole. Using 4-mm needles cast on 147[159] sts. K 9 rows.
10TH ROW k5, p to last 5 sts, k5.
Rep 9th and 10th rows until work measures 12.5[15] cm (5[6] in) from cast on edge finishing with a k row.
Divide for armholes NEXT ROW k5, p31[34], cast off 6 sts, p to last 42[45] sts, cast off 6 sts, p to last 5 sts, k5.
Cont on first group of 36[39] sts for right front.
1ST ROW k to last 3 sts, k2 tog, k1.
2ND ROW k1, p to last 5 sts, k5.
Rep these 2 rows 4[5] times more (31[33] sts).
NEXT ROW k7[6], (k2 tog, k1) 8[9] times (23[24] sts). Break off wool.
Rejoin wool to group of 63[69] sts.
Rep 3rd and 4th rows of raglan shaping as on sleeve 5[6] times (53[57] sts).
NEXT ROW k1, k2 tog tbl, k3[2], *k2 tog, k2. Rep from * to last 11[8] sts, k2 tog, k4[1], (k2 tog) twice, k1. 40[42] sts.
Break off wool. Rejoin wool to group of 36[39] sts.
1ST ROW k1, k2 tog tbl, k to end.
2ND ROW k5, p to last st, k1.
Rep these 2 rows 4[5] times more.
NEXT ROW (k1, k2 tog tbl) 8[9] times, k7[6] (23[24] sts).
NEXT ROW k (thus making ridge).
Slip a group of sleeve sts on to left hand needle and using needle holding group of 23[24] sts and with wrong side facing, k across sleeve sts, k across sts of back, then sts of 2nd sleeve and finally sts of

right front (132[138] sts).

Yoke

1ST ROW k.

2ND ROW (buttonhole row) k5, p to last 5 sts, k2, wlfwd, k2 tog, k1.

3RD TO 13TH ROWS as 9th and 10th rows at commencement.

14TH ROW as 2nd row.

15TH ROW k6, *sl 1, k2, psso the k2. Rep from * to last 6 sts, k6, (92[96] sts).

16TH ROW k5, p4[3], *p2 tog, p4. Rep from * to last 11[10] sts, p2 tog, p4[3], k5 (79[82] sts).

17TH TO 19TH ROWS k.

20TH ROW k5, *p2 tog, p1. Rep from * to last 5 sts, k5 (56[58] sts).

21ST TO 23RD ROWS k.

24TH ROW k5, *p2 tog, p1. Rep from * to last 9[8] sts, p2 tog, p2[1], k2, wlfwd, k2 tog, k1 (41[42] sts).

25TH ROW k.

26TH TO 27TH ROWS cast off 3 sts, k to end.

28TH ROW p.

29TH ROW k.

Cast off loosely purlwise.

Making up

Using a flat seam join sleeve seams and raglan shapings. Fold over yoke at top ridge and stitch down cast off edge on wrong side. Sew on buttons.

Pressing See page 12.

Zigzag three-tone toddler dress

Measurements To fit 51 cm (20 in) chest.

Materials 2 × 20gm balls each of pink and white, 4 × 20 gm balls of yellow 3-ply baby yarn. Yarn must be used double throughout. 2 buttons.

Needles One pair each 3-mm, 3.5-mm and 4-mm (Nos. 11, 9 and 8) needles.
Tension See page.
Abbreviations See page 12.

Front

Using 4-mm needles and pink wool, cast on 120 sts and k 2 rows. Change to 3.5-mm needles, start pattern:
1ST ROW *k into front, then into back of next st, k7, sl 1, k1, psso, k2 tog, k7, k into front then into back of next st. Rep from * to end.
2ND ROW p. Break off pink.
These 2 rows form the pattern and are repeated throughout the skirt. Cont in pattern working in stripes as follows: 12 rows white, 12 rows pink, 12 rows yellow, 10 rows white, 8 rows pink, 2 rows yellow. Cont in yellow in st st.
1ST ROW k2 tog all along row (60 sts).
2ND ROW p.
3RD ROW *k1, wlfwd, k2 tog. Rep from * to end of row.
4TH ROW p.
Shape raglan Cast off 2 sts at beg of next 2 rows.
NEXT ROW k1, sl 1, k1, psso, k to last 3 sts, k2 tog, k1.
NEXT ROW k1, p to last st, k1.**
Rep the last 2 rows until 40 sts remain, ending with a p row.
Shape neck NEXT ROW k1, sl 1, k1, psso, k12, turn.
NEXT ROW p to the last st, k1.
NEXT ROW k1, sl 1, k1, psso, k to last 3 sts, k2 tog, k1.
NEXT ROW p to last st, k1.
Rep last 2 rows until all sts are worked off. With right side facing, slip centre 10 sts on to a holder. Rejoin yarn to remaining sts and complete to match first side, reversing shapings.

Back

Work as given for front up to **. Rep the last 2 rows until 50 sts remain, ending with a wrong side row.
Divide for back opening K1, sl 1, k1, psso, k24, turn.
NEXT ROW k4, p to last st, k1.

NEXT ROW k1, sl 1, k1, psso, k to end.
NEXT ROW k4, p to last st, k1.
NEXT ROW (make buttonhole) k1, sl 1, k1, psso, k to last 3 sts, wlfwd, k2 tog, k1.
Cont to shape raglan and work 4 sts in garter st at centre edge until 12 sts remain, working 2nd buttonhole as before on the 12th row from 1st buttonhole. Leave the 12 sts on holder for back neck.
With right side facing rejoin wool to remaining sts. Cast on 4 sts. K to last 3 sts, k2 tog, k1.
Complete to match first side reversing all shapings, keeping 4 sts in garter st at centre edge and omitting buttonholes.

Sleeves

Using 3-mm needles and yellow yarn cast on 40 sts. Work 6 rows in k1, p1 rib. Change to 3.5-mm needles and cont in st st for 8 rows.
Shape raglan Cast off 2 sts at beg of next 2 rows.
NEXT ROW k1, sl 1, k1, psso, k to last 3 sts, k2 tog, k1.
NEXT ROW k1, p to last st, k1.
Rep these last 2 rows until 6 sts remain. Leave on stitch holder.

Neckband

Join raglan seams (overstitch). Using 3-mm needles and with right side facing, k across 12 sts on left back holder, k across 6 sts on left sleeve top, k up 11 sts down left front, k across 10 sts on holder at centre front, k up 11 sts up right front, k across 6 sts of right sleeve, and k across 12 sts of right back neck.
K 5 rows. Cast off loosely.

Making up

Join all seams using overstitch. Sew on buttons. Colours can of course be changed. For example, you may like to use one strand of pink and one strand of white, thus making a very pale flecked pink.

Children's Wear

London cardigan in 4-ply

Measurements To fit 51[56/61/66]cm (20[22/24/26]in) chest.

Materials Using a 4-ply yarn in 25 gm balls, 2 balls each in red, white, royal blue, pale blue and 1 ball of dark green. Also, small amounts of pink, black and grey for the motifs. 7 buttons to match the red.

Needles One pair each of 3.25-mm and 3.5-mm (Nos. 10 and 9).

Tension 18 rows and 14 sts to a 5 cm (2 in) square on 3.5-mm needles in st st.

Abbreviations See page 12.

Note With the motifs I have found on the whole that the garment retains its natural stretch better if 2 balls of base colour yarn are used and kept either side of the motifs where 5 or more sts are involved, rather than attempting to weave. I then sew in all ends or just tie the ends and snip them off. This way the garment stretches naturally and the motifs lie completely flat.

Back

Using 3.25-mm needles and red yarn cast on 65[71/77/83] sts and work 4[5/5/6.5]cm (1½[2/2/2½]in) in single rib. Change to 3.5-mm needles.

1ST ROW Using white yarn k2, *sl 1, k2. Rep from * to end.

2ND ROW Using white yarn p2, *sl 1, p2. Rep from * to end.

Work 2 rows in red in st st.

5TH ROW Using green yarn work as 1st row.

6TH ROW Using green yarn work as 2nd row.

Work 28[28/30/32] rows in st st in white yarn.

NEXT 2 ROWS Using red yarn work as for 1st and 2nd rows.

In white work 2 rows in st st.

In green work 2 rows as for 1st and 2nd rows.

Using royal blue work 20[24/28/32] rows in st st.

Shape armhole Cast off 4[4/5/5] sts at the beg of the next 2 rows. Change to red yarn and work 2 rows as 1st and 2nd rows, but k2 tog at each end of the first of these rows to cont armhole shaping.

In green work 2 rows in st st and again k2 tog at each end of the 1st row.

In white work 2 rows as 1st and 2nd rows, still k2 tog at each end of 1st row.

In pale blue yarn k2 tog, k to last 2 sts, k2 tog.

In pale blue yarn p 1 row then work 26[28/30/32] rows in st st.

Shape shoulders Cast off 10[11/12/13] sts at the beg of the next 2 rows. Cast off.

Sleeves

Using 3.25-mm needles cast on 38[38/41/41] sts in red and work 4[5/5/6.5]cm (1½[2/2/2½]in) in single rib increasing to 44[47/50/53] sts in the last row. Change to 3.5-mm needles.

Work as for back until armhole shaping.

In royal blue cast off 3 sts at start of next 2 rows.

In red work 2 rows as 1st and 2nd row of back, k2 tog at each end of the 1st row.

Again knitting 2 tog at each end of the 1st row, work 2 rows in green.

Again knitting 2 tog at each end of the 1st row, work 2 rows in white.

In pale blue k2 tog, k to last 2 sts, k2 tog.

In pale blue work 9 more rows in st st, and continuing in pale blue shape top of sleeve by knitting 2 tog at each end of every row until 12[15/16/15] sts remain. Cast off.

THE HAT AND SCARF SHOWN WITH THE STRIPED CARDIGAN IN DOUBLE-KNIT ON THE RIGHT ALSO MATCH THE LONDON CARDIGAN

Collar

Using red yarn and 3.25-mm needles cast on 97[101/105/109] sts and work in single moss st for 5 rows (sl 1, *k1, p1. Rep from * to last 2 sts, k1, k1 tbl on every row).

NEXT ROW cast off 13 sts, moss st to the last 13 sts, cast off 13 sts. Break off yarn. Change to 3.5-mm needles and rejoin yarn working in single rib for 5[6/6.5/6.5] cm (2[2¼/2½/2½]in). Cast off. Stitch overlapping moss st border to sides of collar.

Frontbands

Using red and 3.25-mm needles cast on 9 sts and work in single moss st (i.e. sl 1, *k1, p1. Rep from * to last 2 sts, k1, k1 tbl every row). On the 5th row make a buttonhole thus: sl 1, k1, p1, k1, wlfwd, k2 tog, p1, k1, k1 tbl.

Cont in moss st, working a buttonhole every 4.5 cm (1¾ in) until the band fits up the front of the cardigan to start of neck shaping (very slightly stretched). Work another band without buttonholes.

Right front with motifs

Using 3.25-mm needles cast on 32[35/38/41] sts and work 4[5/5/6.5] cm (1½[2/2/2½]in) in single rib. Change to 3.5-mm needles and work 1st to 6th rows as for back. Change to white yarn and work 2[2/4/4] rows in st st. Work motif for guardsman as follows:

1ST ROW k13[14/16/18] white, 2 black, 1 white, 2 black, 14[16/17/18] white.

2ND ROW p14[16/17/18] white, 2 black, 1 white, 2 black, 14[14/16/18] white.

3RD TO 6TH ROWS Rep the last 2 rows twice more.

7TH ROW k11[12/14/16] white, 1 pink, 1 white, 5 red, 1 white, 1 pink, 12[14/15/16] white.

8TH ROW p11[13/14/15] white, 2 pink, 1 white, 5 red, 1 white, 2 pink, 10[11/13/15] white.

9TH ROW k10[11/13/15] white, 2 red, 1 white, 5 red, 1 white, 2 red, 11[13/14/15] white.

10TH ROW p10[13/14/15] white, 2 red, 1 white, 5 red, 1 white, 2 red, 10[11/13/15] white.

11TH ROW k10[11/13/15] white, 2 red, 1 white, 5 black, 1 white, 2 red, 11[13/14/15] white.

12TH ROW as 10th row.

13TH AND 14TH ROWS as 9th and 10th rows.

15TH ROW k10[11/13/15] white, 11 red, 11[13/14/15] white.

16TH ROW p12[14/15/16] white, 9 red, 11[12/14/16] white.

17TH ROW k14[15/17/19] white, 3 pink, 15[17/18/19] white.

18TH ROW p14[16/17/18] white, 5 pink, 13[14/16/18] white.

19TH ROW k13[14/16/18] white, 5 pink, 14[16/17/18] white.

20TH ROW p14[16/17/18] white, 5 black, 13[14/16/18] white.

21ST ROW k12[13/15/17] white, 7 black, 13[15/16/17] white.

22ND ROW p13[15/16/17] white, 7 black, 12[13/15/17] white.

23RD ROW k as 21st row.

24TH ROW p as 20th row.

Now work 2[2/2/4] rows in st st in white.

Change to red yarn and work as 1st and 2nd rows of back.

Change to white and work 2 rows in st st.

Change to green and work as 1st and 2nd rows of back.

Change to royal blue and work 2[4/6/8] rows in st st.

Work motif for bus as follows:

1ST ROW k9[10/12/14] royal, 1 black, 12 royal, 1 black, 9[11/12/13] royal.

2ND ROW p6[8/9/10] royal, 2 red, 3 black, 10 red, 3 black, 2 red, 6[7/9/11] royal.

3RD ROW k6[7/9/11] royal, 3 red, 1 black, 12 red, 1 black, 3 red, 6[8/9/10] royal.

4TH ROW p6[8/9/10] royal, 20 red, 6[7/9/11] royal.

5TH ROW k6[7/9/11] royal, 20 white, 6[8/9/10] royal.

6TH ROW p6[8/9/10] royal, (2 white, 2 grey) 3 times, 2 white, 4 grey, 2 white, 6[7/9/11] royal.

7TH ROW k6[7/9/11] royal, 2 white, 4

grey, (2 white, 2 grey) 3 times, 2 white, 6[8/9/10] royal.

8TH ROW p6[8/9/10] royal, 20 white, 6[7/9/11] royal.

9TH ROW k6[7/9/11] royal, 20 red, 6[8/9/10] royal.

10TH ROW p6[8/9/10] royal, 20 red, 6[7/9/11] royal.

11TH ROW k6[7/9/11] royal, 20 red, 6[8/9/10] royal.

12TH ROW p6[8/9/10] royal, 20 white, 6[7/9/11] royal.

13TH ROW as 7th row.

14TH ROW as 6th row.

15TH ROW k6[7/9/11] royal, 20 white, 6[8/9/10] royal. 16TH ROW as 10th row.

Continuing in royal, work 1[3/5/7] rows in st st.

Shape armholes Cast off 4[4/5/5] sts at the beg of the next row.

Change to red yarn and work as for 1st and 2nd rows of back, but p2 tog at start of the 2nd row to cont armhole shaping.

In green, work 2 rows of st st again p2 tog at start of 2nd row.

In white work 2 rows as 1st and 2nd rows of back, but p2 tog at start of 2nd row.

In pale blue work 2 rows st st but p2 tog at start of 2nd row.

Work 14[14/16/16] rows in st st in pale blue.

Shape neck as follows Cast off 2 sts at beg of next row (neck edge), k to end. P 1 row.

NEXT ROW k2 tog, k to end.

Rep last 2 rows once more. Then, still continuing in pale blue and st st, work until armhole measures same as back to shoulder.

Shape shoulders Cast off 10[11/12/14] sts at the beg of the next 2 rows, starting at the armhole edge.

Left front

Work exactly as for right front, reversing all shapings.

Making up

Sew up garment using overstitch or flatstitch. Sew buttonhole frontband to left or right side of front according to whether you want the garment for a boy or a girl. Pin collar into position round neck and then sew on using a flat seam. Sew on buttons.

Pressing If you wish press very lightly with a cool iron and dry cloth; but do be very careful about acrylic yarns as pressing can take all life from the yarn, making it go limp and shapeless. It is better to just press the garment into shape with your hands and fold it carefully.

London cardigan in double-knit

Measurements To fit 66-81.5cm (26-32 in) chest.

Materials Using double-knitting weight yarn in 25 gm balls, 3[4/4/4] balls each of red, white and royal, 2[3/3/3] balls of blue, 1 ball dark green and small amounts of pink, black and grey for motifs, 7 buttons to match.

Needles One pair each 3.5-mm and 4.5-mm (Nos. 9 and 7) needles.

Tension See page 10.

Abbreviations See page 12.

Exactly follow the pattern for the 4-ply London cardigan on page 45 but use 3.5-mm needles instead of 3.25-mm and 4.5-mm needles instead of 3.5-mm — this will automatically bring the size of the cardigan up by 3 sizes (i.e. the 51 cm pattern will become a 66 cm, the 61 cm a 76 cm and the 66 cm a 81.5 cm). THE ONE ALTERATION NECESSARY is to adjust the sleeve length to be in proportion to the larger sizes, and this is done by simply working 6 extra rows in the white and the royal blue, and 4 extra rows in blue at the top of the sleeve after the armhole shaping and before the top shaping (13 rows instead of 9 after armhole shaping of sleeve). Also you may prefer to have the buttonholes further spaced to be, on these larger sizes, 5-6 cm (2-2¼ in) apart.

Make up as for the 4-ply cardigan. Also note pressing instructions for the 4-ply version.

Matching hat and scarf

Measurements Scarf 122 cm (48 in) long + fringe (2nd size 132 cm (52 in) long + fringe).
Materials Using 4-ply, 6 × 25 gm balls colour A — small amounts of other colours that hopefully may be left over from other garments.
Needles One pair of 5.5-mm (No. 5) needles.
Tension See page 10.
Abbreviations See page 12.
For colour suggestions see page 51.

There are instructions for two sizes here. The first should fit younger children, say up to about 6 years of age and the second size should fit all older children covered by the cardigans in this book. Being in a double rib it is stretchy and adaptable.

Hat

Using the yarn DOUBLE and with 5.5-mm needles and A cast on 66[74] sts and work in double rib (k2, p2) always slipping the first st and knitting into the back of the last st, to give neat edges. Work 2 rows in A, 6 rows in B, 6 rows in C and 6 rows in D. Then cont in A until work measures 19[23] cm (7½[9]in). Change to garter st and shape top as follows:

1ST ROW sl 1, *k6, k2 tog. Rep from * to last st, k1.
2ND AND ALT ROWS k.
3RD ROW sl 1, *k5, k2 tog. Rep from * to last st, k1.
5TH ROW sl 1, *k4, k2 tog. Rep from * to last st, k1.
7TH ROW sl 1, *k3, k2 tog. Rep from * to last st, k1.
9TH ROW sl 1, *k2, k2 tog. Rep from * to last st, k1.

11TH ROW sl 1,. *k1, k2 tog. Rep from * to last st, k1.
12TH ROW k2 tog all along row then draw wool through the remaining sts.
Sew up with flatstitch or overstitch. Fold back brim to depth required.

Scarf

Using yarn DOUBLE, with 5.5-mm needles and A cast on 26[30] sts and work in double rib as with the hat, again making sure to sl first st and k into back of last st to give neat edges. Work 2 rows in A, 8 in B, 8 in C and 8 in D. Then work in A until the scarf measures 112[122]cm (44[48]in). Work 8 rows in D, 8 in C, 8 in B and 2 in A. Cast off. Fringe in A (or any colour you prefer) using 15-20.5 cm (6 to 8 in) strands 7[9] times at each end of scarf.

Striped cardigan in 4-ply

Without the motifs the same cardigan can be made in a lovely variety of colours: soft colours, rich colours, tone on tone, and so on. There are so many exciting colours available to knitters now, that a cardigan like this could be made again and again looking totally different each time. For this pattern without motifs I shall call the base colour used for welts and collar A, first contrast colour B, 2nd contrast C and 3rd contrast D. There are just the 4 colours used.

Measurements To fit 51[56/61/66]cm (20[22/24/26]in) chest.
Materials Using 4-ply 2[2/2/2] × 25gm balls in colours A, B and C, 1[2/2/2] × 25 gm balls in D, 7 buttons to match.
Needles One pair each 3.25-mm and 3.5-mm (Nos. 10 and 9) needles.
Tension See page 10.
Abbreviations See page 12.

Back

Using 3.25-mm needles and A cast on

<table>
<tr><th colspan="3">Colour suggestions</th></tr>
<tr><td>1</td><td></td><td>2</td></tr>
</table>

Colour suggestions

1		2
Red = **A** =	French navy
White = **B** =	White
Royal = **C** =	Mid blue
Pale blue = **D** =	Camel

3		4
Navy = **A** =	Navy
Rust = **B** =	Royal blue
Camel = **C** =	Emerald
Cream = **D** =	Silver grey

5		6
Bottle green = **A** =	Burgundy
White = **B** =	Air force blue
Pale blue = **C** =	Dusky pink
Beige = **D** =	Pinky beige tone

7		8
Yellow = **A** =	Navy
Bottle green = **B** =	Rust
Camel = **C** =	Mid blue
Cream = **D** =	Cream

These colour blends are only suggestions — but they may help. They can also be used for the matching sleeveless slipover and the hat and scarf set, pages 52 and 50.

65[71/77/83] sts and work 4[5/5/6.5]cm (1½[2/2/2½]in) in single rib. Change to 3.5-mm needles.
1ST ROW using B, k2, *sl 1, k2. Rep from * to end.
2ND ROW using B, p2, *sl 1, p2. Rep from * to end.
Work 2 rows in A in st st.
5TH ROW using D work as 1st row.
6TH ROW using D work as 2nd row.
Work 28[28/30/32] rows in B in st st.
NEXT 2 ROWS using A work as for 1st and 2nd rows.
Using B work 2 rows in st st.
Using D work 2 rows as 1st and 2nd rows.
Using C work 20[24/28/32] rows in st st.
Shape armholes Cast off 4[4/5/5] sts at beg of next 2 rows.
Change to A and work 2 rows as 1st and 2nd rows, knitting 2 sts tog at each end of the 1st of these 2 rows to cont armhole shaping.

Again k2 tog at each end of 1st row using D, work 2 rows in st st.
Again k2 tog at each end of 1st row using B, work 2 rows as 1st and 2nd rows.
Using D k2 tog, k to last 2 sts, k2 tog.
Using D p 1 row.
Continuing in D and in st st work 26[28/30/32] rows.
Shape shoulders Cast off 10[11/12/13] sts at beg of next 2 rows. Cast off.

Fronts
Using 3.25-mm needles and A cast on 32[35/38/41] sts and work in single rib for 4[5/5/6.5]cm (1½[2/2/2½]in). Change to 3.5-mm needles.
Work as for the back working armhole shaping on one side only (reversing shaping for 2nd front). Cont to work as for back until 14 rows of the yoke in D have been worked. Still working in D, shape neck as follows:

Cast off 2 sts at the neck edge (reverse sides for each front) at the beg of the 15th or 16th row according to which side neck shaping is, and work 2 sts tog at this same side on the following row. Then work in st st until the armhole measures same as for back. Shape shoulder by casting off 10[11/12/13] sts at beg of next 2 rows starting at the armhole edge.

Sleeves
Using 3.25-mm needles cast on 38[38/41/41] sts in A and work 4[5/5/6.5]cm (1½[2/2/2½]in) in single rib increasing to 44[47/50/53] sts in last row. Change to 3.5-mm needles and work as for back until armhole shaping reached.
Shape armholes Cast off 3 sts at beg of next 2 rows and then k2 tog at each end of the next 4 alt rows while still continuing pattern as on back. Work 9 more rows in D and then shape top of sleeve by knitting 2 tog at each end of every row until 12[15/16/15] sts remain. Cast off.

Collar

Using A and 3.25-mm needles cast on 97[101/105/109] sts and work in single moss st for 5 rows (sl 1, *k1, p1. Rep from * to last 2 sts, k1, k1 tbl, every row).
NEXT ROW Cast off 13 sts, moss st to last 13 sts, cast off these 13 sts. Break off yarn. Change to 4.5-mm needles and rejoin yarn working in single rib for 5[6/6/6.5]cm (2[2¼/2½/2½]in). Cast off. Stitch overlapping moss st border to sides of collar.

Frontbands

Using A and 3.25-mm needles cast on 9 sts and work in single moss st (i.e. sl 1, *k1, p1. Rep from * to last 2 sts, k1, k1 tbl, every row). On the 5th row make a buttonhole thus: sl 1, k1, p1, k1, wlfwd, k2 tog, p1, k1, k1 tbl. Cont in moss st work a buttonhole every 4.5 cm (1¾ in) until band fits up the front of the cardigan to start of neck shaping (very slightly stretched).
For making up and pressing follow instructions given for cardigan with motifs.

Striped cardigan in double-knit

Measurements To fit 66[71/76/81.5]cm (26[28/30/32]in) chest.
Materials Of double-knitting yarn 3[4/4/4] × 25 gm balls in colours A, B and C. 2[3/3/3] × 25 gm balls in D. 7 buttons.
Needles One pair each 3.5-mm and 4.5-mm (Nos. 9 and 7) needles.
Tension See page 10.
Abbreviations See page 12.

Follow pattern exactly as for 4-ply cardigan, using 3.5-mm needles instead of 3.25-mm and 4.5-mm needles instead of 3.5-mm. This will automatically bring the size of the cardigan up by 3 sizes as for the one with motifs on page 49. As

with that pattern THE ONE ALTERATION NECESSARY is to adjust the sleeve length to be in proportion with the larger sizes, simply by working 6 extra rows in B and C, and 4 extra rows in D at the top of the sleeve after the armhole shaping, and before top shaping (13 rows instead of 9). Again, you may prefer to place the buttonholes a little further apart.
Follow making up and pressing instructions as for London cardigan, see page 49.

Matching sleeveless slipover in 4-ply

Measurements To fit 51[56/61/66]cm (20[22/24/26]in) chest. Instructions for larger sizes given in brackets.
Materials Of 4-ply yarn 1 × 25 gm ball each of colours B, C and D, 1 + balls of A.
Needles One pair each of 3.25-mm and 3.5-mm (Nos. 10 and 9) needles.
Abbreviations See page 12.
Tension See page 10.
Colours see page 51, 4-ply cardigan.

Back and front alike

Work as for the back of the 4-ply striped cardigan (page 50) up to the armholes
WITH ONE ALTERATION. ONLY WORK 18[20/22/24] rows of st st in both colours B and C, and then in A. Work 2 rows as 1st and 2nd rows.
Shape armholes Using D cast off 3 sts at the beg of the next 2 rows.
NEXT ROW k2 tog, k23[26/28/31] sts, cast off next 9[9/11/11] sts, k to last 2 sts, k2 tog. Work on the last set of sts remaining with D. Dec 1 st at the armhole edge on the next 6[7/8/9] rows and AT THE SAME TIME dec 1 st at the neck edge on the next 7[8/8/9] rows (11[12/13/14] sts).
Work without shaping until armhole measures 11[12/13.5/14.5]cm

(4¼[4¾/5¼/5¾]in) ending with
a k row.
With wrong side facing rejoin yarn to
remaining sts and work to match first
side.

Neckband

Join right shoulder seam. With right side
facing, using 3.25-mm needles and A,
join yarn at the top of left side and k up
34[38/42/46] sts down side of neck,
10[10/12/12] sts from cast off centre
front sts, 34[38/42/46] sts up 2nd side
of neck, 34[38/42/46] sts up one side of
back neck, 10[10/12/12] sts across cast
off sts at centre back and 34[38/42/46]
sts up other side of back
(156[172/192/208] sts). Work 6 rows in
single rib and cast off ribwise.

Armhole Bands

Join shoulder seams. With right side
facing and using 3.25-mm needles and A
join yarn at beg of armhole and k up
62[70/78/86] sts evenly all round edge.
Work 6 rows in single rib. Cast off ribwise.
Sew up rest of garment and for making
up and pressing instructions follow those
for London cardigan, page 49.

Rugby-style sweater

Measurements To fit
51[56/61/66/71]cm
(20[22/24/26/28]in) chest.
Materials Sweater: In each of colours A
and B 4[4/5/5/6] × 25 gm balls double-
knitting yarn. 3 buttons.
Needles One pair each 4-mm, 5-mm,
5.5-mm and 6-mm (Nos. 8, 6, 5 and 4)
needles.
Tension See page 10.
Abbreviations See page 12.

Front

Using 4-mm needles and colour A cast
on 46[50/56/60/66] sts and work in
single rib for 8 rows. Change to 5-mm

needles and work in st st in stripes of 8
rows B and 8 rows A until work
measures 19[20.5/23/25.5/28]cm
(7½[8/9/10/11]in) from beg. Mark ends
of last row with a coloured thread to
show end of side seam.
NEXT ROW work 21[23/26/28/31] sts,
turn. Cont working on these sts in same
stripes until work measures 6.5[6.5/
7.5/9/10]cm (2½[2½/3/3½/4]in)
from row marked with threads finishing
at centre (neck) edge. Shape neck by
casting off 2[2/2/3/3] sts and p to end.
NEXT ROW k to last 2 sts, k2 tog tbl.
NEXT ROW p.
Rep last two rows 2[2/2/3/3] times
more, then cont without shaping until
work measures 10[11.5/13/14/15]cm
(4[4½/5/5½/6]in) from start of neck
opening, ending at armhole edge.
To shape shoulders Cast off at shoulder
edge:
size 51 cm: 5 sts twice, then 6 sts
size 56 cm: 6 sts 3 times
size 61 cm: 7 sts 3 times
size 66 cm: 7 sts 3 times
size 71 cm: 8 sts 3 times.
Rejoin yarn to centre front. Cast off 4 sts
and then work on remaining sts to match
1st side, reversing all shapings.

Back

Work as for front until row marked with
threads and cont without shaping until
work measures 29[32/35.5/39.5/43]cm
(11½[12½/14/15½/17]in) and shape
shoulders as on fronts. Cast off
remaining sts.

Sleeves

Using 4-mm needles cast on
33[33/35/37/41] sts and work in single
rib for 5 cm (2 in), increasing 10 sts on
last row. Work in stripes as for back and
front until sleeve measures
21.5[23/25.5/28/30.5]cm
(8½[9/10/11/12]in). Cast off VERY
LOOSELY.

Front buttonhole band

Using 3.5-mm needles and colour A, cast

on 7 sts.
1ST ROW sl 1, *k1, p1. Rep from * to end.
2ND ROW sl 1, *p1, k1. Rep from * to end. Rep these 2 rows once more.
NEXT ROW (Make buttonhole): sl 1, *k1, wlfwd, k2 tog, p1, k1, k1 tbl.
Cont in rib making 2 more buttonholes 2.5 cm (1 in) apart. When band measures 7.5 cm (3 in) cast off ribwise. Make another band the same length but - without the buttonholes.

Collar
Using 3.5-mm needles and colour A cast on 70[70/74/78/82] sts and work in single rib for 2.5 cm (1 in). Change to 5-mm needles and cont in rib until work measures 6.5[6.5/7/7/7.5]cm (2½[2½/2¾/2¾/3]in), ending with a wrong side row. Cast off loosely in rib.

Making up
Using flatstitch or overstitch join shoulder side seams and sleeve seams. Set in sleeves. Stitch buttonhole and button bands into position (boy's buttoning) placing base of bands to cast off section at centre front so that bands neatly overlap. Stitch collar into position.

Matching hat and scarf

Hat
Materials Of 25 gm balls double-knitting yarn 2 balls in A and 1 ball in B.
Crown Using 5.5-mm needles, cast on 72 sts and work in single rib for 5 rows. Change to st st until work measures 9 cm (3½ in) from start.
Shape top
1ST ROW *k6, k2 tog. Rep from * to end.
2ND AND EVERY ALT ROW p.
3RD ROW *k5, k2 tog. Rep from * to end.
5TH ROW *k4, k2 tog. Rep from * to end.
7TH ROW *k3, k2 tog. Rep from * to end.
9TH ROW *k2, k2 tog. Rep from * to end.
11TH ROW *k1, k2 tog. Rep from * to end.
13TH ROW k2 tog all along row.

14TH ROW p.
15TH ROW k.
16TH ROW p.
17TH ROW k2 tog all along row.
Draw thread through remaining sts and fasten off.
Brim Using 6-mm needles, cast on 22 sts in colour A.
1ST ROW k.
2ND ROW k3, p to last 3 sts, k3. Carry on in stripes of 8 rows A and 8 rows B until brim fits LOOSELY round cast on edge of crown, finishing with a B stripe. Cast off. Stitch seam of crown. Sew brim to cast on edge of hat without stretching, Make a pom-pon for top as on scarf. Fold brim over.

Scarf
Materials Of 25 gm balls double-knitting yarn in each of colours A and B 2[2/3/3/3] balls.
Using 5-mm needles and colour A, cast on 44 sts and work in st st, 8 rows A and 8 rows B until scarf measures 91.5[91.5/96.5/107/122]cm 36[36/38/42/48]in) (Treat these measurements as a guide, working so that scarf finishes with 8 rows of colour A, as it started). Sew scarf up to form a tube. Gather ends and finish with a pom-pom in colour B at each gathered end.

Jacquard cardigan

Measurements To fit 51[56/61/66/71/76]cm (20[22/24/26/28/30]in) chest. Instructions for larger sizes given in brackets.
Materials Of 25 gm balls double-knitting yarn 6[6/7/8/10/12] balls in main colour and 1 ball in each of 5 contrast colours. 4[4/5/5/6/6] buttons.
Needles One pair each 3.5-mm, 5-mm and 5.5-mm (Nos. 9, 6 and 5) needles.
Tension See page 10.
Abbreviations See page 12.

Boy's style

Back

Using 3.5-mm needles and main shade cast on 49[53/61/65/73/81] sts and work in single rib for 5[6.5/6.5/7.5/7.5/9]cm (2[2½/2½/3/3/3½]in). Change to 5.5-mm needles and beg with a k row work in st st from the chart from row 1 to row 36[40/40/44/50/54] until work measures 24[24/25.5/28/29/30.5]cm (9½[9½/10/11/11½/12]in). Rep from row 1 if needed to get correct length.

Shape armholes Still working pattern as from the chart cast off 2[2/3/3/4/4] sts at start of next 2 rows and then 1 st at each end of next 2[2/3/3/2/4] rows. Cont without further shaping, still following the chart until work measures 33[35.5/38/40.5/43/46]cm (13[14/15/16/17/18]in) from beg.

Shape shoulders Cast off 6[6/7/8/8/9] sts at the beg of the next 4 rows. Cast off.

First front

Using 3.5-mm needles cast on 25[25/29/33/37/41] sts and work in single rib for 5[5/6.5/7.5/7.5/9]cm (2[2/2½/3/3/3½]in). Change to 5.5-mm needles and beg with a k row work in st st from chart as on back up to armholes.

Shape armhole Cast off 2[2/3/3/4/4] sts at the armhole edge of the next 2 alt rows and then k2 tog at the armhole edge of the next 2[2/3/3/2/4] rows AT THE SAME TIME shaping the front slope by knitting 2 tog at the front edge on first armhole shaping row and every following 3rd row (front edge) until 12[12/14/16/16/18] sts remain. Cont without shaping until work measures same as back.

Shape shoulders Cast off 6[6/7/8/8/9] sts at the armhole edge of the following 2 alt rows. Work second front to match, reversing all shapings.

90	0	0	0	0	0
89	5	0	5	0	5
88	5	0	5	0	5
87	5	5	5	5	5
86	4	5	4	5	4
85	4	5	4	5	4
84	0	0	0	0	0
83	0	0	0	0	0
82	0	0	0	0	0
81	2	2	1	2	2
80	1	2	2	2	1
79	2	2	1	2	2
78	1	2	2	2	1
77	1	1	2	1	1
76	1	1	2	1	1
75	1	2	2	2	1
74	2	2	1	2	2
73	1	2	2	2	1
72	2	2	1	2	2
71	1	2	2	2	1
70	0	0	0	0	0
69	0	0	0	0	0
68	0	0	0	0	0
67	3	0	0	0	3
66	3	3	0	3	3
65	4	3	3	3	4
64	4	4	3	4	4
63	4	3	3	3	4
62	4	3	3	3	4
61	3	3	5	3	3
60	3	5	5	5	3
59	3	3	5	3	3
58	3	3	5	3	3
57	4	3	3	3	4
56	4	4	3	4	4
55	4	3	3	3	4
54	3	0	0	0	3
53	3	0	0	0	3
52	0	0	0	0	0
51	0	0	0	0	0
50	2	2	1	1	2
49	1	2	2	1	1
48	1	1	2	2	1
47	2	1	1	2	2
46	2	2	1	1	2
45	1	2	2	1	1
44	3	3	3	3	3
43	3	3	3	3	3

Row					
42	4	4	4	4	4
41	4	4	4	4	4
40	0	0	0	0	0
39	5	0	0	0	5
38	0	5	0	5	0
37	2	2	5	2	2
36	0	2	2	2	0
35	0	0	2	0	0
34	0	2	2	2	0
33	2	2	5	2	2
32	0	5	0	5	0
31	5	0	0	0	5
30	0	0	0	0	0
29	3	3	4	3	3
28	3	4	4	4	3
27	3	3	4	3	3
26	3	4	4	4	3
25	4	3	4	3	4
24	0	0	0	0	0
23	0	0	0	0	0
22	2	2	2	2	2
21	2	2	2	2	2
20	1	1	1	1	1
19	2	1	1	1	2
18	1	2	1	2	1
17	2	1	2	1	2
16	1	2	2	2	1
15	2	2	2	2	2
14	0	2	2	2	0
13	2	0	2	0	2
12	0	2	0	2	0
11	2	0	0	0	2
10	0	0	0	0	0
9	1	0	0	0	1
8	0	1	0	1	0
7	1	0	1	0	1
6	0	1	1	1	0
5	1	1	1	1	1
4	2	2	2	2	2
3	2	2	2	2	2
2	1	1	1	1	1
1	1	1	1	1	1

4 pattern sts.

Last st on knit rows./
First st on purl rows.

Sleeves

Using 3.5-mm needles cast on 32[32/34/34/36/36] sts and work in single rib for 5[5/5/6.5/6.5/7.5]cm (2[2/2/2½/2½/3]in).

NEXT ROW rib, inc 6 sts evenly across the row (38[38/40/40/42/42] sts).

Colour Suggestions

Natural base		Navy base
Natural =	0	= Navy
Brown =	1	= Sky blue
Sky blue =	2	= Cream
Burgundy =	3	= Cream
School grey =	4	= Red
Gold =	5	= Burgundy

Grey base		Sky blue base
School grey =	0	= Sky blue
Red =	1	= Mid blue
Navy =	2	= Natural
White =	3	= School grey
Mid blue =	4	= Gold
Yellow =	5	= Dark green

Brown base		Red base
Chocolate =	0	= Red
Sky blue =	1	= Navy
Natural =	2	= White
Natural =	3	= School grey
Camel =	4	= Mid blue
Gold =	5	= Gold

Change to 5-mm needles and work in st st, increasing 1 st at each end of 6th and every following 6th row until there are 46[46/50/54/60/66] sts on needles. Cont on these sts until work measures 23[24/24/29/32/35.5]cm (9[9½/9½/11½/12½/14]in).

Shape top Cast off 3 sts at the beg of the next 2 rows and then 2 sts at the beg of next 10 rows, then 1 st at beg of next 8 rows. Cast off.

Frontband
Using 3.5-mm needles cast on 12 sts and work in single rib, always slipping the first st and knitting into the back of the last st to give nice neat edges. On the 3rd row make a buttonhole (rib 5, wlfwd, work 2 tog, rib 5). Cont to work a buttonhole every 5 cm (2 in) until 4[4/5/5/6/6] in all have been worked then cont in single rib until the band is the right length to fit round the cardigan. Cast off ribwise.

Making up
When stitching on the front band PIN CENTRE OF BAND TO CENTRE OF NECK so that there is even length of band both sides of the cardigan. Buttoning can be either boy's or girl's way, whichever is required.

Basket stitch sleeveless slipover

Measurements 56[61/66/71/76]cm (22[24/26/28/30]in).
Materials 5[5/6/7/8] × 25 gm balls of double-knitting yarn.
Needles One pair each 3.25-mm and 5-mm (Nos. 10 and 6) needles.
Tension See page 10.
Abbreviations See page 12.

Back
Using 3.25-mm needles cast on 58[58/66/74/82] sts and work 6[6.5/7/7.5/7.5]cm (2¼[2½/2¾/3/3]in) single rib.
Change to 5-mm needles and basket st pattern as follows.
ROW 1 k1* k4, p4. Rep from * to last st, k1 tbl.
Rep this row 3 times.
ROW 5 sl 1, *p4, k4. Rep from * to last st, k1 tbl.
Rep this row 3 times.
These 8 rows form the basket st pattern which is used throughout the garment other than welts, neckband and armbands.
Cont without shaping until back measures 15[16.5/18/19/20.5]cm (6[6½/7/7½/8]in) from beg.

Shape armhole Cast off 6[6/6/7/7] sts at beg of the next 2 rows.
Cont without further shaping and keeping pattern correct until work measures 30.5[33/35.5/38/40.5]cm (12[13/14/15/16]in) from beg.
Shape shoulders Cast off 8[8/10/11/13] sts at beg of next 4 rows, leave remaining 14[14/14/16/16] sts on spare needle.

Front
Work as for back until armhole shaping.
Shape armhole Cast off 6[6/6/7/7] sts at beg of next 2 rows. Work without further dec until front measures 20.5[21.5/24/25.5/28]cm (8[8½/9½/10/11]in) from beg.
Shape 'V' as follows.
Pattern 23[23/27/30/34] sts, turn. Work 1 row.
Dec 1 st at 'V' edge (inside edge) on every alt row until 16[16/20/22/26] sts remain. Cont without shaping until front measures 30.5[33/35.5/38/40.5]cm (12[13/14/15/16]in) from beg ending at armhole edge.
Shape shoulder Cast off 8[8/10/11/13] sts at beg of next and following alt row. Rejoin yarn to other group of sts and work to correspond with first side, reversing all shapings.
Sew left shoulder seam.

Neckband

Using 3.25-mm needles pick up 23[27/27/31/31] sts down left front, 1 st from centre (mark this st), 23[27/27/31/31] sts from right front and sts from back of neck. Work 6 rows in single rib, dec 1 st each side of centre st on every row. Cast off ribwise.

Armbands

Stitch other shoulder seam. Using 3.25-mm needles pick up 85[92/96/100/102] sts round armhole and work 4[4/4/6/6] rows in single rib. Cast off ribwise.

Making up

Sew side seams and neckband. Sew in all ends.

Tyrolean-style cardigan

Measurements 56/61/66 cm (22/24/26 in) (For 66 cm size follow 61 cm pattern using 3.25-mm and 4-mm needles)
Materials 8[9/10] × 25 gm balls of double-knitting yarn. 7 buttons.
Needles One pair each 3-mm and 3.5-mm (Nos. 11 and 9) needles. For size 66 cm use 3.25-mm and 4-mm (Nos. 10 and 8) needles.
Tension See page 10.
Abbreviations See page 12.

Right front

Using 3-mm needles cast on 34[38] sts and work in single rib for 5[6]cm (2[2¼]in). Change to 3.5-mm needles and work in pattern as follows:
1ST ROW k23, (p1, k3) 2[3] times, p1, k2.
2ND AND ALT ROWS (p3, k1) 3[4] times,p22.
3RD ROW k2, MB, (MB = p1, k1, p1, k1 into next st making 4 sts out of this st, turn, k4, turn, p4, sl 2nd, 3rd and 4th st over first st), k18, (p1, k3) 3[4] times, p1.
5TH ROW k4, MB, k18, (p1, k3) 2[3] times, p1, k2.

7TH ROW k2, MB, k3, MB, k14, (p1, k3) 3[4] times, p1.
9TH ROW k8, MB, k14, (p1, k3) 2[3] times, p1, k2.
11TH ROW k2, MB, k7, MB, k10, (p1, k3) 3[4] times, p1.
13TH ROW k5, MB, k6, MB, k3, MB, k6, (p1, k3) 2[3] times, p1, k2.
15TH ROW as 11th row.
17TH ROW as 9th row.
19TH ROW as 7th row.
21ST ROW as 5th row.
22ND ROW (p3, k1) 3[4] times, p22.
LARGER SIZES ONLY — 23rd row as 3rd row
                    — 24th row (p3, k1) 4
                        times, p22.
Note Rows 3-22 inclusive form pattern on smaller size.
Rows 1-24 inclusive form pattern on larger size.
BOTH SIZES: Rep rows 3-22 [1-24] once then rep rows 3-19 [1-19] once keeping pattern correct.
Shape armhole Cast off 3[4] sts at beg of next row. Dec 1 st at armhole edge on every row until 26[28] sts remain. Work 21[22] rows, thus finishing at the end of a 6th [24th] row of pattern. Omitting bobbles but keeping remainder of pattern correct
Shape neck Work as follows.
Cast off 4[4] sts at beg of next row. Dec 1 st at neck edge on every row until 18[20] sts remain. Cont on these sts until work measures 11[11.5]cm (4¼[4½]in) from beg of armhole shaping, finishing at armhole edge.
Shape shoulder Work as follows.
1ST ROW cast off 6[7] sts, work to end.
2ND ROW work across row.
Rep these 2 rows once. Cast off.

Left front

Work to match right front reversing all shapings and noting the pattern rows should read from end to beg i.e. — k2, p1, (k3, p1) 2[3] times, k23.
2ND AND ALT ROWS p22, (k1, p3) 3[4] times.
3RD ROW p1 (k3, p1) 3[4] times, k18, MB, k2, etc.

Back

Using 3-mm needles cast on 64[68] sts and work in single rib for 5[6]cm (2[2¼]in) increasing 1 st at end of last row.

Change to 3.5-mm needles and work pattern as follows:

1ST ROW *k3, p1. Rep from * to last st, k1.
2ND ROW p2, *k1, p3. Rep from * to last 3 sts, k1, p2.
3RD ROW k1, *p1, k3. Rep from * to end.
4TH ROW p2, *k1, p3. Rep from * to last 3 sts, k1, p2.

These 4 rows form the pattern. Cont in pattern until work measures same as front to armhole.

Shape armholes Keeping pattern correct cast off 3[4] sts at beg of next 2 rows. Dec 1 st at both ends of every row until 51[53] sts remain. Cont without shaping until work measures same as front to shoulder shaping.

Shape shoulders Cast off 6[7] sts at beg of next 4 rows and 5[6] sts at beg of next 2 rows. Cast off.

Sleeves

Using 3-mm needles cast on 32[36] sts and work in single rib for 5[6]cm (2[2¼]in) increasing 1 st at end of last row.

Change to 3.5-mm needles and work in

pattern as for back increasing 1 st at both ends of 7th and every following 10th row until there are 41[47] sts.

Cont on these sts until work measures 21.5[24]cm (8½[9½]in) from beg.

Shape top Cast off 3 sts at beg of next 2 rows, then dec 1 st at both ends of next and every alt row until 21[21] sts remain, and at both ends of each row until 15[15] sts remain. Cast off 4 sts at beg of next 2 rows. Cast off.

Work another sleeve in the same way.

Right frontband

Using 3-mm needles cast on 7 sts.

1ST ROW k2, (p1, k1) twice, k1.
2ND ROW (k1, p1) 3 times, k1.
3RD ROW rib 3, wlfwd, k2 tog, rib to end.
4TH ROW as 2nd row.

Cont in rib, working a buttonhole on the following 13th[15th] row from previous buttonhole until 7 buttonholes have been worked.

Work 1 row. Cast off in rib.

Left frontband

Omitting buttonholes, work to match right frontband.

Neckband

Using overstitch or flatstitch join shoulders of back and fronts. With a flat seam sew on frontbands. Using 3.5-mm needles, with right side of work facing and commencing at centre of cast off sts on right frontband, k up 63[63] sts round neck to centre of band and cast off sts on left frontband.

1ST ROW p.
2ND ROW k1, *wlfwd, k2 tog, k2. Rep from * to last 2 sts, wlfwd, k2 tog.
3RD ROW p.
4TH ROW k.
5TH ROW p.
6TH ROW k1, *wlfwd, k2 tog. Rep from * to end.
7TH AND 9TH ROWS as 2nd and 3rd rows. Cast off.

This cardigan can be embroidered.

Making up

Join side and sleeve seams. Stitch sleeves in position. Fold neckband over at centre row of holes, stitch to knitted edge on wrong side of work to make a picot edge. Sew on buttons to correspond with buttonholes.

Also see page 12.

Lacy cardigan

Measurements To fit 56[61/66/71/76]cm (22[24/26/28/30]in) chest.

Materials 4[5/6/6/7] × 25 gm balls of 4-ply yarn. 5 or 6 buttons according to size.

Needles One pair each 3-mm and 4-mm (Nos. 11 and 8) needles.

Tension See page 10.

Abbreviations See page 12.

Back

Using 3-mm needles cast on 62[68/74/80/86] sts and work 6[6.5/7/7.5/8.5]cm (2¼[2½/2¾/3/3¼]in) in single rib.

Change to 4-mm needles and 1 row pattern.

PATTERN ROW sl 1, *k1, wlfwd, k2 tog.
Rep from * to last st, k1 tbl.

Rep this pattern row until back measures 18[19/21.5/24/25.5]cm (7[7½/8½/9½/10]in) from cast on edge.

Shape raglan Keeping pattern correct, cast off 4[4/4/6/6] sts at beg of next 2 rows.

1ST ROW sl 1, k1, sl 1, k1, psso, pattern to last 4 sts, k2 tog, k1 tbl.
2ND ROW sl 1, p2, pattern to last 3 sts, p2, k1 tbl.
3RD ROW sl 1, k2, pattern to last 3 sts, k2, k1 tbl.
4TH ROW as 2nd row.

Rep these 4 rows until 44[56/62/64/74] sts remain.

Now work rows 1 and 2 only until 24[26/28/30/32] sts remain. Cast off loosely.

Left front

Using 3-mm needles cast on
26[29/32/35/38] sts and work 6[6.5/
7/7.5/8.5]cm (2¼[2½/2¾/3/3¼]
in) in single rib.
Change to 4-mm needles and 1 row
pattern as on back until front measures
18[19/21.5/24/25.5]cm (7[7½/8½/
9½/10]in) from cast on edge.
Shape raglan and front Keeping pattern
correct, cast off 4[4/4/6/6] sts at beg of
the next row. Work 1 row.
1ST ROW sl 1, k1, sl 1, k1, psso, pattern to
last 3 sts, k2 tog, k1 tbl.
2ND ROW sl 1, pattern to last 3 sts, p2,
k1 tbl.
3RD ROW sl 1, k2, pattern to last st, k1 tbl.
4TH ROW as row 2.
Rep these 4 rows 8[9/9/10/11] times
then dec at front edge on every 4th row,
working raglan dec on every alt row until
2 sts remain. Work any rows needed to
bring to same length as back raglan. K2
tog, fasten off.

Right front

Work as for left front, reversing all
shapings and working the raglan dec by
k2 tog at raglan dec and k2 tog tbl at
front shaping.

Sleeves

Using 3-mm needles cast on
32[34/36/38/40] sts and work
6[6.5/7/7.5/8.5]cm (2¼[2½/2¾/
3/3¼]in) in single rib, inc evenly on last
rib row to 41[44/47/47/50] sts.
Change to 4-mm needles and work in
1 row pattern as on back until sleeve
measures 19[20/21.5/24/25.5]cm
(7½[7¾/8½/9½/10]in) from cast on
edge.

Shape raglan Cast off 4[4/4/6/6] sts at
beg of the next 2 rows.
Work the 4 raglan shaping rows as on
back until 23[24/25/17/20] sts remain,
ending on a 4th row. Then work rows 1
and 2 until 5[6/7/7/8] sts remain.
Work any rows needed to bring to same
length as back raglan. Cast off.

Frontband

Using 3-mm needles cast on 8 sts and
work in single rib throughout. Work a
buttonhole (sl 1, k1, p1, k2 tog, wlfwd,
k1, p1, k1 tbl.) on 5th row then at
32 mm (1¼ in) intervals until 5[5/
5/5/6] in all have been worked. Cont in
rib until band fits nicely round cardigan
front slightly stretched. Cast off ribwise.

Making up

Join raglan seams. Sew side and sleeve
seam. Pin front band centre to centre
back and pin in place. Sew into place
with boy's or girl's buttoning.

School cardigan

Measurements To fit
61[66/71/76/81.5/86.5]cm (24[26/
28/30/32/34]in) chest.
Materials In 4-ply yarn
8[9/11/13/14/15] × 25 gm balls. 6 or 7
buttons.
Needles For 4-ply garment one pair each
2.5-mm and 3.25-mm (Nos. 12 and 10)
needles.
Tension and Abbreviations See pages 10
and 12.
4-ply version

Back

Using 2.5-mm needles cast on 90[98/
112/118/126] sts and work in single rib
for 5[5/6.5/6.5/7.5/7.5]cm (2
[2/2½/2½/3/3]in) Change to 3.25-mm
needles and work in st st until work
measures 24[27/29/32/34.5/37]
cm (9½[10½/11½/12½/13½/
14½]in) from beg ending with a p row.
Shape raglan sleeve shaping Cast off 4 sts
at the beg of the next two rows.
NEXT ROW k2, sl 1, k1, psso, k to last 4
sts, k2 tog, k2.
NEXT ROW sl 1, p to last st, k1 tbl.
Rep last 2 rows until 28[32/34/36/38/
40] sts remain. Cast off.

Pocket linings (make two)

Using 3.25-mm needles cast on 22[22/

24/26/26/30] sts and work in st st for 6.5[6.5/7/7.5/8.5/9]cm (2½[2½/ 2¾/3/3¼/3½]in). Leave sts on a length of thread or safety pin.

Left front

Using 2.5-mm needles cast on 40[44/ 48/51/54/58] sts and work in single rib for same length as back rib. Change to 3.25-mm needles and work in st st until work measures 11.5[11.5/12/13/13.5/ 14]cm (4½[4½/4¾/5/5¼/5½]in) from beg, ending with a p row.

Pocket K9[11/12/12/13/13] sts, sl next 22[22/24/26/26/30] sts on to a length of thread or safety pin, k across the first pocket lining sts, k to end. Cont in st st until work measures same length as back to start of raglan shaping.

Shape raglan and front slope Cast off 4 sts, k to last 3 sts k2 tog, k1 tbl.
2ND ROW sl 1, p to last st, k1 tbl.
3RD ROW sl 1, k1, sl 1, k1, psso, k to last st, k1 tbl.
4TH ROW as 2nd row (and for all alt rows).
Cont to dec at the armhole edge on every alt row and AT THE SAME TIME dec 1 st at front edge as before on next and every following 6th[5th/5th/5th/5th/5th] row until 8[8/9/8/8/8] sts remain.
Keeping front edge straight cont to dec at armhole edge until 1 st remains. Fasten off.

Right front

Follow instructions for left front, reversing all shapings and working raglan decreases k2 tog, k2. Place the pockets as follows: k9[11/12/13/15/15] sts, sl next 22[22/24/26/26/30] sts on to a length of thread or safety pin, k across sts for second pocket lining, k to end.

Sleeves

Using 2.5-mm needles cast on 40[44/ 48/50/54/56] sts and work in single rib for 6.5 cm (2½ in) increasing 6 sts evenly along the last row of rib. Change to 3.25-mm needles and work in st st,

increasing 1 st at each end of every following 6th row until there are 68[74/80/84/90/96] sts on the needle then cont without further shaping until work measures 27[30.5/33/35.5/38/43]cm (10½[12/13/14/15/17]in) or the desired length, ending on a p row.
Shape raglan as for back until 6[6/8/8/10/10] sts remain. Cast off.

Pocket tops

Slip the sts from the pocket top on to a 2.5-mm needle and work in single rib for about 13 mm (½ in). Using 3.25-mm needle cast off in rib.

Right frontband (left for girls)

Sew up the raglan seams.
Cast on 10 sts with 2.5-mm needles and work in single rib, always remembering to slip first st, and k into back of last st, on every row until the band fits nicely up right front, across shoulder and to halfway point across back — very slightly stretched. Cast off.

Left frontband (right for girls)

Work this band same way, making buttonholes starting one on 5th row thus: sl 1, rib 3, wlfwd, k2 tog, rib to end. Mark on the band already made the number of buttons required, the last one being where the front slope begins. Then work further buttonholes opposite the points marked.

Making up

Join side and sleeve seams. Using flatstitch stitch frontbands into position, joining bands at centre back. Stitch pocket linings neatly into position and sew sides of pockets tops down. Sew on buttons to correspond with buttonholes.

Double-knit school cardigan

Measurements To fit 61[66/71/76/81.5/86.5]cm (24[26/28/30/32/34]in) chest.

Materials 13[14/16/17/19/22] × 25 gm balls double-knitting yarn. 6 or 7 buttons.

Needles One pair each 3-mm and 3.5-mm (Nos. 11 and 9) needles.

Tension and Abbreviations See pages 10 and 12.

Back

Using 3-mm needles cast on 78[84/90/96/102/106] sts. Work exactly as for the 4-ply version changing to 3.5-mm needles instead of 3.25-mm and shaping raglan as follows

Shape raglan Cast off 3 sts at beg of next 2 rows.

NEXT ROW k2, sl 1, k1, psso, k to last 4 sts, k2 tog, k2.

NEXT ROW sl 1, p to last st, k1 tbl.

Rep these last 2 rows until 24[26/28/30/32/34] sts remain. Cast off.

Pocket linings

Using 3.5-mm needles cast on 18[18/22/22/24/26] sts and work in st st for 6.5[6.5/7/7.5/8.5/9]cm (2½[2½/2¾/3/3¼/3½]in). Leave sts on a spare needle.

Left front

Using 3-mm needles cast on 35(38/41/44/47/49) sts and work in single rib for 5[5/6.5/6.5/7.5/7.5]cm (2[2/2½/2½/3/3]in) Change to 3.5-mm needles and work in st st until work measures 11.5[11.5/12/13/13.5/14]cm (4½[4½/4¾/5/5¼/5½]in) ending on a p row.

Fit in pocket K 8[10/9/11/11/11] sts, slip the next 18[18/22/22/24/26] sts on to a safety pin, k across the pocket lining sts and k to end. Cont until work measures 24[27/29/32/34.5/37]cm (9½[10½/11½/12½/13½/14½/]in) from start ending with a p row.

Shape raglan and front slope Cast off 3 sts, k to the last 3 sts, k2 tog, k1 tbl.

2ND ROW sl 1, p to last st, k1 tbl.

3RD ROW k2, sl 1, k1, psso, k to end.

4TH ROW and every alt row — as 2nd.

Cont to dec at armhole edge on alt rows and AT THE SAME TIME dec 1 st at front edge as before on next and every following 6th[6th/6th/5th/5th/5th] row until 8[7/6/9/9/7] sts remain. Keeping front edge straight cont to dec at armhole edge until 1 st remains. Fasten off.

Right front

Work as for left front, reversing all shapings and working the raglan dec k2 tog, k2. Place the pocket as follows: k9[10/10/11/12/12] sts, sl next 18[18/22/22/24/26] sts on to a safety pin, k across pocket lining sts, k to end.

Sleeves

Using 3-mm needles cast on 36[38/40/42/42/44] sts and work in single rib for 6.5 cm (2½ in) increasing 4 sts evenly along last row. Change to 3.5-mm needles and working in st st, inc 1 st at each end of the 7th and every following 6th row until there are 58[62/68/72/78/82] sts on the needle. Cont without further shaping until work measures same length as for 4-ply cardigan ending on a p row. Shape raglans as for back until there are 4[4/6/6/8/10] sts remaining. Cast off.

Pocket tops

Slip sts on to a 3-mm needle and work in single rib for 13 mm (½ in). Cast off ribwise.

Work frontbands as for 4-ply but cast on 7 sts on 3-mm needle.

Making up

Sew side and sleeve seams. Flatstitch frontbands into place joining bands together at centre back. Stitch pocket linings neatly into position and sew sides of pocket tops down. Sew on buttons to correspond with buttonholes.

RIGHT: GARMENTS FOR ALL AGES: LADY'S LONG SLEEVED BASKET STITCH SWEATER

Belted jacket in speciality yarn

Measurements To fit 56[61/66/71/76/
81.5/86.5]cm (22[24/26/28/30/
32/34]in) chest.
Materials 8[8/10/12/14/16/16] × 50
gm balls in chenille (double-knitting
weight) or any other speciality yarn.
Buttons optional.
Needles One pair each 3.5-mm and
4.5-mm (nos 9 and 7) needles.
Tension 7 sts to a 5 cm (2 in) square
using 4.5-mm needles.
Abbreviations See page 12.

Back

Using 3.5-mm needles cast on 39[43/
47/51/55/59/63] sts and work 8[8/8/
8/10/10/12] rows in single rib.
Change to 4.5-mm needles and work in
st st until back measures 25.5[28/32/
34.5/37/39.5/39.5]cm (10[11/12½/
13½/14½/15½/15½]in) from cast on
edge.
Shape raglan and armholes Cast off 2 sts
at beg of next 2 rows.
Dec 1 st at each end of next row and
every following 4th row until 33[35/37/
39/43/47/51] sts remain and then dec
on every alt row until 9[11/13/15/17/
19/21] sts remain. Work 1 row straight.
Cast off loosely.

Pocket linings (make two)

Using 4.5-mm needles cast on 10[12/
14/15/17/17/19] sts and work 23[25/
27/27/29/31] rows in st st. Slip sts on
to a stitch-holder.

Left front (frontband is worked in with front)

Using 3.5-mm needles cast on 24[26/
28/30/32/34/36] sts and work as
follows:
1ST ROW rib to last 6 sts, k5, k1 tbl.

LADY'S CLASSIC DOUBLE-KNIT CARDIGAN

2ND ROW sl 1, k5, rib to end.
Rep these 2 rows 3[3/3/3/4/4/5] times
more.
Change to 4.5-mm needles and work in
st st keeping the 6 st garter st border at
front edge correct for rest of front.
Work 18[20/22/22/24/24/26] rows in
st st (with garter st front border).
NEXT ROW k4[4/4/5/5/7/7] sts, rib 10
[12/14/15/17/17/19] sts, k to end.
NEXT ROW sl 1, k5, p 4[4/4/4/4/4/4],
rib 10[12/14/15/17/17/19], p to end.
Rep these 2 rows once more.
NEXT ROW k4[4/4/5/5/7/7] sts. Cast off
10[12/14/15/17/17/19] sts, k to end.
NEXT ROW sl 1, k5, p 4[4/4/4/4/4/4], p
across sts from first pocket lining, p to
end.
Keeping border correct cont until front
measures same as back to raglan shaping.
Shape raglan/armhole and front Cast off
2 sts at beg of next row.
2ND ROW sl 1, k5, p to end.
3RD ROW k2 tog, k to last 8 sts, k2 tog,
k5, k1 tbl.

4TH ROW as row 2.
5TH ROW k.
6TH ROW as row 2.
Rep rows 3-6 inclusive until 12[14/16/
18/20/22/24] sts remain. Finish on
6th row.
NEXT ROW k2 tog, k to last 8 sts, k2 tog,
k5, k1 tbl.
NEXT ROW as row 2.
NEXT ROW k2 tog, k to end.
NEXT ROW as row 2.
Rep these 4 rows until 8 sts remain (all
sizes). Then dec at armhole edge only
every alt row until 6 sts remain. Work
5 cm (2 in) in garter st on remaining 6
sts. Leave on spare needle.

Right front
Work as for left front, reversing all
shapings.
Optional Buttonholes should be worked
evenly up this front if a buttoned jacket is
prefered.

Sleeves
Using 3.5-mm needles cast on 22[24/
26/28/30/32/34] sts and work 12[12/
14/16/16/18/18] rows in single rib.
Change to 4.5-mm needles and working
in st st, inc 1 st at each end of next and
every following 8th row until there are
32[34/36/38/40/42/46] sts. Cont
without shaping until sleeve measures 23
[29/34.5/38/38/43/43]cm (9[11½/
13½/15/15/17/17]in) from cast on
edge.
Shape raglan top Cast off 2 sts at beg of
next 2 rows.
Dec 1 st at each end of next and every
following 4th row until 20[22/24/26/
30/32/36] sts remain then on every alt
row until 6 sts remain. Work any rows
needed to bring to same length as back
raglan seam. Work 1 row. Cast off
loosely.

Belt
Using 4.5-mm needles cast on and work
in garter st until belt measures approx
99[104/109/114.5/119.5/124.5/
129.5]cm (39[41/43/45/47/49/51]in)

from beg. Cast off.

Making up
Sew raglan seams, join sleeve and side
seams. Sew pocket linings neatly in
position on wrong side of fronts.
Sew the extra rows of garter st worked
on each front across sleeve tops and back
neck to join together at back left raglan
seam, working any extra rows needed.

Hooded jacket

Measurements To fit 61[66/71]cm
(24[26/28]in) chest.
Materials 12[15/18] × 25 gm balls
double-knitting yarn USED DOUBLE.
Needles One pair each 4.5-mm and
5.5-mm (Nos. 7 and 5) needles.
Tension See page 10.
Abbreviations See page 12.

Front
Using 4.5-mm needles cast on 42[46/50]
sts and work 4 rows in single rib thus:
sl 1, *k1, p1. Rep from * to last st, k1
tbl.
5TH ROW sl 1, k1 *wlfwd, k2 tog, p1, k1.
Rep from * to end.
6TH ROW as 1st row.
Change to 5.5-mm needles and work 4
rows in st st.
NEXT ROW k7[8/9] sts, sl next 28[30/
32]sts for pocket front on to a stitch-
holder, cast on 28[30/32] sts, k to end.
Cont in st st until work measures 14[15/
18]cm (5½[6/7]in). Slip sts from stitch-
holder on to a 5.5-mm needle. Cast on 4
sts (for pocket edge), k across the
28[30/32] sts, cast on 4 sts, k across
these 36[38/40] sts and work for
14[15/18]cm (5½[6/7]in).
NEXT ROW k4, p to last 4, k4, break
off yarn.
Using a 5.5-mm needle and working
from first needle or stitch-holder, k4,
place the needle containing the
36[38/40] sts in front of sts on left hand
needle and k 1 st from each needle tog. K
to end, k4.

Cont in st st until work measures 26.5[29/32]cm (10½[11½/12½]in). NEXT ROW k21[23/25], turn (for neck opening).
Cont on these sts until work measures 35.5[39.5/43]cm (14[15½/17]in) finishing at neck edge.
Shape neck as follows Cast off 2 sts, work to end.
NEXT ROW k to last 2 sts, k2 tog.
NEXT ROW k2 tog, work to end.
Rep last 2 rows once more (16[18/20] sts).
Shape shoulders Cast off 5[6/6] sts at beg of next and following alt row, and then 5[6/7] sts at beg of next alt row.
Work other side of neck opening to match. Cast off.

Back

Work rib and row of holes as for front, then change to 5.5-mm needles and work in st st until work measures same as for front up to shoulders.
Shape shoulders Cast off 5[6/6] sts on next row and 5[6/7] sts on next alt row. Cast off.

Sleeves

Using 4.5-mm needles cast on 28[28/30] sts and work in single rib for 5 cm (2 in) increasing evenly along last row to 34[36/38] sts. Change to 5.5-mm needles and work in st st until sleeve measures 24[27/29]cm (9½[10½/11½]in).
Cast off.

Hood

Using 4.5-mm needles cast on 69[72/75] sts and work in garter st for 5 rows.
Change to 5.5-mm needles and work in st st until work measures 10[11.5/13]cm (4[4½/5]in) from beg.
NEXT ROW cast off 23[24/25] sts and work across centre 23[24/25] sts. Cast off remaining 23[24/25] sts.
Work 5 rows on centre sts.
NEXT ROW k2, sl 1, k1, psso, k to last 4 sts, k2 tog, k2.
Cont dec in this manner every 4th row 4

times and then work without shaping until centre measures same as cast off sides of hood.
Cast off.

Making up

Sew sides of centre to cast off sides.
Make a cord of two strands to go through holes on jumper.

Aran sweater

Measurements To fit 61[66/71/76]cm (24[26/28/30]in) chest.
Materials 7[7/8/8] × 50 gm balls of Aran yarn.
Needles One pair each 3.5-mm and 5.5-mm (Nos 9 and 5) needles
Tension See page 10.
Abbreviations See page 12.

Cable — sl 3 sts, on to a cable needle, leave at back of work, k 3 sts, k 3 sts, from cable needle.
T3R — slip 1 st on to cable needle, leave at front of work, k 2 sts, k sts on cable needle.
T3L — sl 2 sts on to cable needle, leave at back of work, k1 st, k sts on cable needle.

Back

Using 3.5-mm needles cast on 54[60/66/70] sts. Work 12[12/14/14] rows in single rib.
Change to 5.5-mm needles and Aran pattern as follows:
1ST ROW moss st 3[6/9/11] sts k4, p1, k6, p1, k4, p16, k4, p1, k6, p1, k4, moss st to end.
2ND ROW moss st 3[6/9/11] sts p4, k1, p6, k1, p4, (p3 tog, k1, p1, k1 into next st) 4 times, p4, k1, p6, k1, p4, moss st to end.
3RD ROW moss st 3[6/9/11] sts k1, T3R, p1, k6, p1, T3L, k1, p16, k1, T3R, p1, k6, p1, T3L, k1, moss st to end.
4TH ROW moss st 3[6/9/11] sts, p4, k1, p6, k1, p4, (k1, p1, k1, into next st, p3 tog) 4 times, p4, k1, p6, k1, p4, moss st.

to end.

5TH ROW moss st 3[6/9/11] sts, k4, p1,
C 6, p1, k4, p16, k4, p1, C 6, p1, k4,
moss st to end.

6TH ROW as row 2.

7TH ROW as row 3.

8TH ROW as row 4.

9TH ROW as row 1.

10TH ROW as row 2.

11TH ROW moss st 3[6/9/11] sts, k1,
T3R, p1, C 6, p1, T3L, k1, p16, k1, T3R,
p1, C 6, p1, T3L, k1, moss st to end.

12TH ROW as row 4.

These 12 rows form the pattern. Cont in
pattern until back measures
23[25.5/28/30.5]cm (9[10/11/12]in)
from beg.

Shape raglan Keeping pattern correct, cast
off 2 sts at beg of next 2 rows.

NEXT ROW k2, sl 1, k1, psso, pattern to
last 4 sts, k2 tog, k2.

NEXT ROW p2, pattern to last 2 sts, p2.

Rep these 2 rows until 16[18/20/24] sts
remain.

Leave these sts on a holder for neckband.

Front

Work as for back until there are 26[28/
30/34] sts.

Keeping pattern correct, shape neck as
follows.

NEXT ROW k2, sl 1, k1, psso, pattern
6[7/8/8] sts. Cast off 6[6/6/8] sts,
pattern last 4 sts, k2 tog, k2.

Work 1 row.

NEXT ROW k2 tog, pattern to last 4 sts, k2
tog, k2.

NEXT ROW Work in pattern.

Rep these 2 rows until 3 sts remain, right
side facing.

NEXT ROW k2 tog, k1, k2 tog. Fasten off.

Rejoin yarn to other group of sts and
work to correspond, reversing all
shapings.

Sleeves

Using 3.5-mm needles cast on 28[30/
32/34] sts and work 10[10/12/12]
rows in single rib, increasing evenly
along last row to 36[38/40/42] sts.

Change to 5.5-mm needles and pattern as

follows (AT THE SAME TIME increasing 1 st at each end of every 6th row until there are 46[50/54/58] sts, the extra sts being worked into moss st border):

1ST ROW moss st 2[3/4/5] sts, p2, k6, p1,k1,p12,k1, p1,k6,p2, moss st to end.

2ND ROW moss st 2[3/4/5] sts, k2, p6, k1, p1, (p3 tog, k1, p1, k1, into next st) 3 times, p1, k1, p6, k2, moss st to end.

3RD ROW as row 1.

4TH ROW moss st 2[3/4/5] sts, k2, p6, k1, p1 (k1, p1, k1, into next st p3 tog) 3 times, p1, k1, p6, k2, moss st to end.

5TH ROW moss st 2[3/4/5] sts, p2, C 6, p1,k1,p12,k1, p1. C 6, p2, moss st to end.

6TH ROW as row 2.

7TH ROW as row 1.

8TH ROW as row 4.

9TH ROW as row 1.

10TH ROW as row 2.

11TH ROW as row 5.

12TH ROW as row 4.

These 12 rows form the pattern. Cont in pattern until sleeve measures 25.5[28/30.5/33]cm (10[11/12/13]in) from beg.

Shape raglan Keeping pattern corrrect work as for back until 8 sts remain. Leave on a holder for neckband.

Neckband

Using 3.5-mm needles and with right side facing, k 8 sts from first sleeve, 14 sts down left front, cast off sts from centre front, 14 sts up centre front, 2nd sleeve and back. Work 6 rows in single rib. Cast off loosely ribwise.

Making up

Sew up in normal way, neatly and firmly.

Side stripe jacket

Measurements To fit 61[66/71]cm (24[26/28]in) chest.

Materials Double-knitting yarn used double. 4 × 25 gm balls each of cream, brown and grey. For sewing up cream and grey double-knitting.

Needles One pair each 5.5-mm, 6.5-mm and 7.5-mm (Nos. 5, 3 and 1) needles.

Tension Using 6.5-mm needles 6 sts and 4 rows to a 6.5 × 2.5 cm (2½ × 1 in) rectangle.

Abbreviations See page 12.

Colour Ideas

| Brown = Dark Grey = Navy = White |
| Cream = Light Grey = Red = Grey |
| Grey = White = Cream = Red |

Back

Using 6.5-mm needles and brown yarn cast on 32[36/40] sts and starting with a p row work in reverse st st throughout in stripes as follows:

2[4/6] rows brown, 4 rows cream, 2 rows brown, 2 rows grey, 2 rows cream, 4 rows brown, 4 rows cream, 6 rows grey, 4 rows cream, 4 rows brown, 2 rows cream, 2 rows grey, 2 rows brown, 4 rows cream, 2[4/6] rows brown. Cast off using 7.5-mm needle and brown yarn (a 7.5-mm needle is used as this yarn is difficult to cast off loosely).

Front

Using a 6.5-mm needle and brown yarn cast on 32[36/40] sts and, starting with a p row work in reverse st st as on back and in stripes as follows: 2[4/6] rows brown, 4 rows cream, 2 rows brown, 2 rows grey, 1 row cream.

NEXT ROW in cream — cast off 4[6/6] sts, k to end.

NEXT ROW in brown — p.

NEXT ROW in brown — k2 tog, k to end.

Rep these 2 rows in brown.

Rep these 2 rows in cream (end of shaping).

Now work 2 rows in cream and 1 in grey

ROW OF HOLES *k2 tog, wrn in grey. Rep from * 3[4/4] times, k to end.

NEXT ROW p to last 6[8/8] sts in grey. Cast off these sts.

Break yarn.

NEXT ROW rejoin grey yarn to remaining sts. Cast on 6[8/8] sts, k to end.

ROW OF HOLES in grey — p to last 6[8/8] sts, k2 tog, wrn 3[4/4] times.

Work 2 rows in cream.
NEXT ROW in cream — p to last st, inc into this st once.
NEXT ROW in cream — k.
Rep these 2 rows twice more in brown.
P to end in cream. Cast on 4[6/6] sts.
Now cont in stripes as follows:
1 row cream, 2 rows grey, 2 rows brown, 4 rows cream, 2[4/6] rows brown, cast off in brown using a 7.5-mm needle as on back.

Sleeves

Using 6.5-mm needles and grey cast on 30 sts and work in garter st for 4 rows. Change to reverse st st for rest of sleeve, starting with a p row and stripes as follows:
2[6/10] rows cream, 2 rows brown, dec 1 st at each end of 1st of 2 brown rows, 4 grey rows, 2 cream rows, dec 1 st at each end of 1st of 2 cream rows, 2 brown rows, 2 grey rows. Dec 1 st at each end of 1st of 2 grey rows, 4 cream rows, 4 brown rows, 2 cream rows, 2 brown rows, 2 cream rows and 2 brown rows. Cast off in brown, using a 7.5-mm needle.

Collar

Using 6.5-mm needles and grey cast on 40 sts. K 1 row. Cont in garter st, working 6 rows and dec 1 st at each end of these 6 rows. Work 1 row with no dec. Cast off using a 7.5-mm needle.

Waistband

Using 5.5-mm needles and grey yarn cast on 6 sts and work entirely in garter st making a hole on every 4th row as follows:
sl 1, k1, wrn, k2 tog, k1, k1 tbl. Work until waistband measures 66 cm (26 in). Cast off.

Garments fo

This next section covers garments for all ages. I originally designed them for adults and then thought how delightful they would look in tiny sizes. So I scaled them down, some of them through all sizes.

Hooded bouclé oversweater with mittens

Measurements Ladies' small, medium and large.
Materials 17 × 50 gm balls bouclé or like yarn. If striped as in pattern use 5 × 50 gm balls in colour A, 3 balls in colours B and D and 6 balls in colour C.
Needles One pair each 4-mm, 4.5-mm, 5-mm and 6-mm (Nos. 8, 7, 6 and 4) needles.
Tension 6 sts to a 5 cm (2 in) square using 6-mm needles.
Abbreviations See page 12.
Note Bouclé knits up more loosely than flat yarn so if using a different yarn check tension carefully.

Colour suggestions

These 'earthy' colours are extremely attractive for this garment and depending upon which colour is preferred for the hood (C) the 4 basic colours can be changed.

Brown = **A** = Light grey	**A** = Camel
Stone = **B** = Dark grey	**B** = Brown
Grey = **C** = White	**C** = Cream
Cream = **D** = Black	**D** = Gold

Oversweater

STRIPE ORDER Rib in A and then work straight in stripes of: *4 rows B, 8 rows C, 2 rows B, 4 rows A, 10 rows D, 4

All Ages

rows C, 8 rows B, 4 rows D, 10 rows A. Repeat from *.

Back

Using 5-mm needles and A cast on 50[54/60] sts and work in single rib for 10 cm (4 in) increasing to 52[56/62] sts on last row. Change to 6-mm needles and work in stripes as below in reverse st st until work measures 43 cm (17 in) from beg. Mark each end of last row with a coloured thread to indicate end of side and then cont until work measures 67.5 cm (26½ in). Cast off.

Front

Work as for back until work measures 61 cm (24 in).
Divide for neck Work 22[24/27] sts, leave these sts on spare needle, cast off 8 sts, work to end. Cont on these 22[24/27] sts, dec at neck edge on next and following 3 alt rows. Then cont without shaping until front measures same as back. Cast off. Rejoin yarn to inside edge of remaining sts on spare needle and work other side to match first.

Sleeves (both alike)

With 6-mm needles cast on 50 sts in A and work 10 rows in single rib. Change to reverse st st and work in stripes as on body until sleeve measures 43 cm (17½ in) from start. Cast off very loosely (this is best done by using a larger needle, i.e. 7-mm in right hand as you cast off). This yarn is inclined to pull tight when casting off, and top of sleeve must lie flat and not be narrowed at the top.

Pockets (make two)

Using 6-mm needles cast on 52[56/62] sts and working in stripes as on body in reverse st st (pocket to come immediately after rib). Work 26 rows of stripe. Cast off in D. Work last 6 rows in garter st.
Sew pockets on front (before sewing up sides) immediately above rib, making sure stripes correspond. Sew bottom of pocket to first row of reverse in st st on body (front). Sew down centre of pocket to make it divide and give a double pocket.

Making up

Make up using double-knitting yarn.

Balaclava hood
Back

Using C, 4.5-mm needles and with right side of back of sweater facing pick up 20 sts from across the centre back. Work 18 rows in garter st.
NEXT ROW sl 1, (inc in next st, k3) 4 times, inc in next st, k2, (25 sts).
K 7 rows.
NEXT ROW sl 1, k1, (inc in next st, k4) 4 times, inc in next st, k2, (30 sts).
K 28 rows.
Shape top Continuing in garter st dec 1 st at both ends of next and every following 3rd row twice more (24 sts). K 1 row.
Dec 1 st at both ends of next 4 rows.
Cast off 4 sts at beg of next 2 rows.
Cast off.

Front

With right side of front of sweater facing, using C and 4.5-mm needles pick up 32 sts evenly round front of neck.
K 12 rows.
NEXT ROW k15, k twice into next 2 sts, k15. K next and every alt row.
NEXT ROW k16, k twice into next 2 sts, k16. K 1 row.
NEXT ROW k17, k twice into next 2 sts, k17. K 1 row.
NEXT ROW k18, k twice into next 2 sts, k18. K 1 row (40 sts).
NEXT ROW k16, cast off 8 sts, k16. Work on last set of 16 sts. Dec on inside (face) edge of next row (15 sts).
K 26 rows.
Inc 1 st on inside edge of next and every following 4th row until there are 19 sts on the needle and then work without shaping until work measures 32 cm (12½ in) from the beg of the front of the helmet. Leave these sts on a spare needle. Work the other side to match and then cast off knitting 1 st from each side tog, (ie. CASTING OFF 1 st from each side).

Making up

You will find it much easier to sew up this garment using a flat yarn (that is, if you have used bouclé). Since this is a heavy overgarment take special care to fasten off seams securely.

Mittens

Using 4-mm needles cast on 28 sts and work in single rib for 9 cm (3½ in). Change to st st and work for another 2.5 cm (1 in).
NEXT ROW inc in 1st st, k12, inc in next 2 sts, k12, inc in last st (32 sts).
Cont in st st until work measures 19 cm (7½ in).
NEXT ROW k2 tog, k12, (k2 tog) twice, k12, k2 tog. Work 3 rows.
NEXT ROW k2 tog, k10, (k2 tog) twice, k10, k2 tog. Work 3 rows.
NEXT ROW k2 tog, k8, (k2 tog) twice, k8, k2 tog. Work 3 rows.
NEXT ROW k2 tog, k6, (k2 tog) twice, k6 k2 tog. Cast off.
Sew up side seam, making sure not to pull it too tight and that sewn up side seam is same length as fold over side.
Using 3 strands of yarn either crochet a chain cord or plait a cord 152.5 cm (60 in) long, and attach it to the mittens.

Child's hooded oversweater with mittens

Measurements To fit 56[61/66/71/76]cm (22[24/26/28/30]in) chest.
Materials Of 50 gm balls bouclé (or like yarn):
colour A — 2[2/2/3/3] balls
colour B — 2[2/2/2/2] balls
colour C — 3[3/3/3/3] balls
colour D — 2[2/2/3/3] balls
(2 balls extra for mittens in colour C)
Needles One pair each 4-mm, 4.5-mm, 5-mm and 6-mm (Nos. 8, 7, 6 and 4) needles.

See tension note on lady's pattern,
page 78.
BASIC STRIPE PATTERN. Rib in A, 4 rows B,
2 rows C, 6 rows D, 4 rows A, 2 rows C,
4 rows B, 2 rows A, 4 rows D, 6 rows C
and 2 rows A.
Abbreviations See page 12.

Balaclava hood
Back
Using 4.5-mm needles, C and with right
side facing pick up and
k 11[13/15/17/19] sts across back of
sweater.
Work 8[10/12/14/16] rows in garter st.
NEXT ROW k, increasing 3 sts evenly along
row (14[16/18/20/22] sts). K 5 rows.
NEXT ROW k, increasing 4 sts evenly along
row (18[20/22/24/26] sts).
K 14[18/20/22/26] rows.
Shape top (still in garter st) Dec 1 st at
each end of next and following 3rd row.
K 1 row. Dec 1 st at each end of the next
2 rows. Cast off 3 sts at the beg of the
next 2 rows. Cast off remaining sts.
Front
Using 4.5-mm needles, C and with right
side facing pick up 32[32/34/34/38] sts
evenly round front of neck.
K 4[4/6/6/8] rows.

Back
Using 5-mm needles and colour A cast
on 31[34/37/40/43] sts and work in
single rib for 5 cm (2 in) increasing 1 st
at each end of the last row. Change to
6-mm needles and work in stripe pattern
as above in reverse st st (starting with a p
row) until work measures
20.5[23/25.5/28/33]cm
8[9/10/11/13]in) from the beg. Mark
each end of this row with a piece of
coloured thread to indicate start of
armhole and cont without shaping in
stripe pattern until work measures
32[35.5/39.5/43/49.5]cm
(12½[14/15½/17/19½]in) from beg.
Cast off.

Front
Work as for back until work measures

27[29/32/35.5/39.5]cm
(10½[11½/12½/14/15½]in) from beg.
Shape neck as follows:
P14[15/16/17/18], cast off 5 sts,
p to end. Work on second group of sts as
follows. Dec 1 st at neck edge on next
4[4/5/5/6] rows and then work without
shaping until work measures same length
as back. Cast off.
Rejoin yarn to other group of sts and
work to correspond with the first side,
reversing shapings.

Pockets (make two)
Using 6-mm needles and B cast on
33[36/39/42/45] sts and work in
reverse st st in stripe pattern for
7.5[7.5/9/10/11.5]cm
(3[3/3½/4/4½]in). Work another 4
rows in garter st. Cast off.

Sleeves
Using 5-mm needles and A cast on
24[24/26/28/28] sts and work in single
rib for 6.5 cm (2½ in) increasing to
30[30/32/34/36] sts in the last row.
Change to 6-mm needles and work in
stripe pattern in reverse st st until sleeve
measures 25.5[28/33/37/42]cm
(10[11/13/14½/16½]in).
Cast off loosely.
Join shoulder seams.
NEXT ROW k12[12/13/13/14] sts, inc
once in next 2 sts, k to end.
K the next and every following alt row.
NEXT ROW k13[13/14/15/15/16] sts, inc
as before, k to end.
NEXT ROW k14[14/15/15/16] sts, inc as
before, k to end. K 1 row.
NEXT ROW k13, cast off 6[6/8/8/10] sts,
k to end.
Work on the last group of sts as follows.
Dec 1 st at inside (face) edge on next row
(12 sts).
K 6[8/10/12/14] rows.
Inc 1 st at inside edge on next and every
following 4th row until there are 16 sts
on needle. Work without shaping until
this piece fits nicely to the centre front of
the back piece of hood. Leave sts on a
spare needle.

Rejoin yarn to other group of sts and work to correspond with first side, reversing all shapings. When correct length cast off both halves of front together (i.e. knitting 1 st from each side tog and casting off together).

Making up
Place sleeves between coloured threads on back and front and set in so that sleeve seam lies flat and is not pulled or gathered. With wrong side of pocket to right side of sweater front sew bottom edge of pocket to first row above welt. Sew side seams, sewing pocket sides in with the seam. Sew sleeve seams. Carefully stitch down the centre of the pocket to the body (this divides the pocket). Sew in all ends.

Mittens
Using 4-mm needles and C cast on 16[18/20/20/22] sts and work in single rib for 5[5/6.5/7/7.5]cm (2[2/2½/2¾/3]in).
Change to reverse st st (starting with a p row) and work for another 2.5 cm (1 in).
NEXT ROW inc into 1st st, p 6[7/8/8/9], inc in next 2 sts, p to last st, inc in last st. Cont in reverse st st until work measures 11.5[14/16.5/16.5/18]cm (4½[5½/6½/6½/7]in) from beg.
NEXT ROW p2 tog, p6[7/8/8/9], (p2 tog) twice, p6[7/8/8/9], p2 tog.
Work 3 rows.
NEXT ROW p2 tog, p4[5/6/6/7], (p2 tog) twice, p4[5/6/6/7], p2 tog.
Work 3 rows.
NEXT ROW p2 tog, p2[3/4/4/5], (p2 tog) twice, p2[3/4/4/5], p2 tog. Work 1 row.
Cast off.

Making up
Fold mitten in half and sew side seam without any tightness or pull. Using 3 strands of yarn either plait or crochet a chain cord 76[89/102/114.5/127]cm (30[35/40/45/50]in) long to attach to mittens.

Lady's lacy mohair sweater

Measurements To fit 86.5-91.5 cm (34—36 in) chest. Length 71 cm (28 in) (adjustable).
Materials 12 × 25 gm balls mohair.
Needles One pair each 4-mm, 5.5-mm and 6.5-mm (Nos 8, 5 and 3) needles.
Tension 7 sts to a 5 cm (2 in) square on 6.5-mm needles in pattern.
Abbreviations See page 12.

Back and front alike
Using 4-mm needles cast on 71 sts.
1ST ROW k2, *p1, k1. Rep from * to last st, k1.
2ND ROW *k1, p1. Rep from * to last st, k1.
Rep these 2 rows until work measures 9 cm (3½ in).
NEXT ROW p.
Change to 6.5-mm needles and pattern as follows:
1ST ROW k1, *wlfwd, k3, sl 1, k2 tog, psso, k3, wlfwd, k1. Repeat from * to end.
2ND ROW p.
3RD ROW k1, *k1, wlfwd, k2, sl 1, k2 tog, psso, k2, wlfwd, k2. Rep from * to end.
4TH ROW p.
5TH ROW k1, *k2, wlfwd, k1, sl 1, k2 tog, psso, k1, wlfwd, k3. Rep from * to end.
6TH ROW p.
7TH ROW k1, *k3, wlfwd, sl 1, k2 tog, psso, wlfwd, k4. Rep from * to end.
8TH ROW p.
These 8 rows form the pattern. Work in pattern until work measures 67.5 cm (26½ in) from beg.
Change to 5.5-mm needles and work 11 rows in garter st.
Cast off loosely.

Sleeves
Using 4-mm needles cast on 61 sts. Work rib as for back/front for 10 cm (4 in).
Change to 6.5-mm needles and work 5

patterns. Cast off loosely.

Making up
Join shoulder seam leaving 25.5 cm
(10 in) open for neck. Sew sleeves into
place without gathering or pulling.
Sew side and sleeve seams.

Child's lacy mohair sweater

Measurements To fit
56[61/66/71/76/81.5]cm
(22[24/26/28/30/32]in) chest.
Materials Of 25 gm balls mohair
6[7/7/8/8/9] balls.
Needles One pair each 4-mm, 5.5-mm
and 6-mm (Nos. 8, 5 and 3) needles.
Tension See note on lady's pattern.
Abbreviations See page 12.

Back/front
Using 4-mm needles cast on
36[42/44/48/52/56] sts and work in
single rib for 5[5/6/6/6.5/6.5] cm
(2[2/2¼/2¼/2½/2½]in).
Change to 6.5-mm needles and pattern as
follows:
1ST ROW k3[1/2/4/1/3] *wlfwd, k3, sl 1,
k2 tog, psso, k3, wlfwd, k1. Rep from

* to last 3[1/2/4/1/3] sts, k to end.
2ND, 4TH, 6TH AND 8TH ROWS — p.
3RD ROW k3[1/2/4/1/3], *k1, wlfwd,
k2, sl 1, k2 tog, psso, k2, wlfwd, k2. Rep
from * to last 3[1/2/4/1/3] sts, k to end.
5TH ROW k3[1/2/4/1/3], *k2, wlfwd,
k1, sl 1, k2 tog, psso, k1, wlfwd, k3. Rep
from * to last 3[1/2/4/1/3] sts, k to end.
7TH ROW k3[1/2/4/1/3], * k3, wlfwd, sl
1, k2 tog, psso, wlfwd, k4. Rep from * to
last 3[1/2/4/1/3] sts, k to end.
These 8 rows form the pattern. Cont in
pattern until work measures
37[39.5/40.5/41.5/42/43]cm
(14½[15½/16/16¼/16½/17]in)
from beg.
Change to 5.5-mm needles and work
5[7/7/9/9/11] rows in garter st.
Cast off loosely.

Sleeves
Using 4-mm needles cast on
28[28/32/32/34/34] sts and work in
single rib for 5[6/6/7/7.5/7.5]cm
(2[2¼/2¼/2¾/3/3]in). Inc on last row
to 48[52/52/56/56/56] sts. Change to
6.5-mm needles and work in pattern as
for back/front working 4[1/1/3/3/3] sts
on each side of pattern on k rows.
Work in pattern until sleeve measures
23[24/25.5/30/31.5/33]cm
(9[9½/10/11½/12½/13]in) from beg.
Cast off loosely.

Making up
Leave neck opening
19[23/23/25.5/25.5]cm
(7½[9/9/10/10]in). Join shoulder seam
when opening is measured, set sleeves
into place without gathering or pulling.
Sew side and sleeve seams.

Polo neck sweater with Jacquard yoke and cuffs

Measurements To fit children/ladies

66[71/76/81.5/86.5/91.5]cm
(26[28/30/32/34/36]in) chest.
Materials In main colour (M)
8[10/12/14/15/16] × 25 gm balls
double-knitting yarn,
2[3/3/3/4/4] × 25 gm balls in 1st
contrast and 1 × 25 gm ball in each of
2nd and 3rd contrast colours.
Needles One pair each 3.25-mm, 3.5-mm
and 4.5-mm (Nos. 10, 9 and 7) needles.
Tension See page 10.
Abbreviations See page 12.

Back
**Using 3.25-mm needles and M cast on
60[66/70/76/80/86] sts and work in
single rib for 5[6/6.5/7.5/7.5/7.5] cm
(2[2¼/2½/3/3/3]in) increasing 1 st at
end of last row 61[67/71/77/81/87]
sts. Change to 4.5-mm needles and work
in st st until work measures
27[29/32/34.5/37/38] cm
(10½[11½/12½/13½/14½/15]in)
from beg.
Shape armholes Cast off 3[3/3/3/3/4]
sts at beg of next 2 rows then dec 1 st at
each end of next and every alt row until
47[51/57/61/67/71] sts remain. Work
1[1/1/1/3/5] rows, ending on wrong
side. Work from 1st to 17th rows of:

Chart C	Chart D
for 66 cm	for 71 cm
76 cm	81.5 cm
86.5 cm	91.5 cm

Working the bracketed portions
4[5/5/6/6/7] times and working extra
sts at beg and end of each row as marked
on the chart**.

Using 1st contrast only beg with a p row
and proceed in st st until work measures
43[46/48.5/53.5/56/58.5]cm
(17[18/19/21/22/23]in) from beg
ending with a wrong side row.
Shape shoulders Cast off
7[8/9/9/10/11] sts at beg of next 2
rows, then 7[7/8/9/10/10] sts at beg of
following 2 rows. Place the remaining
19[20/23/25/27/29] sts on
stitch-holder.

Colour Suggestions

Base	= M =	Cream
1st contrast	= O =	Emerald
2nd contrast	= X =	Navy
3rd contrast	= Y =	Red

Base	= M =	Soft blue
1st contrast	= O =	Burgundy
2nd contrast	= X =	Dusky pink
3rd contrast	= Y =	Grey

Base	= M =	Navy
1st contrast	= O =	White
2nd contrast	= X =	Camel
3rd contrast	= Y =	Rust

Base	= M =	Grey
1st contrast	= O =	Cream
2nd contrast	= X =	Navy
3rd contrast	= Y =	Gold or camel

C

Rows

17	O O O X O O O O X O O O O X O O O
16	O O X O X O O X O X O O X O X O O
15	X X O O O X X O O X X O O X X
14	O O O Y O O O O Y O O O O Y O O O
13	O O Y O Y O O Y Y Y O O Y O Y O O
12	Y Y O O O Y Y Y Y Y Y O O O Y Y
11	O Y O O O Y O Y Y O Y O O O Y O
10	Y Y Y O Y Y Y O Y O Y Y Y O Y Y Y
9	Y Y Y Y Y Y Y Y O Y Y Y Y Y Y Y
8	Y Y Y M Y Y M Y Y M Y Y Y M Y M Y
7	M Y M M M Y M Y Y M Y M M M Y M
6	Y Y M M M Y Y Y Y Y Y M M M Y Y
5	M M Y M M Y Y Y M M Y Y M Y M M
4	M M M Y M M M Y M M M M M Y M M M
3	X X M M M X X M M M X X M M M X X
2	M M X M X M M X M X M M X M X M M
1	M M M X M M M M X M M M M X M M M

ODD STS   10 ST REPEAT   ODD STS

D

Rows

17	X O O O O X O O O O X
16	O X O O X O O X O O X O
15	O O X X O O O X X O O
14	Y O O O O Y O O O O Y
13	O Y O O Y Y Y O O Y O
12	O O Y Y Y Y Y Y O O
11	O O Y O Y Y Y O Y O O
10	O Y Y Y O Y O Y Y Y O
9	Y Y Y Y O Y O Y Y Y
8	M Y Y Y M Y M Y Y Y M
7	M M Y M Y Y M Y M M
6	M M Y Y Y Y Y Y M M
5	M Y M M M Y Y M Y M
4	Y M M M M Y M M M M Y
3	M M X X M M M X X M M
2	M X M M M X M M X M
1	X M M M M X M M M M X

ODD ST   10 ST REPEAT

Front

Work from ** to ** as given for back.
Using 1st contrast only and starting with a p row proceed in st st until work measures 39.5[42/44.5/49.5/51.5/53.5]cm (15½[16½/17½/19½/20¼/21]in) ending with front facing.

Shape neck K18[20/22/23/25/26] sts, sl remaining sts on to a stitch-holder. Working on this first set of sts only proceed as follows.

Dec 1 st at neck edge on next 5 rows then cont without further shaping until work measures same as back to shoulder shaping ending at side edge.

Shape shoulder. Cast off 7[8/9/9/10/11] sts at beg of next row, then 6[7/8/9/10/10] sts at beg of following alt row.

Sl next 11[11/13/15/17/19] sts on to a thread or spare needle for picking up for neck. Rejoin yarn to remaining sts and work to match first side, reversing all shapings.

Sleeves

Using 3.25-mm needles and M cast on 34[36/38/40/40/42] sts and work in single rib for 5[5/6/6.5/7.5/7.5] cm (2[2/2¼/2½/3/3]in).

NEXT ROW rib 8[10/12/10/10/10], inc in each of next 17[15/13/20/20/19] sts, rib 9[11/13/10/10/9] sts (51[51/51/61/61/61] sts).

Using 4.5-mm needles work from 1st to 17th rows of Chart D, then break off contrast yarns and working rest of sleeve only in M, inc 1 st at each end of next and every following 10th row until there are 55[55/57/63/67/73] sts on needle. Cont without further shaping until work measures 30.5[33.5/38/43/44.5/44.5]cm (12[13¼/15/17/17½/17½]in) from start.

Shape top Cast off 3[3/3/3/3/4] sts at beg of next 2 rows. Dec 1 st at each end of next and every following alt row until 29[29/31/31/37/39] sts remain, then at each end of every row until 11[11/11/13/15/17] sts remain.
Cast off.

Collar (use 1st contrast only)

Polo neck Sew up right shoulder seam with right side of work facing. Using 3.25-mm needles pick up and k 11[11/11/13/13/13] sts down left side of front neck, 11[11/13/15/17/19] sts from front neck stitch-holder, 11[11/11/13/13/13] sts up right front neck and 19[20/23/25/27/29] sts from back neck stitch-holder (52[53/58/66/70/74] sts).

NEXT ROW *k1, (p1, k1) into next st, p1, (k1, p1) into next st. Rep from * to last 2 sts, (k1, p1) into next st, k1. Now work in single rib for 18[18/20/20/22/22] rows. Change to 3.5-mm needles and work another 12[12/14/16/18/20] rows in rib. Cast off ribwise.

Making up

Using overstitch or flatstitch join all seams, fit in sleeves and attach collar using relevant colours on multicolour bands and collar.

Adult's long sleeved basket stitch sweater

Measurements To fit 86.5-91.5[91.5-96.5/96.5-102/102-107]cm (34-36[36-38/38-40/40-42]in) chest.

Materials 20[21/21/22/23/24] × 25 gm balls double-knitting yarn.

Needles One pair each 3.25-mm and 5-mm (Nos. 10 and 6) needles.

Tension See page 10.

Abbreviations See page 12.

Back

Using 3.25-mm needles cast on 88[96/104/112] sts and work in single rib for 9 cm (3½ in) increasing 1 st at each end of last row (90[98/106/114] sts). Change to 5-mm needles and work in basket st as follows.

1ST ROW sl 1, *k4, p4. Rep from * to last st, k1 tbl. Rep this row 3 times.

5TH ROW sl 1, *p4, k4. Rep from * to last st, k1 tbl. Rep this row 3 times.

These 8 rows form the pattern. Use this throughout the garment other than welts and neckband.

Cont working without shaping until work measures 43[44.5/44.5/46]cm (17[17½/17½/18]in) from beg, finishing with right side facing.

Shape raglan Cast off 4[4/5/6] sts at beg of the next 2 rows.

3RD ROW sl 1, k2 tog, pattern to last 3 sts, k2 tog, k1 tbl.

4TH ROW sl 1, k2 tog, pattern to last 3 sts, k2 tog, k1 tbl.

For the 2 larger sizes rep these 2 rows twice more.

ALL SIZES

NEXT ROW sl 1, k2 tog, pattern to last 3 sts, k2 tog, k1 tbl.

NEXT ROW sl 1, pattern to last st, k1 tbl.

Rep these last 2 rows until 26[26/28/28] sts remain. Leave these sts on a spare needle to pick up for the neckband.

Front

Work as for back to the beg of the raglan shaping.

Raglan and 'V' neck shaping Cast off 4[4/5/6] sts, pattern until 41[45/48/51] sts are on the needle.

Turn and pattern back.

3RD ROW sl 1, k2 tog, pattern to last st, k1 tbl.

4TH ROW sl 1, k2 tog, pattern to last 3 sts, k2 tog, k1 tbl.

For the 2 larger sizes work the raglan shaping on EVERY row for the next 4 rows, and then cont the raglan shaping on every ALT ROW as on back. For the 2 smaller sizes go straight into shaping raglan on every ALT ROW and on all sizes dec 1 st as on 4th row on every 4th row 10 more times (11 dec in all on the neck side). Then stop shaping the neck side and carry on shaping the raglan until 2 sts remain. Fasten off. Work second half to match first half of front.

Sleeves

Using 3.25-mm needles cast on
39[39/41/43] sts and work in single rib
for 9 cm (3½ in) increasing in every st
on the last row of welt 78[78/82/86]
sts. Change to 5-mm needles and work in
basket st pattern increasing at each end of
9th and every following 8th row until
there are 90[98/106/114] sts on needle.
Then cont without shaping until work
measures 46[48.5/51/51]cm
(18[19/20/20]in) from beg ending with
right side facing.

Shape raglan Cast off 6[6/8/8] sts at beg
of the next 2 rows.
3RD ROW sl 1, k2 tog, pattern to last 3 sts,
k2 tog, k1 tbl.
4TH ROW sl 1, k2 tog, pattern to last 3 sts,
k2 tog, k1 tbl.
Rep the last 2 rows 7 times more then
cont to shape raglan on every ALT (right
side) row as on back until there are 8 sts
left. Leave these sts on a spare needle to
pick up for the neckband.

Making up and neckband

Sew up side and sleeve seams carefully.
Leaving the left back raglan seam open
join up the three other raglan shapings
using a flat seam and joining the notches.
With 4-mm needles and right side of
work facing pick up 8 sts from top of left
sleeve, 52[52/56/56] sts down left side
of neck, 1 st from centre (marking this st
with a piece of coloured thread),
52[52/56/56] sts up right side of front
neck, 8 sts from top of right sleeve and
26[26/28/28] sts from back. Dec 1 st at
each side of the centre st on every row
and work 7 rows of single rib. Cast off
loosely ribwise.
Join remaining raglan seam and
the neckband.
Make sure when sewing up to thoroughly
oversew bottoms of welts and ribs.

Child's long sleeved basket stitch sweater

Measurements To fit
56[61/66/71/76]cm
(22[24/26/28/30]ins) chest.
Materials 5[5/6/7/9] × 25 gm balls of
double-knitting yarn.
Needles One pair each 3.25-mm and
5-mm (Nos. 10 and 6) needles.
Tension See page 10.
Abbreviations See page 12.

Back

Using 3.25-mm needles cast on
58[58/66/74/82] sts and work
6[6.5/7/7.5/7.5]cm
(2¼[2½/2¾/3/3]in) in single rib.
Change to 5-mm needles and work in
basket st pattern as follows.
1ST ROW sl 1, *k4, p4. Rep from * to last
st, k1 tbl.
Rep this row 3 times more.
5TH ROW sl 1, *p4, k4. Rep from * to last
st, k1 tbl.
Rep this row 3 times more.
These 8 rows form the pattern which is
used throughout, except for the welts and
neckband.
Cont working without shaping until work
measures 21.5[23/21/25.5/26.5]cm
(8½[9/9½/10/10½]in).
Shape raglan Keeping pattern correct, cast
off 2[2/4/4/6] sts at beg of next 2 rows.
3RD ROW sl 1, k2 tog, pattern to last 3 sts,
k2 tog, k1 tbl.
4TH ROW sl 1, pattern to last st, k1 tbl.
5TH ROW as 4th row.
6TH ROW as 4th row.
Rep these 4 rows 4[4/3/2/2] times.
NEXT ROW sl 1, k2 tog, pattern to last 3
sts, k2 tog, k1 tbl.
NEXT ROW sl 1, pattern to last st, k1 tbl.
Rep these 2 rows until 4[4/6/6/8] sts
remain. Leave these sts on a holder for
the neckband.

Front

Work as for back to armhole shaping.
Shape raglan Cast off 2[2/4/4/6] sts at beg of next 2 rows.
NEXT ROW sl 1, k2 tog, pattern 22[22/25/30/32] sts, turn and work on this group of sts as follows.
Work 1 row. Carry on shaping raglan exactly as on back and AT THE SAME TIME start shaping the 'V' neck by dec 1 st on every 4th[5th/3rd/3rd/3rd] row 7[6/9/11/13] times.
Cont raglan shaping until 2[2/2/3/3] sts remain, leaving remaining sts on a pin for neckband.

Sleeves

Using 3.25-mm needles cast on 33[33/35/37/40] sts and work in single rib for 6.5 cm (2½ in) increasing evenly to 50[54/58/62/66] sts on the last row. Change to 5-mm needles and basket st pattern as on back and front working until sleeve measures 23[25.5/29/33/35.5]cm (9[10/11½/13/14]in) from the beg.
Shape raglan Keeping pattern correct, cast off 2[2/4/4/6] sts at the beg of the next 2 rows.
3RD ROW sl 1, k2 tog, pattern to last 3 sts, k2 tog, k1 tbl.
Work 3 rows without shaping as on back, and then rep these 4 rows 3[3/2/2/0] times.
NEXT ROW sl 1, k2 tog, pattern to last 3 sts, k2 tog, k1 tbl.
NEXT ROW sl 1, pattern to last st, k1 tbl.
Rep these last 2 rows until 24[24/24/28/28] sts remain. Leave these sts on a spare needle for neckband.

Neckband

Using 3.25-mm needles and with right side of work facing pick up sts from top of 1st sleeve, 34[36/36/38/40] sts down left front, 1 st from centre of 'V' neck, marking this st with a piece of coloured thread, 34[36/36/38/40] sts up other side of neck, sts from top of 2nd sleeve, and sts from back. Work 6 rows in single rib decreasing 1 st at each side

CHILD'S THREE-BAND SWEATER WITH MOHAIR

of centre st on every row.
Cast off ribwise.

Making up
As for adults.

Three-band sweater with mohair

Measurements Lady's small, medium and large.
Materials Of double-knitting yarn 9 × 25 gm balls in A, 7 balls in B, 5 balls in C. 2 × 25 gm balls of mohair.
Needles One pair each of 4-mm and 6-mm (Nos. 8 and 4) needles.
Tension See page 10.
Abbreviations See page 12.

Back
Using 4-mm needles and A cast on 72[76/80] sts and work 9 cm (3½ in) in single rib, inc evenly along last rib row to 82[86/90] sts. Change to 6-mm needles using A and M (mohair).
1ST ROW using M, k2 *sl 1, k2. Rep from * to last st, k1 M tbl.
2ND ROW using M, p3, *sl 1, p2. Rep from * to end.
Work 2 rows in st st in A.
Using M rep rows 1 and 2 once more.
Cont in A and in moss st until work measures 28.5 cm (11¼ in) from beg.
Using M rep rows 1 and 2.
NEXT ROW k in A.
NEXT ROW p in B.
Using M rep rows 1 and 2 again.
Cont in B and garter st until work measures 48.5 cm (19 in) from beg.
Using M rep rows 1 and 2.
NEXT ROW k in B.
NEXT ROW p in C.
Using M rep rows 1 and 2 again.
Cont in C and in moss st until work

THE THREE-BAND SWEATER HAS A 'V' NECK IN THE ADULT'S PATTERN AND A BOAT NECK IN THE CHILD'S PATTERN. IF YOU WISH TO MAKE A DIFFERENT NECKLINE FOR THE ADULT VERSION AS SHOWN IN THIS PHOTOGRAPH, FOLLOW THE INSTRUCTIONS GIVEN ON PAGE 9 FOR ALTERING BASIC PATTERNS

measures 68.5 cm (27 in) from beg.
Shape shoulders Cast off 10[10/11] sts at beg of the next 6 rows, leave remaining sts on holder for neckband.

Front

Work as for back until 4 rows of moss st in C have been worked.
Shape 'V' Moss st 41[43/45], turn.
Work on first group of sts as follows:
k2 tog, moss st to end.
Dec 1 st at 'V' edge on next and every following alt row 5 times.
Work 2 rows.
Now dec on next then every following 3rd row until 30[30/33] sts remain. Cont until front measures same as back to shoulder.
Shape shoulders Cast off 10[10/11] sts at beg of next and following 2 alt rows.
Rejoin yarn to other group of sts and work to correspond with first side, reversing all shapings.

Sleeves

Using 4-mm needles and A cast on 40 sts and work 9 cm (3½ in) in single rib. On last row inc into every st (80 sts). Change to 6-mm needles and work rows 1 and 2 in M from back.
NEXT ROW k in A.
NEXT ROW p in A.
In M work rows 1 and 2 again.
Cont in A and moss st until work measures 26.5 cm (10½ in) from beg.
In M work rows 1 and 2.
NEXT ROW k in A.
NEXT ROW p in B.
In M work rows 1 and 2.
Cont in B and garter st until sleeve measures 40.5 cm (16 in) from beg.
In M work rows 1 and 2.
NEXT ROW k in B.
NEXT ROW p in C.

In M work rows 1 and 2.
Cont in C and in moss st until sleeve measures 49.5 cm (19½ in) from beg.
Cast off in moss st.

Neckband

Join right shoulder seam.
Using 4-mm needles and M pick up 40 sts down left front, 1 st from centre, 40 sts up right front and 30 sts from back.
Work 6 rows in single rib, dec 1 st each side of centre st on EVERY row. Cast off ribwise.

Making up

Sew left shoulder seam, pin and sew sleeves into place, join side to sleeve seams strongly and firmly. Neaten all ends.

Child's three-band sweater with mohair

Measurements To fit
56[61/66/71/76/81.5]cm
(22[24/26/28/30/32]in) chest.
Materials Of 25 gm balls double-knitting
yarn 3[4/5/6/7/8] balls in A,
2[2/3/3/4/5] in B, 1[2/2/2/3/4] in C
and 1[1/1/1/2/2] balls mohair yarn.
Needles One pair each 4-mm and
6.5-mm (Nos. 8 and 3) needles.
Tension See page 10.
Abbreviations See page 12.

Back and front alike

Using 4-mm needles and A cast on
41[45/49/53/57/61] sts and work in
single rib for 5 cm (2 in), inc evenly
along last row to 47[51/55/59/63/
67] sts.
Change to 6.5-mm needles using A and
mohair (M).
1ST ROW In M k2, *sl 1, k2. Rep from *
to last st, k1 tbl.
2ND ROW p3 *sl 1, p2. Rep from * to end.
Work 2 rows st st in A.
Using M rep rows 1 and 2 again (these 6
rows are colour band).
Cont in A and work in moss st until
work measures 16.5[16.5/17/18/18.5/
19]cm (6½[6½/6¾/7/7¼/7½]in)
from beg.
Using M rep rows 1 and 2.
NEXT ROW k in A.
NEXT ROW p in B.
Using M rep rows 1 and 2.
Cont in B and work in garter st until
work measures 28[28/29/30/30.5/
31]cm (11[11/11½/11¾/12/12¼]in)
from beg.
Using M rep rows 1 and 2.
NEXT ROW k in B.
NEXT ROW p in C.
Using M rep rows 1 and 2.
Cont in C and work in moss st until work
measures 39.5[39.5/40.5/41.5/42/
42.5]cm (15½[15½/16/16¼/16½/

16¾]in) from beg.
Change to M and k 4 rows. Cast off.

Sleeves
Using 4-mm needles and A cast on
22[26/30/32/34/34] sts and work in
single rib for 5 cm (2 in), inc evenly
along last row to 28[32/36/40/42/
44] sts.
Change to 6.5-mm needles.
Work in pattern as for body working to
last colour band.
Work 1 row in C (after colour band).
Cast off evenly.

Making up
Join shoulder seam leaving
7.5[7.5/9/9.5]cm (3[3/3½/3¾]in) on
each side of centre open.
Pin sleeves into place and sew without
pulling or gathering.
Sew side and sleeves seams in
correct colours.
Neaten all ends.

Lady's double-knit sweater with mohair cuffs and polo collar

Measurements Lady's small, medium
and large.
Materials 16 × 25 gm balls of double-
knitting yarn, 3 × 25 gm balls mohair.
Needles One pair each 4-mm and
6.5-mm (Nos. 8 and 3) needles.
Tension See page 10.
Abbreviations See page 12.

Back and front alike

Using 4-mm needles and double-knitting
cast on 66[74/82] sts and work 10 cm
(4 in) in single rib, inc evenly along last
row to 76[84/92] sts.
Change to 6.5-mm needles and work in
moss st until work measures 28.5 cm
(11¼ in) from beg. Change to garter st
and cont until work measures 47 cm

INSTRUCTIONS ARE ALSO GIVEN FOR MAKING A CHILD'S VERSION OF THIS DOUBLE-KNIT SWEATER WITH MOHAIR CUFFS AND POLO COLLAR, TOGETHER WITH MATCHING SCARVES AND HATS FOR BOTH ADULTS AND CHILDREN

(18½ in) from beg.
Shape armhole Work in moss st for rest of back/front. Dec 1 st at each end of next and following alt rows until 66[74/82] sts remain. Cont in moss st, until work measures 66 cm (26 in) from beg.
Shape neck
1ST ROW moss st to end.
2ND ROW moss st 20[22/24] sts, k2 tog, turn. Work on this first group of sts. Dec 1 st at neck edge on every following alt row until 19[21/23] sts remain. Cont without further dec until work measures 71 cm (28 in) from beg. Cast off remaining sts. Slip centre 22[26/39] sts on to a spare needle for collar. Rejoin yarn to other group of sts and work to correspond with first group, reversing shaping.

Sleeves
Using 4-mm needles and mohair cast on 44 sts and work 9 cm (3½ in) in single rib, inc on last row to 84 sts. Change to 6.5-mm needles and main yarn and moss st until sleeve measures 48.5 cm (19 in) from beg. Cast off evenly.
Join right shoulder seam.

Collar
Using 5-mm needles and mohair pick up 100 sts evenly round neck (50 each half) and work in single rib for 21.5 cm (8½ in). Cast off ribwise.

Making up
Join other shoulder seam and pin and sew sleeves in place.
Join side and sleeve seams.
Turn sweater to right side, join collar seam, fold in half.

Lady's matching hat and scarf

Hat
Measurements The hat will fit the average head.
Materials 4 × 25 gm balls mohair (or similar yarn).
Needles One pair 5-mm (No. 6) needles.
Tension See page 10.
Abbreviations See page 12.

Use 2 strands of yarn together.
With 5-mm needles and double yarn cast on 82 sts and work in moss st for 15 cm (6 in). Shape crown as follows, working in garter st.
1ST ROW *k6, k2 tog. Rep from * to last 2 sts, k2.
2ND AND EVERY ALT ROW k.
3RD ROW *k5, k2 tog. Rep from * to last 2 sts, k2.
5TH ROW *k4, k2 tog. Rep from * to last 2 sts, k2.
Cont in this way until on the 12th row you will k2 tog all along row. Draw yarn through remaining sts, and sew up back seam.
If you want a hat which folds back work in moss st for 30.5 cm (12 in) instead of 15 cm (6 in). This gives you a double thick fold back. Allow twice the amount of yarn.

Scarf
Materials 7 × 25 gm balls of mohair (or similar yarn).
Using 5.5-mm needles cast on 36 sts and work in moss st for 183 cm (72 in).
Cast off in moss st.

Fringe
Cut strands of yarn 35.5 cm (14 in) long and fringe 5 strands at a time, 13 times along each end of the scarf.

Child's double-knit sweater with mohair cuffs and polo collar

Measurements To fit
56[61/66/71/76/81.5]cm
(22[24/26/28/30/32]in) chest
Materials 6[7/8/10/11/12] × 25 gm
balls double-knitting yarn, 1 × 25 gm ball
in mohair yarn.
Needles One pair each 4-mm and
6.5-mm (Nos 8 and 3) needles.
Tension See page 10.
Abbreviations See page 12.

Back

Using 4-mm needles cast on
41[45/49/53/57/61] sts and work in
single rib for 5 cm (2 in), inc evenly
along last row to 47[51/55/59/63/
67] sts.
Change to 6.5-mm needles and work in
moss st until work measures
16.5[16.5/17/18/18.5/19]cm
(6½[6½/6¾/7/7¼/7½]in) from beg.
Change to garter st and cont until work
measures 28[28/29/30/30.5/31]cm
(11[11/11½/11¾/12/12¼]in)
from beg.
Change back to moss st and cont until
back measures 39.5[39.5/40.5/41.5/
42/42.5]cm (15½[15½/16/16¼/
16½/16¾]in) from beg. Cast off.

Front

Work as for back until front measures
34.5[34.5/35.5/36/37/37.5]cm
(13½[13½/14/14¼/14½/14¾] in)
from beg.
Shape neck In moss st throughout.
Pattern 20[21/23/24/25/27], sl the
neck 7[9/9/11/13/13] sts on to a spare
needle, pattern to end.
Working on first group of sts dec 1 st at
neck edge on next 6 rows and cont
without further shaping until work
measures same as back to cast off edge.
Cast off.
Rejoin yarn to other group of sts and
work to correspond with first side,

reversing all shapings.

Sleeves

Using 4-mm needles and M cast on
22[26/30/32/34/34] sts and work in
single rib for 5 cm (2 in) inc on last row
to 28[32/36/40/42/44] sts.
Change to 6.5-mm needles, main yarn
and moss st, work in moss st until sleeve
measures 30.5[30.5/32/32.5/33/34]cm
(12[12/12½/12¾/13/13¼]in) from
beg. Cast off.

Collar

Join right shoulder seam.
Using 4-mm needles and M pick up
55[57/59/66/70/74] sts evenly round
neck and work in st st for 13 cm (5 in)
then moss st for 2.5 cm (1 in). Cast off
loosely.

Making up

K side outside when collar folded over.
Join collar and shoulder seams, pin and
sew sleeves into place without gathering
or pulling seam. Sew side and
sleeve seams.

Child's matching hat and scarf

Measurements 124.5[134.5]cm
(49[53]in) long plus fringe.
Materials For hat 2 × 25 gm balls double-
knitting yarn and 1 × 25 gm ball in
mohair. For scarf 4 × 25 gm balls double
knitting yarn and 1 × 25 gm ball in
mohair.
Needles One pair 6.5-mm (No. 3) needles
Tension See page 10.
Abbreviations See page 12.

Scarf

Using 6.5-mm needles cast on 20[24] sts

with M and work garter st for 6.5 cm (2½ in). Change to double-knitting wool and work in moss st until scarf measures 112[122]cm (44[48]in). Change back to M and garter st for 6.5 cm (2½ in). Cast off.

In M cut 18 strands 20.5 cm (8 in) long and fringe 3 strands tog 6 times at EACH end of scarf (36 strands in all).

Hat

Using 6.5-mm needles and M yarn cast on 64 sts and work 6.5 cm (2½ in) in garter st. Change to double-knitting wool and work in single rib for 5 cm (2 in) then work in moss st until work measures 16.5 cm (6½ in) from beg.

Shape Crown

1ST ROW *k6, k2 tog. Rep from * to end.
2ND ROW AND EVERY ALT ROW k.
3RD ROW *k5, k2 tog. Rep from * to end.
5TH ROW *k4, k2 tog. Rep from * to end.
7TH ROW *k3, k2 tog. Rep from * to end.
9TH ROW *k2, k2 tog. Rep from * to end.
11TH ROW *k1, k2 tog. Rep from * to end.
12TH ROW k2 tog all along row. Draw thread through these sts and sew up side seam wrong side of work on the wool part, right side of work on mohair part. Fold back mohair brim.

Adult's heavy multistitch sweater with boat neck and drop sleeves

Measurements Flat measurements about 96.5 cm (38 in) and 107 cm (42 in). To be worn loose on ladies, more fitting on men.
Materials 42 × 25 gm balls of double-knitting yarn or equivalent.
Needles One pair each 4-mm and 6.5-mm (Nos. 8 and 3) needles.
Tension See page 10.
Abbreviations See page 12.

Back and front alike

Use yarn DOUBLE

Using 4-mm needles cast on 68[74] sts and work in single rib for 5 cm (2 in). Change to 6.5-mm needles and work in pattern as follows:

Work 4 rows in garter st, starting with a k row.
**5TH ROW sl 1, *wlfwd, k2 tog tbl, k3. Rep from * to last 2[3] sts, k1[2], k1 tbl.
P back.
7TH ROW sl 1, k1 *wlfwd, k2 tog tbl, k3. Rep from * to last 1[2] sts, k0[1], k1 tbl.
P back.
9TH ROW sl 1, k2, *wlfwd, k2 tog tbl, k3. Rep from * to end [to last st, k1 tbl].
P back.
P 2 rows.
13TH ROW (A) sl 1, *p2, k2. Rep from * to last 3[1] sts, k2[0], k1 tbl.
14TH ROW (B) sl 1, k2[0] *p2, k2. Rep from * to last st, k1 tbl.
15TH ROW (C) sl 1, *k2, p2. Rep from * to last 3[1] sts, k2[0], k1 tbl.
16TH ROW (D) sl 1, k2[0], *k2, p2. Rep from * to last st, k1 tbl.
Rep 5th and 6th rows again.
K 3 rows.
NEXT PATTERN
1ST ROW (wrong side) *p1, k1 tbl. Rep from * to end.
2ND ROW p.
Rep these 2 rows twice more.
P 3 rows.
NEXT PATTERN
1ST ROW sl 1, *wlfwd, k2 tog, k1. Rep from * to last 2 sts, wlfwd, k2 tog.

2ND ROW p back.
Rep these 2 rows twice more.
Work 4 rows in st st.
Work 8 rows in moss st.
Work 4 rows in garter st.
NEXT PATTERN (basket st)
1ST ROW sl 1, *k4, p4. Rep from * to last 3[1] sts, k2[0], k1 tbl.
2ND ROW sl 1, k2[0], *k4, p4 to last st, k1 tbl.
Rep these 2 rows once more.
NEXT ROW sl 1, *p4, k4. Rep from * to last 3[1] sts, k2[0], k1 tbl.

A HAT TO MATCH THE MULTSTITCH SWEATER
AND SCARF CAN BE MADE FOLLOWING THE
INSTRUCTIONS ON PAGE 104

ABOVE: LADY'S ARAN-STYLE CARDIGAN

NEXT ROW sl 1, k2[0], *p4, k4. Rep from * to last st, k1 tbl. Rep these 2 rows once again, and then rep the first 4 rows again. Work 4 rows in garter st.
Then work from beg of the first pattern, marked ** and cont until work measures 68.5 cm (27 in).
Work 5 rows in garter st. Cast off knitwise.

Sleeves

Using 3.5-mm needles cast on 38 sts and work 7.5 cm (3 in) in single rib. Change to 7.5-mm needles.
1ST ROW k5, work twice into next 28 sts, k5 (66 sts).
P back.
Work 15 more rows in st st, ending with a k row.
*NEXT ROW (wrong side) k.
K 2 more rows.
With right side facing and starting with a k row work 13 rows in st st.
Rep from * until work measures 48.5[53.5]cm (19[21]in), ending with a right side row.
Cast off knitwise.

Making up

Using single double-knitting yarn join all seams carefully making sure that the seams are secure as this is a heavy garment. When sewing shoulder leave a 30.5 cm (12 in) opening for the head to go through.

Matching hat and scarf

Hat

Measurements To fit the average head.
Materials 6 × 25 gm balls of double-knitting yarn, or similar. Yarn is used double throughout.
Needles One pair 7.5-mm (No. 1) needles.
Tension See page 10.
Abbreviations See page 12.

Using 7.5-mm needles and double yarn cast on 68 sts and work 4 rows in single rib. Change to st st and work for another 10 cm (4 in).

Top

Work in garter st.
1ST ROW k2, *k6, k2 tog. Rep from * to last 2 sts, k2.
2ND ROW AND EVERY ALT ROW k.
3RD ROW k2, *k5, k2 tog. Rep from * to last 2 sts, k2.
5TH ROW k2, *k4, k2 tog. Rep from * to last 2 sts, k2.
7TH ROW k2, *k3, k2 tog. Rep from * to last 2 sts, k2.
9TH ROW k2 *k2, k2 tog. Rep from * to last 2 sts, k2.
11TH ROW k2, *k1, k2 tog. Rep from * to last 2 sts, k2.
12TH ROW k2 tog all along row. Thread yarn through remaining sts and draw up. Sew seam.

Brim

Using 7.5-mm needles and double yarn cast on 22 sts.
Omit row of holes and work as follows:
1ST ROW sl 1, *p2, k2. Rep from * to last st, k1 tbl.
2ND ROW as row 1.
3RD ROW sl 1, *k2, p2. Rep from * to last st, k1 tbl.
4TH ROW as row 3.
5TH ROW p1, k1 tbl. Rep to end.
6TH ROW sl 1, *wlfwd, k2 tog, k1. Rep from * to end.
7TH ROW p3 *k4, p4. Rep from * to last 3 sts, k3.
8TH ROW as row 7.
9TH ROW k3, *p4, k4. Rep from * to last 3 sts, p3.
10TH ROW as row 9.
Rep these 10 rows until brim fits nicely round hat without pulling or gathering, cast off.

Making up

Sew into place, fold back, sew wrong side of brim to right side of hat, fold brim back a third, then a third again.

Scarf
Measurements 183 cm (72 in) long plus fringe.
Materials 12 × 25 gm balls of double-knitting yarn.
Yarn to be used double throughout.
Needles One pair 7.5-mm (No. 1) needles.
Tension See page 10 .
Abbreviations See page 12.

Using yarn double and 7.5-mm needles cast on 27 sts. Always sl 1st st and k into back of last st to keep edges neat.
ROW OF HOLES sl 1, k1 *wlfwd, k2 tog tbl. Rep from * to last 3 sts, k2, wlfwd, k1 tbl.
K 4 rows.
Now proceed as follows:**
6TH ROW sl 1, *wlfwd, k2 tog tbl, k3. Rep from * to last st, k1 tbl.
7TH ROW sl 1, k2, *wlfwd, k2 tog tbl, k3. Rep from * to end.
P 3 rows.
11TH ROW sl 1, *p2, k2. Rep from * to last 2 sts, k2.
12TH ROW sl 1, p1, *p2, k2. Rep from * to last st, k1.
13TH ROW sl 1, *k2, p2. Rep from * to last 2 sts, k2.
14TH ROW sl 1, p1, *k2, p2. Rep from * to last st, k1.
Rep rows 11 and 12 once more.
K 3 rows.

NEXT PATTERN
1ST ROW wrong side — *p1, k1 tbl. Rep from * to last st, k1.
2ND ROW p.
Rep these 2 rows twice more.
P 3 rows.

NEXT PATTERN
1ST ROW right side — sl 1, *wlfwd, k2 tog, k1. Rep from * to last 2 sts, wlfwd, k2 tog.
2ND ROW p.
Rep these 2 rows twice more.
Work 4 rows in st st.
Work 8 rows in moss st.
Work 4 rows in garter st.

NEXT PATTERN (basket stitch)
1ST ROW sl 1, *k4, p4. Rep from * to last 2 sts, k2.
2ND ROW k2, *k4, p4. Rep from * to last st, k1.
Rep these 2 rows once.
5TH ROW sl 1, *p4, k4. Rep from * to last 2 sts, k2.
6TH ROW sl 1, k1, *p4, k4. Rep from * to last st, k1.
Rep these 2 rows once.
Rep the first 4 basket st rows again.
NEXT 4 ROWS garter st **
Rep this pattern from ** to ** until scarf measures 183 cm (72 in) long.
Work row of holes. Cast off.
Fringe
Cut 35.5 cm (14 in) lengths of yarn, allowing for 7 strands into each hole.

Child's multistitch sweater

Measurements To fit 56[61/66/71/76/81.5]cm (22[24/26/28/30/32]in) chest
Materials 8[10/12/12/14/16] × 25 gm balls of double-knitting yarn or similar.
Needles One pair each 4.5-mm and 7.5-mm (Nos. 7 and 1) needles.
Tension See page 10.
Abbreviations See page 12. .
Use yarn DOUBLE.

Back and front alike
Using 4.5-mm needles cast on 37[40/43/46/50/53] sts and work in single rib for 5[5/5/6/6.5/6.5]cm (2[2/2/2¼/2½/2½]in). Change to 7.5-mm needles:
1ST ROW k.
2ND ROW p.
3RD ROW k.
4TH ROW k.
5TH ROW sl 1, k1, *wlfwd, k2 tog tbl. Rep from * to end for sizes 61 cm, 71 cm and 76 cm, to last st, for sizes 56 cm,

66 cm, 81.5 cm, k1 tbl.

6TH ROW p.

7TH ROW as row 5.

8TH ROW as row 6.

9TH AND 10TH ROWS k.

11TH ROW sl 1, *p2, k2. Rep from * to last 0[3/2/1/1/0] sts.

Size 61 cm: p2, k1 tbl, Size 66 cm: k1, k1 tbl. Sizes 71 cm and 76 cm: k1 tbl.

12TH ROW sizes 56 cm and 81.5 cm: *p2, k2. Rep from * to last st, k1 tbl. Size 61 cm: sl 1, k2 *p2, k2. Rep from * to last st, k1 tbl. Size 66 cm: sl 1, k1 *p2, k2. Rep from * to last st, k1 tbl. Sizes 71 and 76 cm: sl 1, *p2, k2. Rep from * to last st, k1 tbl.

Rep these 2 rows once more.

15TH ROW sl 1, *k2, p2. Rep from * to last 0[3/2/1/1/0] sts.

16TH ROW as row 12 but putting p2 instead of k2 and k2 instead of p2.

17TH TO 20TH ROWS k.

Work 8 rows in moss st, 2 rows in st st and 8 rows in garter st.

Rep from row 1 again until work measures 33[37/40.5/44.5/48.5/53.5]cm (13[14½/16/17½/19/21]in) ending with wrong side facing. Cast off knitwise.

Sleeves

USE YARN DOUBLE

Using 4.5-mm needles cast on 28[30/30/32/32/34] sts and work in single rib for 5[5/6.5/6.5/7.5/7.5]cm (2[2/2½/2½/3/3]in) inc 1 st at each end of last row.

Change to 7.5-mm needles and work in 11 rows in st st and 3 rows k, until sleeve measures 20.5[21.5/25.5/29/33/38]cm (8[8½/10/11½/13/15]in) ending with wrong side facing. Cast off knitwise.

Making up

Sew carefully, putting centre of sleeve top to shoulder seam and making sure sleeve top lies flat where sewn to body.

Join sleeve seam and underarm.

Leave a 20.5[20.5/23/23/25.5/25.5]cm (8[8/9/9/10/10]in) slash opening between shoulder seams.

Child's matching hat and scarf

Hat

Measurements To fit sizes 56-61[66-71/76-81.5]cm (22-24[26-28/30-32]in).

Materials 3 × 25 gm balls of double-knitting yarn.

Needles One pair each 5.5-mm and 6-mm (Nos. 5 and 4) needles.

Tension See page 10.

Abbreviations See page 12.

Crown

Using 5.5-mm needles and double yarn cast on 64[64/72] sts and work in single rib for 5 rows. Change to st st until work measures 6.5[9/13]cm (2½[3½/5]in) from beg.

Shape Top 1ST ROW *k6, k2 tog. Rep from * to end.

2ND AND EVERY ALT ROW p.

3RD ROW *k5, k2 tog. Rep from * to end. Cont in this way until you k2 tog all along row. Draw thread through and fasten off.

Brim

Using 6-mm needles and double yarn cast on 18[22/24] sts and work in moss st for 84[88/92] rows. Cast off.

Making up

Stitch seam of crown. Sew brim on to cast on edge of hat and fold over. Make a pompon for top of hat.

Scarf

Measurements 102[117/132]cm (40[46/52]in) long.

Materials 5 × 25 gm balls double-knitting yarn.

Needles One pair 7.5-mm (No. 1) needles

Tension See page 10.

Abbreviations See page 12.

USE YARN DOUBLE

Using 7.5-mm needles cast on 28 sts and

work in moss st until scarf measures
102[117/132]cm (40[46/52]in). Cast off.
Fringe
Cut lengths 23 cm (9 in) long and fringe
4 strands tog 7 times along each end of
scarf.

Lady's multi coloured cardigan

Measurements To fit 81[86.5/91.5]cm
(32[34/36]in) chest.
Materials of 25 gm balls double knitting
yarn 15[16/16] balls in main colour, 1
ball each of colours 1, 2, 3, 5 and 8 and
2 balls each of colours 4, 6, 7 and 9. 6
buttons.
Needles One pair each 3.5-mm, 4.5-mm
and 5-mm (Nos. 9, 7 and 6] needles.

Tension See page 10.
Abbreviations See page 12.

Note Colour suggestions and charts for all
multicoloured garments are on pages
117-19

Back
Using main colour (0 on chart) and
3.5-mm needles cast on 85[91/97] sts
and work in single rib for 10 cm (4 in).
Change to 5-mm needles and, beg with a
k row, working in st st, work rows 15 to
80 inclusive from the chart (60 rows).
Shape armhole Cont working from chart.
Cast off 3 sts at beg of the next 2 rows
then k2 tog at each end of every row
until 61[67/73] sts remain. Cont without
further shaping still working chart (leave
out rows 97, 98, 105, 106) until row
124 has been worked.
Shape shoulders Cast off (using main
colour) 8[8/9] sts at the beg of the next

PATTERNS FOR A HAT AND SCARF TO MATCH
THIS CHILD'S MULTISTITCH SWEATER ARE GIVEN
ON PAGE 106

4 rows.
Cast off remaining sts.

Fronts

Using main colour and 3.5-mm needles
cast on 37[43/49] sts and work in single
rib for 10 cm (4 in). Change to 5-mm
needles and work as back from rows 15
to 80 of chart.

Shape armholes Cast off 3 sts at the beg
of the next row and then k2 tog at the
armhole end of the following 9 rows.
AT THE SAME TIME shape the front slope by
k 2 tog at the front edge on the 1st
armhole shaping row and every
following 3rd row until 16[16/18] sts
remain.

Shape shoulders Cast off 8[8/9] sts at the
armhole edge of the following 2 alt rows.
Work a second front, reversing all
shapings.

Sleeves

These are worked entirely in the main
colour. Cast on 46 sts and work in single
rib for 10 cm (4 in). Change to 4.5-mm
needles and work in st st. Inc at each end
of next and every following 6th row,
until there are 70 sts on the needle. Work
without shaping until work measures
45.5[45.5/48.5]cm (18[18/19]in).
Shape armhole Cast off 3 sts at the beg of
the next 2 rows, and then k2 tog at each
end of every row until 18 sts remain.
Cast off.

Frontband

Using main colour and 3.5-mm needles
cast on 13 sts.
1ST ROW (right side facing) sl 1, k1, *p1,
k1. Rep from * to last st, k1 tbl.
2ND ROW sl 1, *p1, k1. Rep from
* to end.
Rep these 2 rows twice more.
NEXT 2 ROWS (buttonhole rows)
rib 5, cast off 2, rib to end.
Rib 5, cast on 2, rib to end.
Cont working in rib, making a further
buttonhole at a 9 cm (3½ in) interval,
then work until frontband fits all round
front of the cardigan — very slightly
stretched.

Making up

Sew up neatly, sewing in all ends, using
flatstitch or small oversewing.
When stitching on the frontband, pin
centre of band to centre of back of neck
so that there is an even length of band up
both sides of the cardigan. It is most
important that the band should fit well as
it makes the entire garment look good.
Attach buttons to correspond with
buttonholes.

Lady's multicoloured waistcoat

Materials 10[10/10] × 25 gm balls
double-knitting in main colour (O) and
1 × 25 gm ball in each of other colours.
Tension See page 10.
Abbreviations See page 12.
Back and fronts worked as for cardigan
— only work to row 72 of chart, starting
armhole shaping on row 73.
Shape armholes Work exactly as for
cardigan and work same total length to
shoulder as for cardigan (up to row 124).
This just gives a deeper armhole for
waistcoat.

Armbands

Using 3.5-mm needles cast on 9 sts and
work in single rib until band fits nicely
round armhole slightly stretched.

Frontband

Same as for cardigan.

Making up

When sewing on armband use same
method as for frontband, pinning centre
of the band to shoulder seam and
carefully stitching to armhole of cardigan.
Match join of band to side seam.

INSTRUCTIONS FOR A CREW NECK SWEATER,
WAISTCOAT, SLIPOVER AND SCARF TO MATCH
THIS LADY'S MULTICOLOURED CARDIGAN,

Lady's multicoloured sleeveless slipover

Materials 10[10/10] × 25 gm balls double-knitting in main colour (O) and 1 × 25 gm ball in each of other colours.
Tension See page 10.
Abbreviations See page 12.
Work back and armbands as for waistcoat.

Front

Work as for waistcoat back to end of row 72.
Shape armholes and start 'V' shaping at neck Make sure to keep pattern correct.
1ST ROW cast off 6 sts, pattern 36[39/42] sts (including st left from cast off), cast off 1 st.
Pattern to end —
2ND ROW cast off 6 sts, pattern to cast off st.
3RD ROW work 2 sts tog, work to last 2 sts, k2 tog. Cont to dec at armhole edge on every row 5 more times, and AT THE SAME TIME dec at 'V' edge on every 4th row until 16[16/18] sts remain.
Work straight until same length as back to shoulder.
Shape shoulder Cast off 8[8/9] sts at armhole edge on next and following alt row. Rejoin yarn to other side of front and work to match first side, reversing all shapings.
Join right shoulder seam.

Neckband

Using 3.5-mm needles and main colour with right side facing pick up 60 sts down left front, 1 st at centre of 'V', 60 sts up right side and sts from centre back. Work in single rib for 7 rows dec 1 st at EACH side of centre st (mark centre st with a piece of coloured thread) on EVERY row, including cast off row which must be cast off ribwise.

Making up

Sew up all seams and sew in all ends securely.

Lady's multicoloured sweater with crew neck

Measurements To fit 81[86.5/91.5]cm (32[34/36]in) chest.
Materials Of 25 gm balls double-knitting yarn 15[16/16] balls in colour O. 1 ball each in colours 1, 2, 3, 5 and 8 and 2 balls each in colours 4, 6, 7 and 9.
Tension See page 10.
Abbreviations See page 12.
Back and sleeves
Work as for cardigan.

Front

Work as for back to end of row 110.
Then, being careful to keep pattern correct, work across 23[25/27] sts, sl next 15[17/19] sts on to a spare needle for neck, work to end. Working on this side of neck, dec 1 st at neck edge on following 7 rows. Work without shaping until armhole is same length as back.
Shape armhole
Cast off 8[9/10] sts at armhole edge of following 2 alt rows.

Neckband

Sew up right shoulder seam. Using 3.5-mm needles, with right side facing, starting at left front shoulder and in main colour, pick up 20 sts down first side, sts from front centre, 20 sts up 2nd side and sts from centre back. Work 7 rows in single rib. Cast off ribwise.

Multicoloured garments for men

Each of the aforementioned garments can be adjusted to larger sizes simply by using 5.5-mm needles for body instead of 5-mm needles and for sleeves using 5-mm needles instead of 4.5-mm needles. If extra length is needed start pattern at ROW 1 instead of ROW 15. Don't forget to reverse the button band on cardigan and waistcoat to men's buttoning. Sleeves should be made longer, 45.5[48.5/51]cm (18[19/20]in) to armhole shaping.

Matching scarf

Measurements
Materials Of 25 gm balls double-knitting yarn 14[18/19] balls in colour O and 1 ball in each of other colours.
Needles One pair 5.5-mm (No. 5) needles.
Tension See page 10.
Abbreviations See page 12.

Scarf
Using 5.5-mm needles cast on 61 sts and working entirely in st st work 6 rows in the base colour O. Then work rows 21-124 (leaving out 97, 98, 105, 106) from chart. Then work in base colour until scarf measures 152.5 cm (60 in). Then work from chart backwards from row 124 down to row 21. Work 6 rows in base colour and cast off.
Sew up sides of scarf to form a tube (seam at side), making sure not to cause any pull at all as sewn up side must be same length as folded side.
Turn scarf to right side and neatly sew together or crochet together double ends.

Fringe
Cut 45.5 cm (18 in) fringes — 10 fringes, 5 lengths thick at each end.

Child's multicoloured crew neck sweater

Measurements To fit
51[56/61/66/71/76]cm (20[22/24/26/28/30]in) chest.

Materials Of 25 gm balls double-knitting yarn 6[6/7/8/10/12] balls in colour O and 1 ball in each of other colours. 3 buttons.
Needles One pair each 3.5-mm, 5.5-mm (Nos 9 and 5) needles.
Tension See page 10.
Abbreviations See page 12.

Back
Using 3.5-mm needles and O cast on 49[55/61/67/73/79] sts and work in single rib for 5[6.5/6.5/7.5/7.5/9]cm (2[2½/2½/3/3/3½]in).
Change to 5.5-mm needles and work from Fair Isle chart working rows listed below throughout garment rows 15-42, 45-65, 62-77, 86-108 and 111 to end of work inclusive.
Different body lengths will of course end on different rows on the chart, you will find sizes 56[66/76]cm divide with 7 sts over from 12 st rep. In these sizes, work 1st 6 sts again and then the rep st on k rows. Rep st and last 6 sts, then 12 st reps on p rows.
Work in pattern (multicolour) until sweater measures 24[24/25.5/28/29/30.5]cm (9½[9½/10/11/11½/12]in) from beg.
Shape armhole Cast off 2[2/3/3/4/4] sts at beg of next 2 rows. Then dec 1 st at each end of next every following alt row 4 times.
Cont without further dec until back measures 33[35.5/38/40.5/43/45.5]cm (13[14/15/16/17/18]in) from beg.
Shape shoulder Cast off 6[6/7/8/8/9] sts at beg of the next 4 rows, leaving remaining sts on a spare needle for neckband (13[19/19/21/25/27] sts).

Front
Work as for back until work measures 28[30.5/33/35.5/38/40.5]cm (11[12/13/14/15/16]in) from beg.
Shape neck Keeping pattern correct work 16[17/24/26/30/34] sts, leave next 5[9/9/11/11/13] sts on a spare needle for neckband, pattern to end. Work on first group of sts as follows.

Dec 1 st at neck edge on next
4[5/5/5/7/7] rows. Cont without further
dec until same as back to shoulder (finish
at armhole edge).
Shape shoulder Cast off 6[6/7/8/8/9]
sts at beg of next and following alt row.
Rejoin yarn to other group of sts and
work to correspond with other group,
reversing shaping.

Sleeves

Using 3.5-mm needles and O cast on
32[32/34/36/36] sts and work
5[5/5/6.5/6.5/7.5]cm
(2[2/2/2½/2½/3]in) in single rib, inc
on last row to 38[38/40/40/42/42] sts.
Change to 5-mm needles and st st and
inc 1 st at each end of every 6th row
until there are 46[46/50/54/60/66] sts.
Cont on these sts until work measures
23[24/24/29/32/35.5]cm
(9[9½/9½/11½/12½/14]in).
Shape top Cast off 3 sts at beg of next 2
rows, then 2 sts at beg of next 10 rows,
then 1 st at beg of next 8 rows. Cast off
remaining sts.
Stitch right shoulder seam.

Neckband

With right side facing and using 3.5-mm
needles and O pick up 5[6/6/6/8/8] sts
down left front, 5[9/9/11/11/13] sts
across centre front, 5[6/6/6/8/8] sts up
right front and 13[19/19/21/25/27] sts
across back. Work 5[5/6/6/7/7] rows in
single rib. Cast off ribwise.

Making up

Join other shoulder seam leaving seam
open 6.5 cm (2½ in) for buttons. Pin
sleeves into place and sew. Join side and
sleeve seams and neaten all ends. Work
two buttonholes neatly on front of neck
opening.

MAN'S MULTICOLOURED WAISTCOAT

Child's multicoloured slipover

Measurements To fit
51[56/61/66/71/76]cm
(20[22/24/26/28/30]in) chest.
Materials Of 25 gm balls double-knitting
yarn 4[5/5/6/7/9] balls in colour O and
1 ball in each of other colours.
Needles One pair each 3.5-mm, 5.5-mm
(Nos. 9 and 5) needles.
Tension See page 10.
Abbreviations See page 12.

Back
Work back as for child's multicoloured
crew neck sweater.

Front
Work as for back to armhole shaping.
Shape armhole and 'V' front Keep pattern
correct throughout.
Cast off 2[2/3/3/4/4] sts at beg of next
2 rows.
NEXT ROW Count sts and divide in half, k2
tog, work to halfway point, turn. k2 tog,
pattern to end. Cont on first group of sts.
Dec 1 st at armhole edge on next and 4
following alt rows, AT THE SAME TIME dec
1 st at front 'V' on every 3rd row until
12[12/14/16/16/18] sts remain. Cont
without further dec until front measures
same as back to shoulder.
Shape shoulder Cast off 6[6/7/8/8/9]
sts at beg of next and following alt row.
Rejoin yarn to other group of sts and
work to correspond with first half,
reversing all shapings.
Join right shoulder seam.

Neckband
With right side facing, 3.5-mm needles
and main colour, pick up sts evenly
down left front, 1 st from centre front, sts
evenly up right front and sts evenly
across back of neck. Work 6 rows in
single rib. Dec 1 st on each side of centre

st on every row. Cast off ribwise. Sew shoulder seam.

Armbands

Using 3.5-mm needles and main colour cast on 6 sts and work in single rib until band fits nicely round armhole. Cast off ribwise. Sew into place joining under arm.

Making up

Join side seams and neaten all ends.

Child's multicoloured cardigan and waistcoat

Measurements See sweater.
Materials As for sweater plus 4 buttons. Waistcoat as for slipover.
Needles One pair each 3.5-mm and 5.5-mm (Nos. 9 and 5) needles.
Tension See page 10.
Abbreviations See page 12.

Body

Worked in one piece.
Using 3.5-mm needles and 0 cast on 97[109/121/133/145/157] sts and work 5[6.5/6.5/7.5/7.5/9]cm (2[2½/2½/3/3/3½]in) in single rib. Change to 5.5-mm needles and work from Fair Isle chart, working rows listed below throughout garment. Rows 15-42, 45-55, 62-77, 86-108 and 111 to end of work inclusive.
When body measures 24[24/25.5/28/29/30.5]cm (9½[9½/10/11/11½/12]in) from beg. Divide for armhole, this of course will end on different chart row depending upon the size.
Divide for armhole Keeping pattern correct pattern 22[25/27/30/32/35] sts, cast off 4[4/6/6/8/8] sts, pattern 45[51/55/61/65/71] sts, cast off 4[4/6/6/8/8] sts, pattern to end. Work on first group of sts as follows.

Dec 1 st at armhole edge on the next 5 alt rows AT THE SAME TIME shape front edge (starting on first armhole row) by dec 1 st at front edge on every 3rd row until 12[12/14/16/16/18] sts remain. Work without further dec until work measures 33[35.5/38/40.5/43/45.5]cm (13[14/15/16/17/18]in) from beg.
Shape shoulder Cast off 6[6/7/8/8/9] sts at armhole edge on the following 2 alt rows.

Back

Rejoin yarn to centre group of sts and dec 1 st at each end of next and following 4 alt rows. Cont without dec until back measures same as front to shoulder.
Shape shoulder Cast off 6[6/7/8/8/9] sts at beg of next 4 rows. Cast off remaining sts.

Front

Rejoin yarn to last group of sts and work to correspond with first side reversing all shapings. Join shoulder seams and neaten ends.

Frontband

Using 3.5-mm needles and 0, cast on 10 sts and work in single rib. On 3rd row work a buttonhole (rib 4, k2 tog, rib 4). Cont to work a buttonhole every 5 cm (2 in) until there are 4[4/5/5/6/6] in all. Cont in rib until the band is the right length to go round the cardigan, slightly stretched. Cast off ribwise. Sew band into place.

Waistcoat only

Armbands Using 3.5-mm needles and 0 cast on 6 sts and work in single rib until band fits nicely round armhole. Cast off ribwise.

Making up

Sew into place joining under arm.

Cardigan

Sleeves Using 3.5-mm needles and 0 cast on 32[32/34/34/36/36] sts and work in single rib for 5[5/6.5/6.5/7.5]cm

(2[2/2/2½/2½/3]in) inc evenly across last row to 38[38/40/40/42/42] sts. Change to 5-mm needles and work in st st, inc 1 st at each end of every 6th row until there are 46[46/50/54/60/66] sts. Cont on these sts until work measures 23[24/24/29/32/35.5]cm (9[9½/9½/11½/12½/14]in).
Shape top Cast off 3 sts at beg of next 2 rows, then 2 sts at beg of next 10 rows, then 1 st at beg of next 8 rows. Cast off remaining sts.

Making up
Sew sleeves into place neatly and finish garment completely.

Balaclava hood for all ages

Measurements To fit 6-10 year old, average lady's and average man's size.
Materials Using 25 gm balls of double-knitting yarn you will need 5[6/7] balls.
Needles One pair each 3.25-mm and 4-mm (Nos. 10 and 8) needles.

Tension See page 10.
Abbreviations See page 12.

Note This hood (not illustrated) is in single rib and will match any garment

Using 4-mm needles cast on 147[163/175] sts.
1ST ROW (right side) *k1, p1. Rep from * to last st, k1 tbl.
2ND ROW *p1, k1. Rep from * to last st, k1 tbl.
Rep these 2 rows until work measures 16.5[18/19]cm (6½[7/7½]in) from beg, ending with a wrong side row. Now start decreasing.
1ST SIZE (CHILD) (k1, p1) 4 times, (k3 tog, p1, k1, p1, k1, p1) 17 times, k1, p1, k1 (113 sts).
2ND SIZE (LADIES') k1, p1, (k3 tog, p1, k1, p1, k1, p1) 20 times, k1 tbl (123 sts).
3RD SIZE (MEN'S) (k1, p1) twice, (k3 tog, p1,

k1, p1, k1, p1) 21 times, k1, p1, k1 (133 sts).
For all sizes now change to 3.25-mm needles and work for 4 cm (1½ in). Change back to 4-mm needles.
NEXT ROW cast off 17[20/22] sts, rib to end. Work this row once more (79[83/89] sts). Now work on these sts for 9.5[11/12]cm (3¾[4¼/4¾]in) ending with a wrong side row.NEXT ROW cast off 22[24/24] sts, rib to end. Rep this row once more (35[35/41] sts). Work without shaping on these sts for 10[11.5/11.5]cm (4[4½/4½]in). Leave these sts on a spare needle.

Using 3.25-mm needles and with right side facing, pick up and k 17[20/22] sts along first cast off edge, 22[24/28] sts evenly along the straight edge, work across the 35[35/41] sts on the spare needle (leave the 2nd cast off sts and 2nd straight edge on either side of sts on a spare needle to be sewn together), pick up and k22[24/28] sts along straight edge and 17[20/22] sts along remaining cast off edge (113[123/141]sts). Work in single rib for 2.5 cm (1 in).
Cast off ribwise.

Making up
Join centre front and top seams neatly with a flatstitch.

**Colour suggestions for all
multicoloured patterns**

WHITE		PILOT BLUE
White	= 0 =	Pilot blue
White	= 1 =	Pilot blue
Natural	= 2 =	Dull mauve
Camel	= 3 =	Black
Natural	= 4 =	Dull mauve
Blue	= 5 =	Cream
Silver grey	= 6 =	Pale blue
Camel	= 7 =	Grey
Natural	= 8 =	Dull mauve
Blue	= 9 =	Lavender

BLACK		MID BROWN
Black	= 0 =	Mid brown
Black	= 1 =	Mid brown
Camel	= 2 =	Natural
Cream	= 3 =	Cream
Camel	= 4 =	Natural
Gold	= 5 =	School grey
Mid brown	= 6 =	Camel
Cream	= 7 =	Black
Camel	= 8 =	Natural
Rust	= 9 =	Rust

NATURAL		CAMEL
Natural	= 0 =	Camel
Natural	= 1 =	Camel
Rust	= 2 =	Mid brown
Chocolate	= 3 =	Black
Rust	= 4 =	Mid brown
Dark green	= 5 =	Moody blue
Cream	= 6 =	Cream
Gold	= 7 =	School grey
Mid green	= 8 =	Mid brown
School grey	= 9 =	Rust

CREAM		GREY
Cream	= 0 =	Grey
Cream	= 1 =	Grey
Camel	= 2 =	Natural
Orange	= 3 =	Black
Camel	= 4 =	Natural
Mid brown	= 5 =	Cream
Beige	= 6 =	Silver grey
Rust	= 7 =	Rust
Camel	= 8 =	Natural
Black	= 9 =	Burgundy

BURGUNDY		NAVY
Burgundy	= 0 =	Navy
Burgundy	= 1 =	Navy
Silver grey	= 2 =	Cream
Black	= 3 =	Rust
Silver grey	= 4 =	Cream
Camel	= 5 =	Chocolate brown
Cream	= 6 =	School grey
Black	= 7 =	Rust
Silver grey	= 8 =	Cream
Pilot blue	= 9 =	Cream

12 ST. REPEAT

Row													
31	7	5	5	7	7	5	5	7	7	5	5	7	7
30	7	7	5	5	7	7	5	5	7	7	5	5	7
29	5	7	7	5	5	7	7	5	5	7	7	5	5
28	5	5	7	7	5	5	7	7	5	5	7	7	5
27	7	5	5	7	7	5	5	7	7	5	5	7	7
26	9	9	9	9	9	9	9	9	9	9	9	9	9
25	4	4	4	4	4	4	4	4	4	4	4	4	4
24	4	4	4	4	4	4	4	4	4	4	4	4	4
23	9	9	9	9	9	9	9	9	9	9	9	9	9
22	7	7	7	7	7	7	7	7	7	7	7	7	7
21	7	7	7	7	7	7	7	7	7	7	7	7	7
20	6	6	8	6	8	6	6	6	8	6	8	6	6
19	6	6	8	6	8	6	6	6	8	6	8	6	6
18	6	6	8	6	8	6	6	6	8	6	8	6	6
17	6	6	8	6	8	6	6	6	8	6	8	6	6
16	5	5	5	5	5	5	5	5	5	5	5	5	5
15	5	5	5	5	5	5	5	5	5	5	5	5	5
14	4	4	4	4	4	4	4	4	4	4	4	4	4
13	4	4	4	4	4	4	4	4	4	4	4	4	4
12	3	3	0	0	0	3	3	3	0	0	0	3	3
11	3	3	0	0	0	3	3	3	0	0	0	3	3
10	3	0	0	3	0	0	3	0	0	3	0	0	3
9	3	0	0	3	0	0	3	0	0	3	0	0	3
8	0	0	3	3	3	0	0	0	3	3	3	0	0
7	0	0	3	3	3	0	0	0	3	3	3	0	0
6	1	1	1	1	1	1	1	1	1	1	1	1	1
5	1	1	1	1	1	1	1	1	1	1	1	1	1
4	2	2	2	2	2	2	2	2	2	2	2	2	2
3	2	2	2	2	2	2	2	2	2	2	2	2	2
2	1	1	1	1	1	1	1	1	1	1	1	1	1
1	1	1	1	1	1	1	1	1	1	1	1	1	1

END ST.   12 ST. REPEAT

START HERE
WITH K ROW

12 ST. REPEAT

Row													
79	7	7	9	9	9	7	7	7	9	9	9	7	7
78	7	7	9	9	9	7	7	7	9	9	9	7	7
77	9	9	7	7	7	9	9	9	7	7	7	9	9
76	9	9	7	7	7	9	9	9	7	7	7	9	9
75	9	9	7	7	7	9	9	9	7	7	7	9	9
74	7	7	9	9	9	7	7	7	9	9	9	7	7
73	7	7	9	9	9	7	7	7	9	9	9	7	7
72	7	7	9	9	9	7	7	7	9	9	9	7	7
71	1	1	1	1	1	1	1	1	1	1	1	1	1
70	1	1	1	1	1	1	1	1	1	1	1	1	1
69	1	1	1	1	1	1	1	1	1	1	1	1	1
68	2	2	2	2	2	2	2	2	2	2	2	2	2
67	3	3	3	8	3	3	3	3	3	8	3	3	3
66	3	3	8	8	8	3	3	3	8	8	8	3	3
65	3	8	8	3	8	8	3	8	8	3	8	8	3
64	3	8	3	3	3	8	3	8	3	3	3	8	3
63	8	3	3	3	3	3	8	3	3	3	3	3	8
62	9	9	9	9	9	9	9	9	9	9	9	9	9
61	4	4	4	4	4	4	4	4	4	4	4	4	4
60	4	4	4	4	4	4	4	4	4	4	4	4	4
59	9	9	9	9	9	9	9	9	9	9	9	9	9
58	0	0	0	0	0	0	0	0	0	0	0	0	0
57	0	0	0	0	0	0	0	0	0	0	0	0	0
56	0	0	0	0	0	0	0	0	0	0	0	0	0
55	6	6	6	7	6	6	6	7	6	6	6	7	6
54	6	7	6	6	6	7	6	6	6	7	6	6	6
53	6	6	6	7	6	6	6	7	6	6	6	7	6
52	6	9	6	6	6	9	6	6	6	9	6	6	6
51	9	9	9	6	9	9	9	6	9	9	9	6	9
50	9	9	9	6	9	9	9	6	9	9	9	6	9
49	6	9	6	6	6	9	6	6	6	9	6	6	6
48	6	6	6	7	6	6	6	7	6	6	6	7	6
47	6	7	6	6	6	7	6	6	6	7	6	6	6
46	6	6	6	7	6	6	6	7	6	6	6	7	6
45	6	7	6	6	6	7	6	6	6	7	6	6	6
44	0	0	0	0	0	0	0	0	0	0	0	0	0
43	0	0	0	0	0	0	0	0	0	0	0	0	0
42	0	0	0	0	0	0	0	0	0	0	0	0	0
41	1	1	2	2	2	1	1	1	2	2	2	1	1
40	2	2	9	9	9	2	2	2	9	9	9	2	2
39	2	2	9	9	9	2	2	2	9	9	9	2	2
38	2	2	2	2	2	2	2	2	2	2	2	2	2
37	2	2	9	9	9	2	2	2	9	9	9	2	2
36	2	2	9	9	9	2	2	2	9	9	9	2	2
35	1	1	2	2	2	1	1	1	2	2	2	1	1
34	3	3	3	3	3	3	3	3	3	3	3	3	3
33	3	3	3	3	3	3	3	3	3	3	3	3	3
32	5	5	7	7	5	5	7	7	5	5	7	7	5

12 ST. REPEAT   **Chart for all multicoloured patterns**

126					you cast off for shoulder							
125	8	8	8	8	8	8	8	8	8	shoulder		
124	4	4	4	3	4	4	4	4	4	3	4	4	4
123	4	4	3	4	3	4	4	4	3	4	3	4	4
122	4	4	3	4	3	4	4	4	3	4	3	4	4
121	4	4	4	3	4	4	4	4	4	3	4	4	4
120	6	6	6	6	6	6	6	6	6	6	6	6	6
119	6	6	6	6	6	6	6	6	6	6	6	6	6
118	7	7	7	7	7	7	7	7	7	7	7	7	7
117	7	7	7	7	7	7	7	7	7	7	7	7	7
116	6	6	6	6	6	6	6	6	6	6	6	6	6
115	9	0	0	0	0	9	0	0	0	0	0	9	
114	9	9	0	0	0	9	9	9	0	0	0	9	9
113	9	9	9	0	9	9	9	9	9	0	9	9	9
112	9	9	0	0	0	9	9	9	0	0	0	9	9
111	9	0	0	0	0	9	0	0	0	0	0	9	
110	7	7	7	7	7	7	7	7	7	7	7	7	7
109	7	7	7	7	7	7	7	7	7	7	7	7	7
108	9	9	9	9	9	9	9	9	9	9	9	9	9
107	9	9	9	9	9	9	9	9	9	9	9	9	9
106												
105												
104	2	2	1	1	1	2	2	2	1	1	1	2	2
103	2	2	1	1	1	2	2	2	1	1	1	2	2
102	2	1	1	2	1	1	2	1	1	2	1	1	2
101	2	1	1	2	1	1	2	1	1	2	1	1	2
100	1	1	2	2	2	1	1	1	2	2	2	1	1
99	1	1	2	2	2	1	1	1	2	2	2	1	1
98												
97												
96	3	3	3	3	3	3	3	3	3	3	3	3	3
95	6	6	6	6	6	6	6	6	6	6	6	6	6
94	8	8	6	8	8	8	6	8	8	8	6	8	8
93	8	6	6	6	8	6	6	6	8	6	6	6	8
92	8	8	6	8	8	8	6	8	8	8	6	8	8
91	5	5	5	5	5	5	5	5	5	5	5	5	5
90	5	5	5	5	5	5	5	5	5	5	5	5	5
89	8	8	6	8	8	8	6	8	8	8	6	8	8
88	8	6	6	6	8	6	6	6	8	6	6	6	8
87	8	8	6	8	8	8	6	8	8	8	6	8	8
86	6	6	6	6	6	6	6	6	6	6	6	6	6
85	0	0	0	0	0	0	0	0	0	0	0	0	0
84	0	0	0	0	0	0	0	0	0	0	0	0	0
83	9	9	9	9	9	9	9	9	9	9	9	9	9
82	4	4	4	4	4	4	4	4	4	4	4	4	4
81	4	4	4	4	4	4	4	4	4	4	4	4	4
									Armhole			
80	7	7	9	9	9	7	7	7	9	9	9	7	7

Ladies' Wear

Blackberry stitch cardigan with coloured knot stitch yoke

Measurements Small and medium
Materials 18 × 25 gm balls of double-knitting yarn and small pieces of any chosen colours for knots on yoke. 7 buttons.
Needles One pair each 3.25-mm, 3.5-mm and 5-mm (Nos. 10, 9 and 6) needles.
Tension See page 10.
Abbreviations See page 12.

Back
Using 3.5-mm needles cast on 74[82] sts. Work 9 cm (3½ in) in single rib. On last row of rib work as follows:
sl 1, *k1, work twice into next st. Rep from * to last st, k1 tbl (110[122] sts). Change to 5-mm needles and work in blackberry st as follows.
1ST ROW (right side) p.
2ND ROW sl 1, *p3 tog, (k1, p1, k1 into next st). Rep from * to last st, k1 tbl.
3RD ROW p.
4TH ROW sl 1, *(k1, p1, k1 into next st), p3 tog. Rep from * to last st, k1 tbl.
These 4 rows form the pattern. Cont until work measures 32 cm (12½ in).
NEXT ROW sl 1, *k1, k2 tog. Rep from * to last st, k1 tbl (74[82] sts).
Shape armhole Cast off 3 sts at beg of next 2 rows, then 2 sts at beg of next 2 rows.
Now work in knot st working knots in 5 different colours: royal – red – gold – cerise – green, done alternately on background of base colour.
TO MAKE KNOT: p3 tog, leave sts on left and needle, wrn, p same 3 sts tog again.

Knot pattern — 8 rows
1ST ROW p.
2ND ROW k.
3RD ROW p.
4TH ROW *k5, knot 3. Rep from * to end.
5TH ROW p.
6TH ROW k.
7TH ROW p.
8TH ROW *k1, knot 3, k4. Rep from * to end.
Work 6 rows of knots (3 full patterns), or until work measures 51 cm (20 in) from cast on edge.
Shape shoulder Cast off 9 sts at beg of next 4 rows. Leave remaining sts on spare needle for neckband.

Left front
Using 3.5-mm needles cast on 43[49] sts, and work as follows.
1ST ROW sl 1, rib to last 8 sts, k7, k1 tbl.
2ND ROW sl 1, k7, rib to last st, k1 tbl.
Rep these 2 rows until work measures 9 cm (3½ in). On last rib row inc as follows.
Sl 1, k7, work twice into every alt st (55[63] sts). Change to 5-mm needles and, keeping garter st frontband correct, work in blackberry st as on back until front measures 32 cm (12½ in) from cast on edge.
NEXT ROW dec in every other st (excluding band) (43[49] sts). Work 1 row to bring to side edge.
Shape armhole Keep garter st border correct throughout. Cast off 3 sts at beg of next row. Work 1 row. Cast off 2 sts at beg of next row. Work 1 row. Work in knot pattern 5 (first size) as on back until front measures 46 cm (18 in) from cast on edge. End on front edge.
Shape neck Work first 11 sts then slip them on to a spare needle for neckband. Work rest of sts in pattern.
Keeping pattern correct dec 1 st at neck

edge on every row until 18 sts remain.
Work rows needed to bring front to same
length as back to shoulder shaping (end
at armhole edge).
Shape shoulder Cast off 9 sts at beg of
next and following alt rows.

Right front

Work as for left front, reversing all
shapings and working the knot pattern,
reading from right to left.
On this front work buttonholes on 5th
row and last rib row by k3, wlfwd, k2
tog, k3. Work another 4 buttonholes on
frontband at 7.5 cm (3 in) intervals, the
last one to come 5 cm (2 in) below neck

shaping row (6 buttonholes in all).

Neckband
Sew shoulder seams. With right side
facing and 3.25-mm needles pick up
25[28] sts up right front (including the
frontband sts) the sts from across back of
neck and 25[28] sts down left front,
again, including frontband sts. Work 5
rows in garter st. Make a buttonhole on
next row. Work 4 more rows in garter st.
Cast off evenly.

Sleeves
Using 3.5-mm needles cast on 38 sts and
work 7.5 cm (3 in) in single rib. On last

row inc in every st (76 sts).

Change to 5-mm needles and work in blackberry st as on body until sleeve measures 45 cm (17½ in) from cast on edge.

Shape top Working in blackberry st cast off 3 sts at beg of the next 2 rows, then dec 1 st at each end of next and every following alt row, until 46 sts remain. Then dec 1 st at each end of every row until 19 sts remain.

NEXT ROW k1, *k3 tog. Rep from * to end of row. Cast off remaining sts.

Making up

Sew in ends from knot st. Pin sleeves into place, gathering centre top to make a puff sleeve. Sew sleeves into place, sew sleeve and side seams. Sew buttons into place.

The original cardigan was made in black with very bright knots on the yoke. Lurex could be used for the knots, and this cardigan also looks lovely in many other colours with toning knots i.e. burgundy, aubergine (dull mauve), natural, grey, red, royal and shocking pink.

Cable and bobble waistcoat

Measurements Small, medium and large.
Materials 8[8/9] × 25 gm balls double-knitting yarn. 7 buttons.
Needles One pair each 3.25-mm, 3.5-mm, 4-mm, 4.5-mm and 5-mm (Nos. 10, 9, 8, 7 and 6) needles.
Tension See page 10.
Abbreviations See page 12.
Also MB = k1, p1, k1 into next st, turn, k3, turn, p3. Then slip 2nd and 3rd sts over 1st st. C2f = cable 2 front. Sl 2 sts on to a cable needle and leave in front of work, k2 then k2 from cable needle.

Back

Using 3.25-mm needles cast on 74[80/86] sts and work in single rib for 7.5 cm (3 in). Change to 4-mm needles

and work in pattern as follows:
ROW 1 sl 1, k1, p1, (k2, p1) 1[2/3] times, (k3, p1) twice, (k4, p1) 3 times, (k5, p1) twice, k5, (p1, k4) 3 times, (p1, k3) twice, (p1, k2) 1[2/3] times, p1, k1 tbl.
ROW 2 p.

These 2 rows form pattern. Cont until work measures 18 cm (7 in) and then change to 4.5-mm needles until work measures 23 cm (9 in). Change to 5-mm needles and cont until work measures 28 cm (11 in) ending with right side facing.

Now start working garter st armbands.
1ST ROW sl 1, k6, pattern to last 7 sts, k6, k1 tbl.
2ND ROW sl 1, k6, pattern to last 7 sts, k6, k1 tbl.

Cont, keeping 7 sts in garter st at both ends and work pattern until back measures 52 cm (20½ in) from beg.

Shape shoulders Cast off 12 sts at beg of next 2 rows and 11 sts at beg of following 2 rows. Cast off.

Left front

Using 3.5-mm needles, cast on 45[48/51] sts and work in single rib for 7.5 cm (3 in). Change to 4-mm needles and work in pattern as follows:
1ST ROW sl 1, (k2, p1) 2[3/4] times, k3, p1, k4, MB (making only 3 sts out of 1 st), k1, MB, k5, c2f, k5, MB, k1, MB, k2, turn, leaving last 8 sts on pin for frontband.
2ND ROW p.
3RD ROW sl 1, (k2, p1) 2[3/4] times, k3, p1, k to end.
4TH ROW p.
5TH ROW work as for row 1, except c2b instead of c2f (ie leave the 2 sts at back of work instead of front).
6TH ROW p.
7TH ROW as row 3.
8TH ROW p.

These 8 rows form the pattern. Cont until work measures 18 cm (7 in).

Change to 4.5-mm needles and cont until work measures 23 cm (9 in).

Change to 5-mm needles and cont until work measures 28 cm (11 in) finishing at

armhole edge.
NEXT ROW sl 1, k6, pattern to end.
NEXT ROW sl 1, pattern to last 7 sts, k6,
k1 tbl.
Continue, keeping garter st armhole band,
and without shaping until work measures
45 cm (17½ in) from start, finishing at
front edge.
Shape neck Cast off 4 sts at beg of next
row. Work 1 row.
NEXT ROW sl 1, work 2 sts tog, work
to end.
Cont dec in this way on every alt row
until there are 23 sts on the needle. Work
without shaping until front measures
same as back to shoulder, finishing at
armhole edge.
Shape shoulder Cast off 12 sts at beg of
next row and 11 sts at beg of next
alt row.

Right front
Using 3.25-mm needles, cast on
45[48/51] sts and work in single rib for
4 rows. On next row make buttonhole
thus:
1ST ROW rib 3, cast off 2 sts, rib to end.
2ND ROW Rib to cast off sts, cast on 2,
rib to end.
Cont in single rib until work measures
7.5 cm (3 in). On the last row of rib
(wrong side facing) turn before last 8 sts,
leaving these sts on a safety pin. Change
to 4-mm needles. The pattern row will
now read:
sl 1, k1, MB, k1, MB, k5, c2f, k5, MB,
k1, MB, k4, p1, k3, (p1, k2) 2[3/4]
times, k1 tbl. Now cont as for left front
reversing all shapings.

Frontbands
Pick up sts from pin on left front and
using 3.5-mm needles work in single rib
for 45 cm (17¾ in) (this should make
band fit up front nicely, very slightly
stretched). Leave sts on a safety pin to
pick up for neck.

Right frontband
Work another buttonhole 7.5 cm (3 in)
after the first one and then every 8 cm

(3 in) until 6 have been worked. Work
until band measures same as left band
and leave sts on a safety pin for neck.

Neckband
With right side facing pick up 73 sts — 8
from right frontband, 20 sts from side of
neck, 17 across back, 20 sts from other
side of neck and 8 from left band. K 3
rows.
NEXT ROW k4, *wlfwd, k2 tog, k2. Rep
from * to last 5 sts, wlfwd, k2 tog, k3.
K 3 more rows. Cast off loosely (most
easily achieved by holding a needle 2
sizes larger in right hand).

Making Up
Sew up all seams using flatstitch or
overstitch. Make a crochet chain cord
about a yard long to thread through row
of holes round neck attaching little
tassels, or bobbles to each end of the cord
when threaded. Attach buttons to
correspond with buttonholes.

Cable and bobble cardigan

Measurements Small, medium and large.
Materials 16 × 25 gm balls of double-knitting yarn plus 7 buttons.
Needles As for waistcoat.
Tension and abbreviations As for waistcoat.

Back

Work as for back of waistcoat except that after changing to 5-mm needles cont until work measures 32 cm (12½ in) from start (instead of 28 cm (11 in), finishing with right side facing.
Shape armhole Cast off 4 sts at beg of next 2 rows and 2 sts at beg of following 2 rows. Then cont without shaping until work measures 51 cm (20 in) from the start.
Shape shoulders Cast off 12 sts at beg of next 2 rows, 11 sts at beg of following 2 rows. Cast off remaining sts.

Left front

Work as for waistcoat except cont until work measures 32 cm (12½ in).
Shape armhole Cast off 4 sts at beg of next row (at armhole edge) and 2 sts at beg of next alt row. Then cont without shaping until work measures 46 cm (17½ in) from beg ending at front edge. Work neck shaping as for waistcoat to end of shoulder shaping.

Right front

Work as for waistcoat — excluding garter st armhole band as on left front.

Sleeves

Using 3.25-mm needles cast on 39 sts and work in single rib for 10 cm (4 in) increasing 4 sts evenly along last row (43 sts).
Change to 5-mm needles and pattern:
1ST ROW sl 1, k1, p1, (k3, p1) twice, k4, MB, k4, MB, k1, MB, k4, MB, k4, (p1, k3) twice, p1, k1, k1 tbl.
2ND ROW p.

3RD ROW sl 1, k1, p1, (k3, p1) twice, k21, (p1, k3) twice, p1, k1, k1 tbl.
4TH ROW p. Cont in pattern increasing each end of next and every following 6th row until there are 61[67/73] sts on needle, working these increased sts into the broken rib pattern at each side. Cont until work measures 43[43/46]cm (17[17/18]in) from start.
Shape top of sleeve Cast off 4 sts at beg of next 2 rows and 2 sts at beg of next 4 rows. Then dec at each end of every alt row until 21 sts remain. Work 3 sts tog all along next row. Cast off.

Frontbands and neckband

As for waistcoat.

Cable and bobble long sleeved sweater

Measurements, materials, needles, tension and abbreviations As for cardigan, page 126, except 2 buttons only.
Work back and sleeves as for cardigan

Front

Using 3.25-mm needles cast on 74[80/86] sts and work in single rib for 8 cm (3 in). Change to 4-mm needles and pattern as follows:
1ST ROW sl 1, (k2, p1) 2[3/4] times, k3, p1, k4, MB, k1, MB, k5, c2f, k5, MB, k1, MB, k4, MB, k1, MB, k5, c2f, k5, MB, k1, MB, k4, p1, k3, (p1, k2) 2[3/4] times, k1 tbl.
2ND ROW p.
3RD ROW sl 1, (k2, p1] 2[3/4] times, k3, p1, k52, p1, k3, (p1, k2) 2[3/4] times, k1 tbl.
4TH ROW p.
5TH ROW as 1st row except c2b instead of front (see waistcoat).
6TH ROW p.
7TH ROW as 3rd row.
8TH ROW p.
These 8 rows form the pattern. When work measures 18 cm (7 in) from beg change to 4.5-mm needles and after another 5 cm (2 in) (23 cm (9 in) from the start) change to 5-mm needles. Then cont without shaping until work measures 32 cm (12½ in) from the beg.
Shape armholes Cast off 4 sts at beg of next 2 rows, then 2 sts at beg of following 2 rows. Cont without shaping until work measures 45 cm (17½ in) from beg.
Shape neck Pattern 25[28/30] sts, turn. NEXT ROW p2 tog, p to end. Cont working on these sts for left side of neck decreasing at neck edge on every row until 23 sts remain, then work without shaping until work measures same as back to shoulders, finishing at armhole edge.

Shape shoulder Cast off 12 sts at the beg of the next row, 11 sts at beg of following alt row. Rejoin yarn to remaining sts, sl next 12[12/14] sts on to a spare needle for front neck, and pattern across remaining 25[28/30] sts working this side to match first side reversing all shapings.
Join right shoulder seam.

Neckband

With right side facing and 3.25-mm needles and starting at left front shoulder pick up 17 sts down left front, centre front sts, 17 sts up right side front, and sts from centre back. K 6 rows. Cast off loosely holding a 4.5-mm needle in right hand.

Making up

Stitch all seams leaving left shoulder seam open for 7.5 cm (3 in). Make 2 loop buttonholes (either crochet chain, blanket st or chain st) on the front side of opening, and attach 2 buttons on back to correspond.
Do not press these bobble and cable garments as this flattens the texture.

Classic double-knit cardigan

Measurements Medium and large
Materials 17 × 25 gm balls of double-knitting yarn. 8 buttons to match.
Needles One pair each 3.25-mm and 4.5-mm (Nos. 10 and 7) needles.
Tension See page 10.
Abbreviations See page 12.

Back

Using 3.25-mm needles cast on 80[86] sts and work in single rib for 10 cm (4 in).
Change to 4.5-mm needles and work in st st, increasing 1 st at each end of 9th and every following 8th row until 88[94] sts are on needle. Cont without shaping

until work measures 34 cm (13½ in) from beg.

Shape armholes Cast off 4 sts at beg of next 2 rows, then dec 1 st at each end of every row until 72[78] sts are on needle. Cont without shaping until work measures 55 cm (21½ in) from start.

Shape shoulders Cast off 11[12] sts at beg of next 4 rows. Leave remaining sts on a spare needle for neckband.

Left front

Using 3.25-mm needles cast on 45[49] sts and work in single rib with a 7 st garter st at border at front edge as follows:

1ST ROW sl 1, k1 *p1, k1. Rep from * to last 7 sts, k6, k1 tbl.

2ND ROW sl 1, k6, rib to last st, k1 tbl.

Rep these 2 rows until rib measures 10 cm (4 in) on the last row leaving last 7 sts on a safety pin for front border (38[42] sts to work on).

Change to 4.5-mm needles and work in st st, increasing 1 st at the side edge on 9th and every following 8th row 3 times 42[46] sts.

Cont without shaping until work measures 34 cm (13½ in) from the beg ending at side edge.

Shape armhole Cast off 4 sts at beg of next row, then decreasing at this armhole edge on every row 4 times 34[38] sts.

Cont without shaping for 17 rows leaving last 4 sts on a pin (to pick up for neck), turn.

Cont in st st, decreasing at neck edge on next 8[10] rows, then cont without shaping until work measures same as back to shoulder.

Shape shoulder Cast off 11 sts at beg of next and following alt row.

Right front

Using 3.25-mm needles cast on 45[49] sts and work in single rib with 7 st garter st border.

1ST ROW k7, rib to end.

2ND ROW rib to last 7 sts, k7.

Work as for left front BUT MAKING A BUTTONHOLE ON 5TH ROW AS FOLLOWS

k3, wlfwd, k2 tog, k3, rib to end.

Also, work a buttonhole on last but one row of welt.

Sleeves

Using 3.25-mm needles cast on 40 sts and work in single rib for 10 cm (4 in), working last row as follows.

Rib 10, work twice into next 20 sts, rib 10 [60 sts].

Change to 4.5-mm needles and work in st st inc 1 st at each end of every 8th row until 76 sts are on needle. Cont until sleeve measures 43 cm (17 in).

Shape top Cast off 4 sts at beg of next 2 rows, then dec 1 st at each end of every row until 56 sts remain. Now dec 1 st at each end of every alt row for 30 rows. Cast off, working 3 sts tog as you do so.

Left frontband

Rejoin yarn to 7 sts left on pin. With 3.25-mm needles cont in garter st until band fits neatly up front edge, slightly stretched (leave sts on pin for neck).

Right frontband

Work as for left frontband working buttonholes about 7.5 cm (3 in) apart up band, the last to come about 6.5 cm (2½ in) from end (as there will be a buttonhole in neckband.

Neckband

Sew up shoulders. With right side facing and starting at right front pick up 7 sts from frontband, 4 sts from centre front, 25 sts up right side, sts across back, 25 sts down left side, 4 sts from left side centre and 7 sts from left frontband.

Work 4 rows in garter st

5TH ROW k3, wlfwd, k2 tog, k to end.

Cast off.

Making up

This cardigan can be made very special by embroidering it either down the fronts, on the yoke only, or with a small design just here and there on the fronts.

Mohair sweater in three colours with a big cowl collar

Measurements Lady's petite, small, medium, large and outsize.

Materials Of 25 gm balls mohair yarn 5 balls in A, 10 balls in B and 8 balls in C.

Needles One pair each 4-mm and 5-mm (Nos. 8 and 6) needles.

Tension 9 sts to a 5 cm (2 in) square using 5-mm needles.

Abbreviations See page 12.

Back

Using 4-mm needles and B cast on 73 [77/81/85/90] sts and work 6.5 cm (2½ in) in single rib. Change to 5-mm needles and A and work in st st for 20.5[23.5/23/24/25.5]cm (8[8½/9/ 9½/10]in) Change to B and work in st st for same length as A.

Shape raglan 1ST ROW In C sl 1, k1, sl 1, k1, psso, k to last 4 sts, k2 tog, k1, k1 tbl.

2ND ROW p.

Rep these 2 rows until 27[29/31/33/35] sts remain.

NEXT ROW sl 1, k1, sl 1, k2 tog, psso, k to last 5 sts, k3 tog, k1, k1 tbl.

NEXT ROW p. Leave remaining sts on a spare needle for collar.

Front

Work as for back to raglan shaping.

Shape raglan Change to C.

Work rows 1 and 2 as on back then work 2 rows WITHOUT decreasing. Rep these 4 rows once more, then rows 1 and 2 until 31[33/35/37/39] sts remain.

NEXT ROW k1, sl 1, k2 tog, psso, k to last 5 sts, k3 tog, k1, k1 tbl.

NEXT ROW p. Leave remaining sts on a spare needle for collar.

Sleeves

Using 4-mm needles and B cast on 32

Colour suggestions			
A = French navy	Brown	French navy	Wine
B = Brick	Camel	Mid blue	Pink
C = Beige	Cream	Very pale blue	White

[36/40/44/51] sts and work 6.5 cm (2½ in) in single rib, increasing evenly across last row to 39[43/47/51/55] sts. Change to 5-mm needles and A and cont in st st, increasing 1 st at each end of every 8th row until there are 51[55/59/63/67] sts. After 20.5[21.5/23/24/25.5]cm (8[8½/9/9½/10]in) have been worked in A change to B and work for the same length as for A.

Shape raglan Change to C. Work rows 1 to 4 as on front, 6 times, then rows 1 and 2 until 15[17/17/19/19] sts remain. (Should be the same length raglan as on back and front.) Leave these sts for collar.

Collar

Using 5-mm needles and B and with right side facing k up sts from first sleeve, sts from front, sts from second sleeve and those from back. K 1 row working the last st and the first st of each piece tog. Starting with a p row cont in st st for 23 cm (9 in) and then work 2.5 cm (1 in) in moss st to ensure that edge of collar lies flat. Cast off loosely in moss st.

Making up

Join all seams in their correct colours. Turn to right side, join collar seam, and fold collar in half.

Poncho

Measurements To fit average size.
Materials Of 25 gm balls double-knitting yarn used double, 32 balls.
Needles One pair each 4.5-mm, 6-mm and 7.5-mm (Nos. 7, 4 and 1) needles.
Tension See page 10.
Abbreviations See page 12.

Poncho
Back and front
Using 4.5-mm needles cast on 45 sts and

k 1 row.
2ND ROW sl 1, k1, *wlfwd, k2 tog. Rep from * to last st, k1 tbl.
3RD ROW k.
4TH ROW sl 1, k21, wlfwd, k1, wlfwd, k21, k1 tbl.
5TH ROW k.
6TH ROW sl 1, k22, wlfwd, k1, wlfwd, k22, k1 tbl.
7TH ROW k.
8TH ROW sl 1, k23, wlfwd, k1, wlfwd, k23, k1 tbl.
9TH ROW k.
10TH ROW sl 1, k24, wlfwd, k1, wlfwd, k24, k1 tbl (53 sts).
11TH ROW sl 1, wlfwd, *k4, wlfwd. Rep from * to last 4 sts, k3, k1 tbl (66 sts).
Change to 7.5-mm needles. Starting with a p row work 7 rows in st st.
NEXT ROW sl 1, k25, (inc in next st) 7 times, k1, (inc in next st) 7 times, k25, k1 tbl.
Work 7 rows in st st.
NEXT ROW sl 1, k32, (inc in next st) 7 times, k1, (inc in next st) 7 times, k32, k1 tbl.
Work 11 rows in st st.
NEXT ROW sl 1, k39, (inc in next st) 7 times, k1, (inc in next st) 7 times, k 39, k1 tbl.
Work 11 rows in st st.
NEXT ROW sl 1, k47, (inc in next st) 7 times, k1, (inc in next st) 7 times, k47, k1 tbl.
Work 15 rows in st st.
NEXT ROW sl 1, k55, (inc in next st) 7 times, k1, (inc in next st) 7 times, k55, k1 tbl.
Work 15 rows in st st.
NEXT ROW sl 1, k63, (inc in next st) 7 times, k1, (inc in next st) 7 times, k63, k1 tbl.
Cont in st st until work measures 58.5 cm (23 in) from beg then change to garter st and work 12 rows.
NEXT ROW sl 1, *wlfwd, k2 tog. Rep from

* to end.
NEXT ROW k. Cast off.

Making up
Sew up side seams.

Fringe
Cut fringe pieces 51 cm (20 in) long and using 3 strands at a time fringe into every wlfwd space along bottom of poncho.

Tie
Using a 3.5-mm hook and 3 strands of yarn make a crochet chain long enough to thread through neck holes and tie at front of poncho. Make a tassel to go on each end of the chain.

Matching hat and scarf

Hat
Materials 4 × 25 gm balls double-knitting yarn.
Measurements, needles, tension and abbreviations As for poncho, page 131.

Using 6-mm needles cast on 73 sts and work 2 rows in garter st.
3RD ROW sl 1, *(k1, p1) into next st, k1, (k2 tog) twice, k1, (p1, k1) into next st. Rep from * to end.
4TH ROW p.
These 2 rows (3rd and 4th) form the pattern.
Rep until work measures 18 cm (7 in).
Shape crown 1ST ROW *k6, k2 tog. Rep from * to last st, k1.
2ND AND ALT ROWS: k.
3RD ROW *k5, k2 tog. Rep from * to last st, k1.
5TH ROW *k4, k2 tog. Rep from * to last st, k1.
7TH ROW *k3, k2 tog. Rep from * to last st, k1.
9TH ROW *k2, k2 tog. Rep from * to last st, k1.
11TH ROW *k1, k2 tog Rep from * to last st, k1.

12TH ROW k2 tog all along row and then draw yarn through.

Sew up without pulling.

Scarf

Materials 12 × 25 gm balls double-knitting yarn.

Measurements, needles, tension and abbreviations As for poncho, page 131.

Using 6-mm needles cast on 26 sts and work in garter st for 1 row.

NEXT ROW sl 1, k1, *wlfwd, k2 tog to end.

Cont in garter st until work measures 183 cm (72 in).

NEXT ROW sl 1, k1, *wlfwd, k2 tog to end.

Work 1 more row garter st. Cast off.

Fringe as for poncho.

Striped oversweater

Measurements Lady's medium.

Materials Of 25 gm balls double-knitting yarn 12 balls in A, 10 in B, 4 in C, 8 in D, 4 in E, 4 in F and 2 in G.

Needles One pair each 6-mm, 7-mm and 7.5-mm (Nos 4, 2 and 1) needles.

Tension See page 10.

Abbreviations See page 12.

Use double-knitting yarn double

Stripe order for this sweater is:

6 rows B, 4 rows C, 8 rows D, 4 rows A, 4 rows E, 6 rows F, 2 rows G, 6 rows B, 6 rows A.

Back

Using 6-mm needles and A cast on 68 sts and work in single rib for 6.5 cm (2½ in). Change to 7-mm needles and work in st st following the stripe order as above, until work measures 43[44.5/47]cm (17[17½/18½]in) from beg. Mark each end of the last row to indicate end of side seam.

Cont in st st until work measures 63.5 cm (25 in) from beg ending with a k row.

Divide for back neck P 30, leave these sts on a spare needle for left back shoulders, cast off the next 8 sts, p to end. Work on remaining 30 sts for right shoulder. Dec 1 st at neck edge on next and following 3 alt rows. Work 1 row. Cast off.

Left back shoulder With right side facing rejoin yarn to inner end of sts on spare needle and work as for other shoulder.

Front

Work as for back until front measures

Colour suggestions	
	CAMEL
A	= Black
B	= Camel
C	= Cream
D	= Rust
E	= Mid brown
F	= Chocolate
G	= Cream
GREY	BURGUNDY
Black = A	= Currant red
Grey = B	= Burgundy
Oatmeal = C	= Oatmeal
Dull green = D	= Burgundy
Light grey = E	= Grey
Bottle green = F	= Black
Oatmeal = G	= Oatmeal
PILOT BLUE	BLUE
Aubergine = A	= Sky blue
Pilot blue = B	= Burgundy
Medium grey = C	= Pilot blue
Mauve = D	= Navy
Medium grey = E	= Currant red
Navy blue = F	= Aubergine
Sky blue = G	= Sky blue
MINK	YELLOW
Black = A	= Old gold
Mink = B	= Yellow
Caramel = C	= Mid brown
Mocha = D	= Cream
Peacock blue = E	= Black
Chocolate = F	= Orange
Caramel = G	= Mid brown

58.5 cm (23½ in) from beg ending with a k row.

Divide for neck P 30, leave these sts on a spare needle, cast off 8 sts, p to end, working on these 30 sts for left front shoulder.

Dec 1 st at neck edge on next and following 3 alt rows and then work without shaping until work measures same as back to shoulder. Cast off. Rejoin yarn to inner end of sts on spare needle and work as for left front shoulder to end.

Sleeves

Using 7-mm needles and A cast on 60 sts and work 6 rows in single rib. Change to garter st and work in stripes until sleeve measures 40.5 cm (16 in) from beg. Work 6 rows in single rib and cast off.

Pockets (make two)

Using 7-mm needles cast on 20 sts and work in garter st in stripes until work measures 15 cm (6 in). Cast off.
Sew pockets immediately above rib and 2.5 cm (1 in) in from side. Ensure pockets lie flat and square and don't stretch or gather up main body.

Making up

Join shoulder seams using flatstitch or overstitch. Set in sleeves between coloured markers, back and front. Join side seams of body and sleeve. With a size 3.5-mm crochet hook and right side of work facing, rejoin yarn and work 2 rows of double crochet all round neck edge (about 84 double crochet). Fasten off. Alternatively you may wish to have a polo collar.
Using 7.5-mm needles cast on 84 sts and work one whole pattern of stripes in garter st. Cast off loosely.
Sew on to neck using overstitch or flatstitch.

Matching hat and scarf

Tension and Abbreviations See pages 10 and 12.

Crown

Using A yarn double and 7.5-mm needles cast on 68 sts and work in single rib for 4 rows. Change to st st and work 16 more rows.
Shape top *k2, k2 tog. Rep from * to end. Work 3 rows in st st.
NEXT ROW *k1, k2 tog. Rep from * to end. Work 3 rows in st st.
NEXT ROW k2 tog all along row. Work 3 rows in st st.
NEXT ROW k2 tog all along row. Work 3 rows in st st.
Draw yarn through remaining sts.

Brim

Using yarn double and 7.5-mm needles cast on 22 sts and work in garter st and in stripes as on sweater until brim is long enough to be stitched loosely on to cast on edge of crown with no pull on the brim at all, preferably eased on (about 108 rows).

Scarf

Using 7.5-mm needles and A double, cast on 30 sts and working in garter st do one set of stripes as on sweater then work in yarn A double until work measures 163 cm (64 in). Work another set of stripes.

Fringe

In a mixture of the colours, cutting 35.5 cm (14 in) lengths and fringe with 7 lengths at a time 10 times along each short end of scarf.

Mohair short sweater with single cable up centre front

Measurements Medium size. Use one size smaller needles for small, one size larger for large.
Materials 17 × 25 gm balls mohair or similar yarn. 2 buttons.
Needles One pair each 4-mm and 6.5-mm (Nos. 8 and 3) needles.
Tension 7 sts to a 5 cm (2 in) square
Tension See page 10.
Abbreviations See page 12.

Back

Using 4-mm needles cast on 64 sts and work in single rib for 7.5 cm (3 in). Change to 6.5-mm needles and work in st st until work measures 32 cm (12½ in).
Shape armhole Cast off 3 sts at beg of next 2 rows, then dec 1 st at each end of following 3 alt rows (52 sts). Cont without shaping until work measures 51 cm (20 in) from beg finishing with k row. Cast off.

Front

Using 4-mm needles cast on 64 sts and work in single rib for 9 cm (3½ in). Change to 6.5-mm needles and work in st st with centre front cable as follows:
1ST ROW k26, p2, k8, p2, k26.
2ND ROW p26, k2, p8, k2, p26.
3RD ROW as row 1.
4TH ROW as row 2.
5TH ROW k26, p2, slip next 4 sts on to a cable needle and leave at back of work, k4, then k4 from cable needle, p2, k26.
6TH ROW as row 2.
7TH ROW as row 1.
8TH ROW as row 2.
These 8 rows form the pattern. Cont until work measures 32 cm (12½ in) from start then shape armholes as on back. Cont without further shaping until work

measures 44.5 cm (17½ in) from beg.
Shape neck K 18, slip next 16 sts on to a pin to pick up for neck, k18.
Working on last 18 sts only dec 1 st at neck edge 3 times then work without shaping until armhole measures same as back. Cast off.

Sleeves

Using 4-mm needles cast on 40 sts and work 7.5 cm (3 in) in single rib. Change to 6.5-mm needles and inc evenly on first row to 54 sts.
Work in st st until sleeve measures 44.5 cm (17½ in) from cast on edge.
Shape top Cast off 2 sts at beg of next 2 rows, then dec 1 st at each end of next and following 2 alt rows. Work 5 rows. Dec 1 st at each end of next and following 3 alt rows. Work 3 rows. Dec 1 st at each end of next and following alt rows.
Now dec 1 st at each end of next 2 rows.
NEXT ROW k3 tog all along row. Cast off.
Join right shoulder seam.

Neckband

With right side facing and 4-mm needles, pick up 15 sts down left front, 16 sts from centre, 15 sts up right front, 20 sts across back of neck (66 sts). Work 6 rows in single rib, decreasing 1 st on each side of centre front st on every row. Cast off loosely in rib.

Making up

Join left shoulder seam, leaving it open 5 cm (2 in) from neck. Set sleeves into place and stitch. Join side and sleeve seams. Work 2 buttonholes in crochet, blanketstitch or chain stitch on front side of opening and attach 2 buttons on back of opening to correspond.

Dolman cardigan

Measurements To fit small, medium and large.

Materials 12 × 25 gm balls double-knitting yarn and 10 × 25 gm balls mohair, 3 buttons.
Needles One pair each 3.5-mm and 4-mm (Nos. 9 and 8) needles.
Tension See page 10.
Abbreviations See page 12.
The stripe pattern = 12 rows mohair; 2 rows double-knitting yarn; 6 rows mohair; 2 rows double-knitting.
Work in st st throughout.

Back

Using 3.5-mm needles and double-knitting yarn cast on 90[98/102] sts and work in single rib for 15 cm (6 in). Change to 4-mm needles and start working in stripe pattern as above. Knit 2[4/2] rows.
Shape sleeve Work 24[22/24] rows increasing 1 st at each end of EVERY row (138[142/150] sts). Cast on 33 sts at the beg of the next 2 rows (204[208/216] sts).
Work 56 rows without shaping.
Cast off 21[21/22] sts at beg of the next 8[4/8] rows.
Medium size only: cast off 22 sts at beg of next 4 rows.
There are now 36[36/40] sts remaining. Cast off.

Left front

Using 3.5-mm needles and double-knitting yarn cast on 50[54/58] sts and work in single rib for 15 cm (6 in) ending with a wrong side row and leaving last 8 sts on a safety pin to pick up for front-band. Change to 4-mm needles and start working in stripe pattern. Work 2[4/2] rows decreasing 1 st at the end of the 1st row. While continuing to decrease at front edge on 5th[2nd/3rd] row and every following 6th[5th/4th] row until 15[15/19] decreases in all have been worked at this edge, AT THE SAME TIME inc 1 st at the side edge on next 24[22/24] rows. Then cast on 33 sts at beg (side edge) of next row. Work 57 rows straight at armhole edge still shaping front as before. Keeping front edge correct work

6[4/6] rows casting off 21[21/22] sts at beg of next side edge row and following 2[1/2] rows.

Medium size only: work 2 rows, casting off 22 sts at beg of 1st row. For all sizes cast off remaining sts.

Right front

Using 3.5-mm needles and double-knitting yarn cast on 50[54/58] sts and work in single rib for 4 rows.

5TH ROW Work to last 6 sts, wlfwd, k2 tog rib to end (buttonhole).

Cont to work in rib until work measures 15 cm (6 in) working another buttonhole halfway up the rib and one at the end. Finish the rib at the end of a right side row slipping last 8 sts on to a safety pin for frontband. Change to 4-mm needles and start working stripe pattern and work to match first front, reversing all shapings.

Join shoulder and upper sleeve seams.

Cuffs

Using 3.5-mm needles, double-knitting yarn and with right side facing pick up and k 58 sts along sleeve edge and work in single rib for 18 cm (7 in). Cast off in rib.

Left frontband

Using 3.5-mm needles, double-knitting yarn and with wrong side facing rejoin yarn to the 8 sts left on pin for band and work in single rib until band is long enough to fit up the front to centre back, slightly stretched. It is very important to get the band the correct length to hold a cardigan in shape.

Right frontband

Using 3.5-mm needles, double-knitting yarn and with right side facing rejoin yarn to 8 sts left on pin and complete as for left frontband.

Making up

Join side and sleeve seams in the correct matching yarns. Sew frontbands into position and sew on buttons to correspond with buttonholes.

This dolman cardigan is a very basic pattern and could be varied in many ways: different stripes, made in one colour, made with the body in bouclé and welts in double-knitting yarn and so on.

Blazer cardigan

Measurements Medium size. Use 4.5-mm (No. 7) needles to make small size. For a heavier blazer use Aran weight yarn instead of double-knitting. 1 button.

Materials 17 × 25 gm balls of double-knitting yarn. Allow 500 gms Aran yarn.

Needles One pair 5-mm (No. 6) needles 4.5-mm (Nos. 7) for small size.

Tension See page 10.

Abbreviations See page 12.

Pocket lining (make two)

Using 5-mm needles cast on 20 sts and work 10 cm (4 in) in st st.

Leave sts on a thread.

Left front

Using 5-mm needles cast on 52 sts and work as follows:

1ST ROW sl 1, *p2, k2. Rep from * to last 7 sts, (k1, p1) 3 times, k1 tbl.

2ND ROW sl 1, (p1, k1) 3 times, *p2, k2. Rep from * to last st, k1 tbl.

Rep these 2 rows 3 times more (8 rows). Keeping moss st border correct (i.e. 7 sts at end right side row, beg of wrong side row) work remaining 45 sts in st st. Cont as follows:

1ST ROW sl 1, k2 tog, k to last 7 sts, moss st 6, k1 tbl.

2ND, 4TH, 8TH, 10TH ROWS sl 1, moss st 6, p to last st, k1 tbl.

3RD, 5TH, 7TH, 9TH ROWS sl 1, k to last 7 sts, moss st 6, k1 tbl.

6TH ROW sl 1, moss st 6, p to last 3 sts, p2 tog, k1 tbl.

Rep these 10 rows once more (pocket top should be DOUBLE RIB).

NEXT ROW sl 1, k2 tog, k6, work 20 sts in double rib, k to last 7 sts, moss st 6, k1 tbl.

1ST ROW sl 1, moss st 6, p 12, work 20 sts in double rib, p7, k1 tbl.

2ND ROW sl 1, k7, work 20 sts in double rib, k to last 7 sts, moss st 6, k1 tbl.

Rep rows 1 and 2 twice more.

Set in pocket (wrong side)

1ST ROW sl 1, moss st 6, p 12, cast off 20 sts in double rib, p to last st, k1 tbl.

2ND ROW sl 1, k7, k 20 sts from pocket lining, k to last 7 sts, moss st 6, k1 tbl.

Now cont in st st with moss st border until front measures 35.5 cm (14 in) from cast on edge.

Front shaping 1ST ROW sl 1, k to last 9 sts, k2 tog, inc into next st, moss st to last st, k1 tbl.

2ND ROW sl 1, moss st 7, p to last st, k1 tbl.

3RD ROW sl 1, k to last 8 sts, moss st 7, k1 tbl.

4TH ROW as row 2.

5TH ROW as row 3.

6TH ROW sl 1, moss st 6, inc into next st, p to last st, k1 tbl.

7TH ROW sl 1, k to last 9 sts, moss st 8, k1, tbl.

8TH ROW sl 1, moss st 8, p to last st, k1, tbl.

Shape armhole Cast off 5 sts. Work remainder of row as row 7.

10TH ROW sl 1, moss st 8, p to last st, k1 tbl

Cont decreasing 1 st at armhole edge on next 7 rows, AT THE SAME TIME increasing at front edge by repeating rows 1 to 10, 4 times more.

NOTE 9TH ROW will read 7th row and moss st border will be increased by 1 st after every 1st and 5th row.

Cont front shaping, keeping armhole edge straight until 5 front dec (39 sts) in all have been worked then work rows 1 to 5 again.

NEXT ROW Cast off 17 sts in moss st, p to last st, k1 tbl.

Work 3 rows in st st.

Dec 1 st at front edge on next row. Work 2 rows in st st. Armhole depth should be 21.5 cm (8½ in) IF NOT, work any rows needed to bring it to correct length.

Shape shoulder Cast off 7 sts at beg of next and following alt row. Work 1 row.

Cast off remaining sts.

Right front

Work as for left front reversing all shapings, position of pocket and, of course, moss st band for front edge.
After 18 cm (7 in) work a buttonhole on moss st band as follows:
1ST ROW sl 1, moss st 2, cast off 2, moss st 2.
2ND ROW moss st 2, cast on 2, moss st 2, k1 tbl.

Back

Using 5-mm needles cast on 98 sts and work 8 rows in k2, p2 rib. Change to st st and dec 1 st at each end of next and every following 5th row until 88 sts remain.
Cont in st st until back measures same as front to armhole shaping.
Shape armhole Cast off 5 sts at beg of next 2 rows, then dec 1st at each end of every row until 64 sts remain.
Now cont without further decreasing until back measures 60 cm (23½ in) from cast on edge (same length as front to shoulder).
Shape shoulder Cast off 7 sts at beg of next 6 rows. Cast off remaining sts.
Join shoulder seams.

Sleeves

Using 5-mm needles cast on 42 sts and work 10 rows in k2, p2 rib. Change to st st and inc 1 st at each end of next and every following 6th row until there are 48 sts then at each end of every 8th row until there are 60 sts. Cont without shaping until sleeve measures 40.5 cm (16 in) from cast on edge.
Shape top Cast off 5 sts at beg of next 2 rows. Dec 1 st at each end of every 3rd row until 30 sts remain, then dec 1 st at beg of every row until 24 sts remain. Work 6 rows without shaping.
NEXT ROW k4 tog all along row (to pleat top of sleeve).
Cast off remaining sts.

Collar

Using 5-mm needles, with right side facing and starting 6 rows below shoulder seam on right front, pick up 5 sts up front, 24 sts across back of neck, 5 sts down left front finishing at same point as start on right front (34 sts). Work 2 rows in moss st. Still in moss st inc 1 st at each end of every row until there are 62 sts. Work 14 rows in moss st without increasing. Cast off in moss st.
Stitch increase edge of collar to front and lapel leaving last 4 cm (1½ in) unsewn.

Belt

Using 5-mm needles cast on 8 sts and work 112 cm (44 in) in moss st.

Making up

Sew sleeves into place, centre tuck to shoulder seam. Sew pockets into place, flatstitch side and sleeve seams, sew button on.

Mohair bolero

Measurements Medium size.
Materials 5 × 25 gm balls mohair or similar yarn.
Needles One pair 6-mm (No. 4) needles.
Tension Using 6-mm needles 7½ sts to a 5 cm square.
Abbreviations See page 12.

Right front

Using 6-mm needles cast on 48 sts and work in pattern as follows:
1ST ROW p.
2ND ROW k.
3RD ROW p.
4TH ROW *k5, knot 3. Rep from * to end (knot 3 = p3 tog, leave sts on left hand needle, wrn, p to the 3 sts again, take off needle, 3 sts left).
5TH ROW p.
6TH ROW k.
7TH ROW p.
8TH ROW k1 *knot 3, k5. Rep from * to last 4 sts, k4.
Rep these 8 rows until work measures 11.5 cm (4½ in).

Shape front Keep knot st correct throughout.

1ST ROW work to last 2 sts, k2 tog.
2ND ROW p3 tog, work to end.
3RD ROW k2, k2 tog, work to end.
4TH ROW p2 tog, work to last 4 sts, p2 tog, work to end.
5TH ROW k1, k2 tog, work to last 2 sts, k2 tog.
6TH ROW p3 tog, work to last 2 sts, p2 tog.
7TH ROW k2 tog, work to last 3 sts, k3 tog.
8TH ROW p3 tog, work to end.
9TH ROW cast off 3 sts, work to last 2 sts, k2 tog.
10TH ROW pattern complete row.
11TH ROW work to last 2 sts, k2 tog.
12TH ROW p2 tog, work to end.
13TH ROW cast off 3 sts, work to last 2 sts, k2 tog.
14TH ROW p2 tog, work to end.
15TH ROW cast off 2 sts, work to last 2 sts, k2 tog.
16TH ROW p2 tog, work to end.
17TH ROW k2 tog, work to last 2 sts, k2 tog.
18TH ROW p2, p2 tog, work to end.
19TH ROW k2, k2 tog, work to last 3 sts, k2 tog, k1.
20TH ROW p2 tog, work to last 3 sts, p2 tog, p1.
Cast off remaining 11 sts.

Left front

Work as for right front, reversing pattern i.e. work from right to left.
The first row reads — k2 tog, work to end.

Back

Using 6-mm needles cast on 48 sts and work 44.5 cm (17½ in) in st st. Cast off evenly (same length as cast on edge).
Back is worked sideways same as fronts. Join shoulder seams 12.5 cm (5 in) in depth.

Frontbands

With right side facing and 4-mm needles pick up 12 sts along right front bottom edge (starting at the side seam), 69 sts up shaped front, 25 sts across back of neck, 69 sts down left front and 12 sts along left front bottom edge (187 sts). Work 4 rows in single rib. Cast off LOOSELY in rib.

Back band lower edge

Using 4-mm needles and with right side facing pick up 72 sts and work 4 rows in single rib. Cast off loosely in rib.

Armbands

Join side seams for 15 cm (6 in) including rib. Work 1 row of double crochet round armhole opening.

Making up

To make bolero more special the centres of some knots on front can be embroidered.

Slipover in square stitch

Measurements Small, medium and large.
Materials 12 × 25 gm balls of double-knitting yarn.
Needles One pair each 3.25-mm and 4.5-mm (Nos. 10 and 7) needles.
Tension See page 10
Abbreviations See page 12.

Back

Using 3.25-mm needles and double-knitting yarn, cast on 82[92/102] sts and work in single rib for 10 cm (4 in).
Change to 4.5-mm needles and pattern.
1ST ROW k.
2ND ROW sl 1, *p4, k1. Rep from * to last st, k1 tbl.
Rep 1st and 2nd rows once more, then 1st row again.
6TH ROW k.
These 6 rows form the pattern. Cont in pattern until work measures 34.5 cm (13½ in) to armhole. From this point work the 1st and last 6 sts in every row in garter st and change to larger square pattern as follows:

1ST ROW sl 1, k to last st, k1 tbl.

2ND ROW sl 1, k5, *p9, k1. Rep from * to last 6 sts, k5, k1 tbl.

Rep 1st and 2nd rows 4 times, then 1st row again.

12TH ROW k.

These 12 rows form the pattern. Cont without shaping until work measures 56 cm (22 in). Cast off.

Front

Work as for back until work measures 34.5 cm (13½ in), still working pattern as for back, changing now to large square pattern and garter st armhole band. MAKE SURE TO KEEP SQUARES CORRECT.

NEXT ROW work 41[46/51] sts, turn.

NEXT ROW work 2 sts tog, pattern to end. Cont in pattern with 6 st garter st armhole band.

Dec at neck edge on every 4th row until 10 decreases have been made 31[36/41] sts. Cont without shaping until front measures same as back to shoulder. Cast off. Work other side of front to match, reversing shapings. Join right shoulder.

Neckband

Using 4-mm needles and with right side facing pick up 66 sts down left front, 1 st from centre of 'V' (marking this st with a piece of thread), 66 sts up right front and 25 sts across centre back. Work 6 rows in single rib, working 2 sts tog on either side of the st at the centre 'V' on EVERY row. Cast off loosely in rib (the easiest way to ensure this is to hold a larger needle (5-mm) in right hand).

Making up

The squares in this garment make it an obvious garment to decorate i.e. embroider tiny flowers in the larger squares — or decorate with beads (see photograph page 154).

Aran-style cardigan

Measurements To fit bust 81.5[86.5/91.5/96.5]cm (32[34/36/38]ins).

Materials 14[14/15/15] balls × 25 gm balls double-knitting yarn. 3 buttons.

Needles One pair each 3.5-mm and 5.5-mm (Nos. 9 and 5) needles.

Tension See page 10.

Abbreviations See page 12.

Back

Using 3.5-mm needles cast on 76[82/88/92] sts and work in single rib for 10 cm (4 in). Change to 5.5-mm needles and pattern as follows:

1ST ROW sl 1, p7[10/13/15], *p4, k8, p4*, p28. Rep from * to *. P to end.

2ND ROW sl 1, k7[10/13/15], *k4, p8, k4*, (p3 tog, k1, p1, k1 into next st) 7 times. Rep from * to *. K to end.

3RD ROW sl 1, p7[10/13/15] *p4, c8. (c8 thus: sl next 4 sts on to a cable needle, leave at back of work, k next 4 sts, then k4 from cable needle), p4, *p28. Rep from * to *. P to end.

4TH ROW sl 1, k7[10/13/15] *k4, p8, k4*, (k1, p1, k1 into next st, p3 tog) 7 times. Rep from * to *. K to end.

These 4 rows form the pattern for the centre blackberry st panel, with cable panels at each side, for which no more instructions will be given. BUT PLEASE NOTE only do the cable twist every other 4 pattern rows (every 8th row as an 8 row cable).

Cont in pattern until work measures 33[34.5/35.5/37]cm (13[13½/14/14½]in).

Shape armholes Keeping pattern correct cast off 4 sts at the beg of the next 2 rows, then dec 1 st at each end of the next and every alt row, until 64[66/72/76] sts remain. Cont without shaping until work measures 52[54.5/56/57]cm (20½[21½/22/22½]in). Cast off 12 [12/13/14] sts at the beg of the next 4 rows. Cast off.

Left front

Using 3.5-mm needles cast on 46[49/51/53] sts and work in single rib for 10 cm (4 in). On last 2 rows rib to last 8 sts, leave these sts on a pin for frontband. Rib back.
Change to 5.5-mm needles and pattern as follows:
1ST ROW sl 1, p7[10/12/14], p4, k8, p4, p14.
2ND ROW sl 1, k1, (p3 tog, k1, p1, k1 into next st) 3 times, k4, p8, k4, k to end.
3RD ROW sl 1, p7[10/12/14] p4 c8, p4, p14.
4TH ROW sl 1, k1, (k1, p1, k1, into next st, p3 tog) 3 times, k4, p8, k4, k to end.
Cont in pattern as on back until the work measures the same as back to armhole.
Shape armhole Keeping pattern correct cast off 4 sts at the beg of the next row (armhole end), and continuing in pattern dec 1 st at the armhole edge every alt row 2[5/5/7] times, while AT THE SAME TIME decreasing 1 st at front edge on next and every following 4th row until 24 [24/26/28] sts remain. (If the decreasing affects the blackberry st do one blackberry less and work the odd sts in reverse st st). Then cont without shaping until front measures the same as the back to shoulder finishing at the edge.
Shape shoulder Cast off 12[12/13/14] sts at the beg of the next and following alt row.

Right front

Using 3.5-mm needles cast on 46[49/51/53] sts and work in single rib for 4 rows.
NEXT ROW rib 3, cast off 2 sts, rib to end.
NEXT ROW rib to cast off sts, cast on 2, rib to end.
Cont in rib until 2 rows short of the 10 cm (4 in), then work the 2 buttonhole rows again.
NEXT ROW rib 8, leave these sts on a pin for frontband. Change to 5.5-mm needles and work in pattern set as follows:
1ST ROW sl 1, p13, p4, k8, p4, p to end.
2ND ROW sl 1, k7[10/12/14], k4, p8, k4 (k1, p1, k1 into next st, p3 tog) 3 times, k2.

3RD ROW sl 1, p13, p4, p to end.
4TH ROW sl 1, k7[10/12/14], k4, p8, k4, (p3 tog, k1, p1, k1, into next st) 3 times, k2.
Cont to work to match left front, reversing all shapings.

Sleeves

Using 3.5-mm needles cast on 38[40/40/42] sts and work in single rib for 7.5 cm (3 in), increasing on last row as follows.
Rib 10[12/12/13] sts, inc in each of the following 18[16/16/14] sts, rib to end (56 sts).
Change to 5.5-mm needles and pattern as follows:
1ST ROW sl 1, p3, k8, p4, p24, p4, k8, p4.
2ND ROW sl 1, k3, p8, k4 (p3 tog, k1, p1, k1 into next st) 6 times, k4, p8, k4.
3RD ROW sl 1, p3, c8, p4, p24, p4, c8, p4.
4TH ROW sl 1, k3, p8, k4, (k1, p1, k1 into next st, p3 tog) 6 times, k4, p8, k4.
Cont in pattern as for back increasing 1 st at each end of next and every following 6th row until there are 68[72/74/78] sts on needle. Cont without shaping until the sleeve measures 43[44.5/44.5/46]cm (17[17½/17½/18]ins) from beg.
Shape armhole Cast off 4 sts at the beg of next 2 rows, then dec 1 st at each end of every alt row 10[10/12/14] times. Work 12[12/18/24] rows without shaping. Cast off, knitting 3 sts tog all along row (this is to give the fullness at the top of the sleeve).

Left frontband

Rejoin yarn to 8 sts left on pin and work in single rib until band fits up left front and halfway across centre back (slightly stretched). Make it fit nicely as the band makes the shape of the cardigan correct, which is all important for look of finished garment.

Right frontband

Work the same length as for left front band, making one more buttonhole, the same distance apart as the other two.

Making up

Use overstitch or flatstitch to join all the seams easing any extra fullness to top of sleeve to give the 'puff' look.

Norwegian-style cardigan

Measurements To fit bust 91.5[96.5/102]cm (36[38/40]in).
Materials 18×25 gm balls main colour (M), 2 balls of colours A, B and C. 6 buttons.
Needles One pair each 3.25-mm and 5-mm (Nos. 10 and 6) needles.
Tensions See page 10.
Abbreviations See page 12.

Colour suggestions		
1		
Beige	= M	
Red	= A	
Rust	= B	
Blue	= C	
2		**3**
Silver grey	= M =	Cream
Gold	= A =	Red
Red	= B =	Rust
Blue	= C =	Blue

Back

Using 3.25-mm needles cast on 81[87/93] sts and work in colour B. Work in single rib for 2 rows. Change to main colour and cont in single rib until work measures 7.5 cm (3 in). Change to 5-mm needles and colour B and work 2 rows in st st. Change to pattern:
1ST ROW sl 1, k1M, *k1A, k2M. Rep from * to last st, k1A.
2ND ROW sl 1, p2M, *p1 A, p2M. Rep from * to end.
3RD ROW sl 1, k1M, *k1C, k2M. Rep from * to last st, k1C.
4TH ROW sl 1, p2M, *p1C, p2M. Rep from * to end.
Change to spot pattern, decreasing 1 st at end of last row. Work 4 rows in st st.
5TH ROW sl 1, k2M, *k1C, k5M. Rep from

* to last 5 sts, k1C, k4M. Work 5 rows in st st increasing 1 st at each end of last row.
11TH ROW sl 1, *k1A, k5M. Rep from * to last 3 sts, k1A, k2M.
Work 5 rows in st st increasing 1 st at each end of last row.
17TH ROW * k5M, k1C. Rep from * to last 6 sts, k6M.
Work 5 rows in st st increasing 1 st at each end of the last row.
23RD ROW k3M, *k1A, k5M. Rep from * to last 5 sts, k1A, k4M.
Work 5 rows in st st increasing 1 st at each end of last row.
29TH ROW k1M, *k1C, k5M. Rep from * to last 3 sts, k1C, k2M.
Work 5 rows in st st increasing 1 st at each end of last row.
**35TH ROW *k5M, k1A. Rep from * to last 6 sts, k6M.
Work 5 rows in st st.
41ST ROW k2M, *k1C, k5M. Rep from * to last 4 sts, k1C, k3M.
Work 5 rows in st st.**
Rep last 12 rows, from ** to **, until work measures 34.5[35.5/37]cm (13½[14/14½]in) from beg.

RIGHT: MAN'S MULTICOLOURED WAISTCOAT

OVERLEAF: GARMENTS FOR ALL AGES: MAN'S MULTICOLOURED WAISTCOAT, CHILD'S MULTICOLOURED CARDIGAN, LADY'S MULTICOLOURED CARDIGAN.

LEFT: MAN'S HEAVY MOSS STITCH SWEATER
WITH COLLAR

rows, using A instead of C.
21ST AND 22ND ROWS as 17th and 18th
rows.
Rep from rows 5 to 20 again.
Cont in main colour in st st until work
measures 25.5 cm (10 in) from beg of
Jacquard yoke.
Shape shoulder Cast off 18 sts at the beg
of the next 4 rows, and leave remaining
sts on a spare needle for neck.

Right front

Using colour B and 3.25-mm needles cast
on 46 sts and work in single rib with a 7
st garter st border as follows:
ROW 1 rib to last 7 sts, k7.
ROW 2 k7, rib to end. Change to main
colour. Rep these last 2 rows once more.
5TH ROW work in single rib to last 7 sts,
k3, wlfwd, k2 tog, k2.
Work another buttonhole on the last but
one row of the 7.5 cm (3 in) rib.
Change to 5-mm needles and colour B.
K to last 7 sts, leave these 7 sts on a pin.
For frontbands turn and p back in B. On
remaining 39 sts work as for back,
increasing only at side edge until the
20th row of the Jacquard yoke has been
worked.
NEXT ROW Work in pattern to the last 2
sts, k2 tog.
Cont to work in pattern decreasing at
neck edge on next 7 rows, and then
continuing without shaping until work
measures same as back to shoulders,
finishing at side edge.
Shape shoulders Cast off 18 sts at the beg
of the next and following alt rows.

Left front

Work as for right front reversing all
shapings and patterns, working the 7 st
garter st border at the beg of the right
side row instead of at the end.

Sleeves

Using colour B and 3.25-mm needles cast
on 39 sts and work 2 rows in single rib.
Change to main colour and cont in rib
until work measures 7.5 cm (3 in),
working twice into every st on the last

Jacquard yoke

1ST ROW sl 1, k1M, *k1A, k2M. Rep from
* to last st, k1A.
2ND ROW sl 1, *p2M, p1A. Rep from * to
last 2 sts, p2M.
3RD ROW as row 1, using C instead of A.
4TH ROW as row 2, using C instead of A.
5TH ROW *k2M, k4C. Rep from * to end.
6TH ROW p1M, *p2C, p4M. Rep from * to
last 5 sts, p2C, p3M.
7TH ROW k in B.
8TH ROW p in B.
9TH ROW sl 1, *k1M, k1A. Rep from * to
last st, k1M.
10TH ROW *p1A, p1M. Rep from * to
end.
Repeat 9th and 10th rows once more.
13TH AND 14TH ROWS as 7th and 8th rows.
15TH ROW k3M, *k2C, k4M. Rep from *
to last 3 sts, k2C, k1M.
16TH ROW *p4C, p2M. Rep from * to end.
17TH ROW *k2M, k1C. Rep from * to end.
18TH ROW *p1C, p2M. Rep from * to end.
19TH AND 20TH ROWS Rep 17th and 18th

LEFT: SLIPOVER IN SQUARE STITCH

row. Change to 5-mm needles and pattern as follows.

Work as for Jacquard yoke from row 1 -20 inclusive.

Work 4 rows in st st increasing 1 st at each end of last row (80 sts).

Now change to spot pattern, working as for back body from row 5 to row 34 inclusive. Cast off loosely in rib (this is best done by holding a large needle in right hand while casting off).

Frontbands

Using 3.25-mm needles work left frontband first, picking up 7 sts left on pin and working in garter st until band fits nicely up the front to start of neck shaping (have it slightly stretched to keep the cardigan in good shape). Leave sts on a pin.

Now work the right frontband. Count the number of rows worked on left front from the pick up point after the rib, and divide the number of rows equally so that 3 more buttonholes are worked — with the fourth to come in the neckband (6 buttonholes in all). Leave sts on a pin.

Neckband

Using 3.25-mm needles pick up the 7 sts from the right front, 4 sts from centre front, 25 sts up the right side, the sts left on a spare needle from the back, 25 sts down the left side, 4 sts from left centre front, 7 sts from left frontband. Work in garter st for 6 rows, making a buttonhole on the 4th row. Cast off with a 4.5-mm needle in right hand.

Making up

Join shoulder seams. Pin centre of cast off stitches at top of sleeves into place and join all other seams. Attach buttons to correspond with buttonholes.

Heavy sports sweater with cables and bobbles

Measurements Small, medium and large.
Materials 15 × 50 gm balls of Aran weight yarn
Needles One pair each 3.5-mm and 6-mm (Nos. 9 and 4) needles.
Tension See page 10.
Abbreviations See page 12.

Cable 6 Back: C6B: sl next 3 sts on to cable needle and put to back of work, k3, then k3 from cable needle.
Cable 6 Front: C6F: sl next 3 sts on cable needle and put to front of work, k3, then k3 from cable needle.
Make Bobble: MB: (k1, p1, k1, p1) all into next st, turn, k4, turn, p4, then sl 2nd, 3rd and 4th sts over 1st st.

Back
Using 3.5-mm needles cast on 85[89/93] sts and work in single rib for 9 cm (3½ in).
Change to 6-mm needles and pattern as follows:
1ST ROW k7[9/11], p3, k12, p3, k35, p3, k12, p3, k7[9/11].
2ND ROW k10[12/14], p12, k3, p35, k3, p12, k10[12/14].
3RD ROW k7[9/11], p3, C6B, C6B, p3, k7, MB, k19, MB, k7, p3, C6F, C6F, p3, k7[9/11].
4TH ROW as row 2.
5TH ROW k7[9/11], p3, k12, p3, k5, MB, k3, MB, k15, MB, k3, MB, k5, p3, k12, p3, k7[9/11].
6TH ROW as row 2.
7TH ROW k7[9/11], p3, k12, p3, k3, MB, k3, MB, k3, MB, k11, MB, k3, MB, k3, MB, k3, p3, k12, p3, k7[9/11].
8TH ROW as row 2.

9TH ROW as row 5.
10TH ROW as row 2.
11TH ROW as row 3.
12TH ROW as row 2.
13TH ROW k7[9/11], p3, C6F, C6F, p3, k17, MB, k17, p3, C6B, C6B, p3, k7[9/11].
14TH ROW as row 2.
15TH ROW k7[9/11], p3, k12, p3, k15, MB, k3, MB, k15, p3, k12, p3, k7[9/11].
16TH ROW as row 2.
17TH ROW k7[9/11], p3, k12, p3, k13, MB, k3, MB, k3, MB, k13, p3, k12, p3, k7[9/11].
18TH ROW as row 2.
19TH ROW as row 15.
20TH ROW as row 2.
21ST ROW as row 13.
22ND ROW as row 2.
Rows 3 to 22 complete the pattern which is repeated until work measures about 63.5 cm (25 in) (this should finish after 5 full patterns and 5 rows of the sixth). Work 4 rows in garter st. Cast off (holding a 6.5-mm needle in right hand).

Front
Work as for back until work measures 60 cm (23½ in) (5 patterns).
Shape neck as follows:
1ST ROW pattern 37[39/41], turn.
2ND ROW cast off 3 sts, pattern to end.
3RD ROW pattern to last 2 sts, k2 tog.
4TH ROW cast off 3 sts, pattern to end.
5TH ROW pattern to last 2 sts, k2 tog.
6TH ROW cast off 2 sts, pattern to end.
7TH ROW work in pattern, leave sts on spare needle.
Rejoin yarn to centre edge and pattern to end.
NEXT ROW pattern 37[39/41], turn (leave remaining sts on pin). Work on 37[39/41] sts, as for first side.

Neckband
Pick up and k 85[89/93] sts across front. Work 4 rows in garter st. Cast off with a 6.5-mm needle in right hand. Leave neck open 27 cm (10½ in) across for boat neck.

Sleeves

Using 3.25-mm needles cast on 38[42/46] sts and work in single rib for 9 cm (3½ in).

NEXT ROW sl 1, *work twice into next st, k1. Rep from * all along row to last st, k twice into last st 58[62/66] sts). Change to 5.5-mm needles and work in garter st, increasing 1 st at each end of 11th row, and then every 10th row 2 more times (3 increases in all). Then carry on without shaping until sleeve measures 43[44.5/46]cm (17[17½/18]in), finishing with wrong side facing. Cast off holding a 6-mm needle in right hand.

Making up

Make up carefully with flatstitch or overstitch, making sure sleeve lies nice and flat in body.

Broken rib and cable short sleeved sweater

Measurements Small, medium and large.
Materials 8 × 25 gm balls of 4-ply yarn. 3 buttons.
Needles One pair each 2.5-mm and 3.25-mm (Nos. 12 and 10) needles.
Tension See page 10.
Abbreviations Cable 8 = sl next 4 sts on to cable needle and keep at front of work, k next 4 sts, then k 4 from cable needle. for other abbreviations see page 12.

Back

Using 2.5-mm needles cast on 106[114/122] sts and work in single rib for 7.5 cm (3 in) change to 3.25-mm needles and work in broken rib as follows:
ROW 1 sl 1, *k1, p1, work in single rib set as for rib welt. Rep from * to last st, k1 tbl.
ROW 2 sl 1, p to last st, k1 tbl.
These 2 rows form the broken rib pattern which cont until work measures 33 cm (13 in) from beg.
Shape armholes Cast off 5 sts at beg of next 2 rows then k2 tog at each end of next 4[5/5] alt rows (88[94/102] sts. Cont without shaping until work measures 51 cm (20 in).
Shape shoulders Cast off 15 sts at beg of next 4 rows.
Leave remaining sts on safety pin for neckband.

Front

Using 2.5-mm needles cast on 114[120/126] sts and work in single rib for 7.5 cm (3 in). Change to 3.25-mm needles and work in broken moss and cable pattern as follows:
1ST ROW rib 26[29/32] sts as set, (p2, c8) 6 times, p2, rib 26[29/32].
2ND ROW p 26[29/32], (k2, p8) 6 times, k2, p26[29/32].
3RD ROW rib 26[29/32], (p2, k8) 6 times,

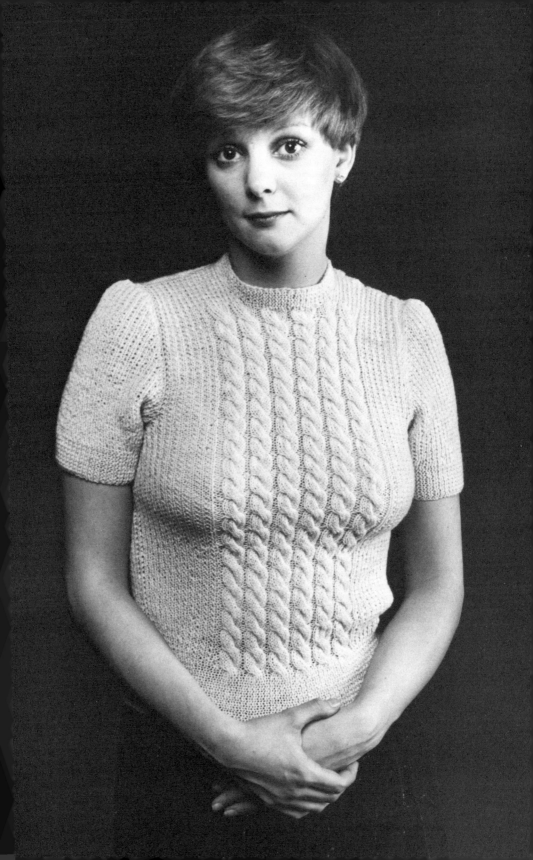

p2, p 26[29/32].
4TH ROW as row 2.
Rep rows 3 and 4 twice more.
These 8 rows form the pattern. Cont until
work measures 33 cm (13 in).
Shape armholes Cast off 5 sts at beg of
next 2 rows and then dec 1 st at each
end of next 6[7/7] alt rows (92[96/
102] sts). Cont without shaping until
work measures 47 cm (18½ in) from
beg. Now stop cable and work only in
broken
moss st.
Shape for neck Rib 33, sl next 26[30/
36] sts on to a pin for neckband, rib 33.
Keeping pattern correct work on this side
of front decreasing 1 st at front (neck)
edge on 3 following alt rows (30 sts).
Cont without shaping until armhole
measures same as back.
Shape shoulder Cast off 15 sts on next
row beg at side edge and following alt row.
Rejoin yarn to remaining 33 sts and work
to match first side.

Sleeves
Using 2.5-mm needles cast on 88 sts and
work in single rib for 16 rows, increasing
at each end of last row (90 sts).
Change to 3.25-mm needles and pattern:
ROW 1 sl 1, rib to last st, k1 tbl.
ROW 2 sl 1, p to last st, k1 tbl.
Rep these 2 rows until sleeve measures
9.5 cm (3¾ in) from beg.
Shape top Keeping rib correct cast off 5
sts at beg of next 2 rows, then dec at
each end of every alt row until 24 sts
remain finishing with right side facing.
K4 sts tog all along row. Cast off. Join
right shoulder seam.

Neckband
Using 3.25-mm needles, with right side
facing and starting at left front shoulder
pick up 21 sts down left front, sts from
centre front, 21 up right side of front and
sts across back. Work 2.5 cm (1 in) in
single rib. Cast off ribwise.

Making up
Leave left shoulder open for 7.5 cm (3 in)

making 3 buttonholes (either crochet,
blanket st or chain st) on front of
opening, then attach 3 buttons to
correspond on back of opening. Join all
other seams. See page 12 for further
sewing and pressing instructions.

Short sleeved sweater with multicoloured yoke

Measurements Small, medium and large.
Materials 4 × 50 gm balls of main colour,
small amounts of colours. 3 small buttons
for shoulder fastening.
Needles One pair each 2.5-mm, 3.25-mm
and 3.5-mm (Nos. 12, 10 and 9) needles.
Tension See page 10.
Abbreviations See page 12.

Colour suggestions
Cream = M = Natural
Mauve = V = Cream
Green = G = Gold
Blue = B = Orange
Pink = P = Apricot
Yellow = Y = Mink
Silver Grey = M = Navy
White = V = White or Cream
Burgundy = G = Blue
Dark Grey = B = Mauve
Pilot Blue = P = Pink
Red = Y = Grey

Back
Using 2.5-mm needles and main colour
cast on 94[98/102] sts and work in
single rib for 10 cm (4 in). Change to
3.25-mm needles and work in st st until
work measures 20.5 cm (8 in). Inc 1 st at
each end of next and every following 4th
row until there are 112[116/120] sts
then cont without shaping until work
measures 33 cm (13 in) from start.

Shape armholes Cast off 4[5/6] sts at beg of next 2 rows, then dec 1 st at each end of every alt row until there are 96 sts on needle. Cont without shaping until work measures 40.5 cm (16 in). Change to 3.5-mm needles and pattern as follows:

1ST ROW k * 1G, 2M, 1G, 2M, 1G, 2M, 1G, 2M. Rep from * to end.

2ND ROW p * 2M, 2G, 3M, 2G, 3M. Rep from * to end.

3RD ROW k * 3M, 3B, 1M, 3B, 2M. Rep from * to end.

4TH ROW p * 2B, 1M, 2B, 1M, 2B, 1M, 3B. Rep from * to end.

5TH ROW k * 1M, 3V, 1M, 1V, 1M, 1V, 1M, 3V. Rep from * to end.

6TH ROW p * 1M, 3V, 1M, 1V, 1M, 3V, 2M. Rep from * to end.

7TH ROW k as row 6.

8TH ROW p as row 5.

9TH ROW k as row 4.

10TH ROW p as row 3.

11TH ROW k as row 2.

12TH ROW p as row 1.

Work 2 rows in main colour in st st.

15TH ROW k * 2M, 1V, 3M, 1V, 3M, 1V, 1M. Rep from * to end.

16TH ROW p * 3V, 1M, 3V, 1M, 3V, 1M. Rep from * to end.

17TH ROW k * 2V, 1P, 3V, 1P, 3V, 1P, 1V. Rep from * to end.

18TH ROW p * 3P, 1V, 3P, 1V, 3P, 1V. Rep from * to end.

19TH ROW k * 2P, 1Y, 3P, 1Y, 3P, 1Y, 1P. Rep from * to end.

20TH ROW p * 3Y, 1P, 3Y, 1P, 3Y, 1P. Rep from * to end.

21ST ROW k * 2Y, 1V, 3Y, 1V, 3Y, 1V, 1Y. Rep from * to end.

22ND ROW p * 3V, 1Y, 3V, 1Y, 3V, 1Y. Rep from * to end.

23RD ROW k * 2V, 1M, 3V, 1M, 3V, 1M, 1V. Rep from * to end.

24TH ROW p * 3M, 1V, 3M, 1V, 3M, 1V. Rep from * to end.

Now using main colour change back to 3.25-mm needles.

Shape back neck K32, sl next 32 sts on to a pin to pick up for neck, k32. Working on these last 33 sts only, work 2 more

rows decreasing 1 st at neck edge on each row.

Shape shoulders Cast off 15 sts at beg of next row and following alt row. Rejoin yarn to other side and work to match.

Front

Work exactly as for back to end of 14th coloured pattern row (ending with the 2 rows in main colour).

NEXT ROW (which will be 15th pattern row) k (2M, 1V, 3M, 1V, 3M, 1V, 1M) 3 times, sl next 24 sts on to a pin to pick up for neck, work pattern 3 times more. Working on this side of front only work remaining 9 rows of pattern. Change to 3.25-mm needles and main colour only.

NEXT ROW (k2 tog, k4) 6 times (30 sts). Work 3 more rows in st st.

Shape shoulders Cast off 15 sts at beg of next and following alt rows. Rejoin yarn to other side and work to match.

Sleeves

Using 3.25-mm needles cast on 80 sts and work in single rib for 2.5 cm (1 in). Now work in st st for 16 rows increasing 1 st at each end of every alt row (96 sts).

Shape armhole Cast off 4 sts at beg of next 2 rows then k2 tog, at each end of every row 8 times then every other row 8 times, finishing with right side facing. Change to 3.5-mm needles and work 24 rows of coloured pattern — still decreasing as follows:

1ST ROW k, k2 tog M, 1M * 1G, 2M. Rep from * to last 2 sts, k2 tog M.

2ND ROW p, 3M * 2G, 3M, 2G, 5M. Rep from * to last 3 sts, 2G, 1M.

3RD ROW k, k2 tog M, 6M, * 3B, 1M, 3B, 5M. Rep from * to last 10 sts, 3B, 1M, 3B, 1M, k2 tog M.

4TH ROW p, 3M * 2B, 1M, 2B, 1M, 5B, 1M. Rep from * to last st, k1 M.

5TH ROW k, k2 tog M, 2V * 1M, 3V, 1M, 1V, 1M, 1V, 1M, 3V. Rep from * to last 12 sts, 1M, 3V, 1M, 1V, 1M, 1V, 1M, 1V, k2 tog V.

6TH ROW p, * 3V, 1M, 1V, 1M, 3V, 3M. Rep from * to last 2 sts, 2V.

7TH ROW k, k2 tog V * 3M, 3V, 1M, 1V,

1M, 3V. Rep from * to last 12 sts, 3M, 3V, 1M, 1V, 1M, 1V, k2 tog V.

8TH ROW p, 1V * 1M, 1V, 1M, 1V, 1M, 3V. Rep from * to last 11 sts, 1M, 1V, 1M, 1V, 1M, 3V, 1M, 2V.

9TH ROW k, k2 tog B, 3B, * 1M, 2B, 1M, 2B, 1M, 5B. Rep from * to last 7 sts, 1M, 2B, 1M, 1B, k2 tog B.

10TH ROW p, 2B * 1M, 3B, 5M, 3B. Rep from * to last 8 sts, 1M, 3B, 4M.

11TH ROW k, k2 tog M, 2M * 2G, 3M, 2G, 5M. Rep from * to last 6 sts, 2G, 2M, k2 tog M.

12TH ROW p, 1M, 1G * 2M, 1G. Rep from * to end.

13TH ROW k, k2 tog M, k to last 2 sts, k2 tog M.

14TH ROW p in main colour.

15TH ROW k, k2 tog M, 1M * 1V, 3M. Rep from * to last 3 sts, 1V, k2 tog M.

16TH ROW p * 3V, 1M. Rep from * to end.

17TH ROW k, k2 tog V * 1P, 3V. Rep from * to last 2 sts, k2 tog V.

18TH ROW p, 1P, * 1V, 3P. Rep from * to end.

19TH ROW k, k2 tog P, * 3P, 1Y. Rep from * to last 4 sts, 2P, k2 tog P.

20TH ROW p, 2P, * 3Y, 1P. Rep from * to last 2 sts, p2Y.

21ST ROW k, k2 tog Y, 2Y, * 1V, 3Y. Rep from * to last 4 sts, 1V, 1Y, k2 tog Y.

22ND ROW p, * 1Y, 3V. Rep from * to last 2 sts, p 2Y.

23RD ROW k, k2 tog V, 1V * 1M, 3V. Rep from * to last 3 sts, 1M, k2 tog V.

24TH ROW p * 3M, 1V. Rep from * to end.

Now work 4 rows in st st in M decreasing at each end of the k rows (28 sts).

NEXT ROW (k4 tog) 7 times.

Cast off.

Neckband

Using main colour join right shoulder seam and sew in ends round neck. Using -mm needles and with right side of work facing, pick up 27 sts down left front, 24 sts across centre front, 27 sts up right front and 46 sts from back of neck

(124 sts). Work in single rib for 2.5 cm (1 in) (8 rows).

CAST OFF AS FOLLOWS

Starting at back (wrong side facing) cast off 68 sts, (k2 tog) 4 times as you cast off (for corner). Cast off 22 sts, (k2 tog) 4 times as you cast off. Cast off remaining sts.

Making up

Join other shoulder seam leaving a 10 cm (4 in) neck opening. Make three buttonholes (either crochet, blanket stitch or chain stitch) on front of opening then attach three buttons to correspond on back of opening. Set and sew in sleeves matching patterns carefully and making sure fullness at top of sleeve is central across shoulder (to make a puff sleeve). Sew side and sleeve seams in correct colours and sew in all ends.

Striped sleeveless slipover and waistcoat

Measurements This garment, being entirely in double rib and in yarns that keep the elasticity of the rib so beautifully, is virtually a one size garment. It naturally fits wearers of most sizes.

Materials Of 25 gm balls double-knitting weight yarn 4 balls in colour B
2 in each colour A and C, 1 ball colour D. 8 buttons.

Needles One pair each 3.25-mm and 4-mm (Nos. 10 and 8) needles.

Tension See page 10.

Abbreviations See page 12.

Colour suggestions

        Rust = A = French navy
Mid brown = B = Blue
    Peach = C = White
     Gold = D = Mauve

    Camel = A = Navy
    Brick = B = Blue
     Navy = C = White
    Cream = D = Dusky pink

            A = Chocolate
            B = Golden brown
            C = Cream
            D = Gold

Garment without front buttoning

Back Using 3.25-mm needles and colour A cast on 98 sts and work in double rib (k2, p2) for 24 rows. Change to 4-mm needles and continuing in the same rib, work 6 rows in C; 8 rows in B; 4 rows in C; 22 rows in B; 6 rows in A; 8 rows in D; 4 rows in C; 10 rows in B. Cont in rib and colour B.

Shape armholes Cast off 4 sts at the beg of the next 2 rows then dec 1 st at each end of every row until 66 sts remain. Work 40 rows without decreasing.

Shape shoulders Cast off 6 sts at beg of next 4 rows. Leave remaining 42 sts on a holder.

Front

Work as for back until armhole shaping.

Shape armholes Cast off 4 sts at beg of the next 2 rows then dec 1 st at each end of every row until 70 sts remain. Keeping armhole edge straight cont as follows. Rib 31, cast off 8 sts, rib 31. Work on 1st group of sts as follows. Dec 1 st at the neck edge on the next 7 rows, then on every alt row until 12 sts remain. Cont without shaping until work measures same as back to shoulder, finishing with right side row. Cast off 6 sts (armhole edge) rib to end. Work 1 row then cast off remaining 6 sts. Rejoin yarn to second group of sts and work to match 1st side reversing all shapings. Join right shoulder seam.

Neckband

With 3.25-mm needles, C and with right side facing pick up 138 sts evenly round neck. Work 5 rows in single rib. Cast off in rib. Join other shoulder seam.

Armbands

Using 3.25-mm needles and C and with right side facing pick up 98 sts evenly round armhole and work 3 rows in singl rib. Cast off in rib. Join side seams.

Garment with front buttoning
Work the back same as for slipover.

Left front

With 3.25-mm needles and A cast on 4⁸ sts and work in double rib (k2, p2) for 2 rows. Change to 4-mm needles and wor stripes as for back to armhole.

Shape armhole (right side facing): Cast o 4 sts at beg of next row. Work one row, then dec 1 st at armhole edge on every row until 36 sts remain. Work 1 more row if necessary so as to end wrong sid facing.

Shape neck Keeping armhole edge straight cast off 9 sts at the beg of the next row and then dec 1 st at the neck edge on every row until 12 sts remain. Cont without shaping until work measures same as back to shoulder ending with right side facing.
Shape shoulders Cast off 6 sts at beg of next row. Work 1 row. Cast off remaining 6 sts.

Right front
Work as for left front reversing all shapings. Join shoulder seams.

Armhole bands
Work bands as for slipover without buttoned front. Join side seams.

Left frontband
With 3.25-mm needles and C cast on 11 sts and work in single rib until band fits left front VERY SLIGHTLY stretched. Leave these 11 sts on a safety pin and sew band into position.

Right frontband
Work as for left band making buttonholes all the way up. It's a good idea to mark position for buttonholes on the left front the 1st about 1.3 cm (½ in) from the cast on edge and the last about 2.5 cm (1 in) below neck shaping making 7 buttonholes on the band evenly. Make buttonhole as follows:
1ST BUTTONHOLE ROW rib 4, cast off 3 sts, rib 4.
2ND BUTTONHOLE ROW rib 4, cast on 3 sts, rib 4. Sew band in position.

Neckband
With 3.25-mm needles and C (right side facing) rib across 11 right band sts, pick up and k 120 sts evenly round the neck (including 42 sts from back) then rib the 11 sts from the left frontband. Work 5 rows in single rib working an 8th buttonhole on the right front on the last 2 rows. Cast off ribwise. Attach buttons to left front.
DO NOT PRESS THIS GARMENT.

4-ply cardigan with cable yoke

Measurements 86.5[91.5] cm (34[36] in) chest. To make smaller size use 3-mm needles.
Materials 12 × 25 gm balls of 4-ply yarn. 6 buttons.
Needles One pair 3.25-mm (No. 10) needles; 3-mm (No. 11) for smaller size.
Tension See page 10.
Abbreviations See page 12.

Pocket lining (make two)
Using 3.25-mm needles cast on 30 sts and work 9 cm (3½ in) in st st. Leave sts on a spare needle.

Left front
Using 3.25-mm needles cast on 60 sts and work in single rib for 10 cm (4 in). Change to pattern as follows:
1ST ROW sl 1, p1 * k6, p3. Rep from * to last 13 sts, k6, rib 6 sts, k1 tbl.
2ND ROW sl 1, rib 6, p6, * k3, p6. Rep from * to last 2 sts, k1, k1, tbl.
3RD ROW inc into 1st st, p1, * k6, p3. Rep from * to last 13 sts, k6, rib 6, k1 tbl.
Rep 2nd and 1st rows, 4 times more (working extra st into pattern).
Rep 2nd and 3rd rows, once (working inc st into pattern).
Rep these 10 rows again then row 1 again (63 sts).
Now work pocket edge as follows:
1ST ROW sl 1, k1, p3, k6, work next 30 sts in single rib, work in pattern to last 7 sts, rib 6, k1 tbl.
2ND ROW sl 1, rib 6, pattern 15, rib 30, p6, k3, p1, k1 tbl.
3RD, 5TH, 7TH, 9TH ROWS as row 1.
4TH, 6TH, 8TH ROWS as row 2.
10TH ROW sl 1, rib 6, pattern 15, cast off 30 sts, in single rib, pattern to end.
11TH ROW sl 1, k1, p3, k6, now work pocket lining sts as follows: p3, k6, p3, k6, p3, k6, p3, k6, p3, k6, rib 6, k1 tbl.
Now work 2nd and 1st rows until work measures 33 cm (13 in) from cast on

edge, finishing at side edge.

Shape armhole

Keeping pattern correct throughout, including single rib border. Cast off 6 sts at beg of next row. Work 1 row.
NEXT ROW k2 tog, pattern to end.
NEXT ROW work in pattern.
Rep these 2 rows until 50 sts remain.
Cont in pattern until front measures 43 cm (17 in) from cast on edge.
Now work in cable pattern as follows:
1ST ROW sl 1, k6, * p3, k6. Rep from * to last 7 sts, rib 6, k1, tbl.
2ND ROW sl 1, rib 6, * p6, k3. Rep from * to last 7 sts, p6, k1, tbl.
3RD ROW as row 1.
4TH ROW as row 2.
5TH ROW sl 1, c6 (sl first 3 sts on to a cable needle and leave at front of work, k3, then k3 sts from cable needle — this will be known as c6) * p3, c6. Rep from * to last 7 sts, rib 6, k1, tbl.
6TH ROW as row 2.
Rep these 6 rows until front measures 49 cm (19¼ in) from cast on edge, ending with a right side row.
Shape neck Work first 10 sts then slip them on to a spare needle, pattern to end. Keeping cable pattern correct, dec 1 st at neck edge on every row until 30 sts remain. Work without further decreasing and keep pattern correct until front measures 53.5 cm (21 in) from cast on edge.
Shape shoulder Keeping pattern correct cast off 10 sts at beg of next row. Work 1 row.
Rep these 2 rows once more, cast off remaining sts.

Right front

Work as for left front, reversing all shapings and position of pocket. Pattern rows 1 and 2 will read:
1ST ROW sl 1, rib 6, k6, * p3, k6. Rep from * to last 2 sts, p1, k1 tbl.
2ND ROW sl 1, p1, * k6, p3. Rep from * to last 13 sts, k6, rib 6, k1 tbl.
On 5th row of right front work a buttonhole as follows:

sl 1, rib 2, k2 tog, wlfwd, rib 2, on this front work a further 5 buttonholes at 7.5 cm (3 in) intervals (about every 28 rows) the last one to come 6.5 cm (2½ in) BELOW start of neck shaping.

Back

Using 3.25-mm needles cast on 110 sts and work 10 cm (4 in) in single rib. Now work in pattern as follows:
1ST ROW sl 1, k3, * p3, k6. Rep from * to last 7 sts, p3, k3, k1 tbl.
2ND ROW sl 1, p3, * k3, p6. Rep from * to last 7 sts, k3, p3, k1 tbl.
Rep these 2 rows inc 1 st each end of next and every following 10th row until there are 116 sts. Pattern rows will then read:
1ST ROW sl 1, k6, * p3, k6. Rep from * to last st, k1 tbl.
2ND ROW sl 1, p6, * k3, p6. Rep from * to last st, k1 tbl.
Rep these 2 pattern rows until back measures 33 cm (13 in) from cast on edge.
Shape armhole Keeping pattern correct, cast off 7 sts at beg of next 2 rows.
1ST ROW k2 tog, pattern to last 2 sts, k2 tog.
2ND ROW sl 1, pattern to last st, k1, tbl.
Rep these 2 rows until 88 sts remain.
Now work without shaping until back measures 43 cm (17 in) from cast on edge.
Work pattern as follows:
1ST ROW sl 1, k1, * p3, k6. Rep from * to last 5 sts, p3, k1, k1 tbl.
2ND ROW sl 1, p1, * k3, p6. Rep from * to last 5 sts, k3, p1, k1 tbl.
5TH ROW sl 1, k1, * p3, c6. Rep from * to last 5 sts, p3, k1, k1 tbl.
Work in cable pattern until work measures 51 cm (20¼ in) from cast on edge.
Neck shaping Keeping pattern correct pattern 33, sl next 21 sts on to a spare needle, pattern to end. Work on this group of sts and dec 1 st at neck edge on next and 2 following alt rows (should be 53.5 cm (21 in) in length). If not work any rows needed.

Shape shoulder Keeping pattern correct cast off 10 sts at beg of next row. Work 1 row. Rep these 2 rows once more. Cast off remaining sts.
Rejoin yarn to other group of sts and work to correspond with first side.

Sleeves

Using 3-mm needles cast on 56 sts and work 5 cm (2 in) in single rib. Change to 3.25-mm needles and pattern as follows:
1ST ROW sl 1, k3, * p3, k6. Rep from * 4 times, p3, k3, k1 tbl.
2ND ROW sl 1, p3, k3, * p6, k3. Rep from * 4 times, p3, k1 tbl.
3RD ROW as row 1
4TH ROW as row 2
5TH ROW sl 1, k3, (p3, k6) twice, p3, c6, (p3, k6) twice, p3, k3, k1 tbl.
6TH ROW sl 1, inc in next st, pattern to last st, inc in last st. Rep these 6 rows until 86 sts are on the needle working the increased sts into the pattern. Then work without shaping until sleeve measures 40.5 cm (16 in) from cast on edge.
Shape top Keeping pattern correct, cast off 6 sts at beg of next 2 rows.
NEXT ROW k2 tog, pattern to last 2 sts, k2 tog.
NEXT ROW sl 1, pattern to last st, k1 tbl.
NEXT 2 ROWS as last row.
Rep these 4 rows until 50 sts remain, then work 1st 2 rows until 26 sts remain. Work 1 row.
NEXT ROW (p4 tog) 6 times. Cast off
Join shoulder seams.

Neckband

Using 3-mm needles, with right side facing and starting at right front, sl first 10 sts on to the needle then pick up 21 sts up right front, 39 sts across back of neck, 21 sts down left front and 10 sts from spare needle (101 sts). Work 3 rows in st st. Work a buttonhole on next row. Work 1 row.
NEXT ROW k1 * wrn, k2 tog. Rep from * to end. P 1 row. Work a buttonhole on the next row. Work 3 rows in st st. Cast off.

Making up

Stitch pocket linings into place. Pin sleeves into armhole making sure the centre tuck is in line with the shoulder seam. Sew carefully into place. Turn the picot neck edge over and slip stitch into place without pulling tight. Sew sleeve and side seams. Sew on buttons.

Matching short sleeved jumper

Measurements 86.5[91.5]cm (34[36]in) chest (use 3-mm needles for smaller size).
Materials 8×25 gm balls of 4-ply yarn. 3 buttons.
Needles One pair 3.25-mm (No. 10) needles (3-mm (No. 11) for smaller size).
Tension See page 10.
Abbreviations See page 12.

Back

Using 3-mm needles cast on 110 sts and work 10 cm (4 in) in single rib. Inc 1 st at each end of last row (112 sts).
Change to 3.25-mm needles and work in pattern as follows:
1ST ROW sl 1, *p3, k6. Rep from * to last 3 sts, p2, k1 tbl.
2ND ROW sl 1, k2, *p6, k3. Rep from * to last st, k1 tbl.
Rep these 2 rows until work measures 33 cm (13 in) from cast on edge.
Shape armhole Keep pattern as correct as possible.
Cast off 5 sts at beg of next 2 rows. Then k2 tog at each end of next and every alt row until 90 sts remain.
Cont without shaping until work measures 40.5 cm (16 in) from cast on edge. K2 at END of last row (finish with right side facing).
Work in cable pattern as follows:
1ST ROW sl 1, *k6, p3. Rep from * to last 7 sts, k6, k1 tbl.
2ND ROW sl 1, p6, *k3, p6. Rep from * to last st, k1 tbl.
3RD ROW as row 1.
4TH ROW as row 2.

5TH ROW sl 1, *c6 (slip first 3 sts on to a cable needle, leave at front of work, k3, k3 sts from cable needle — c6), p3. Rep from * to last 7 sts, c6, k1 tbl.
6TH ROW as row 2.
Rep these 6 rows until work measures 51 cm (20 in) from cast on edge.
Shape shoulder Keep pattern correct.
Cast off 10 sts at beg of next 6 rows.
Leave remaining 29 sts on a spare needle for neckband.

Front

Work as for back until 3 cable patterns have been worked.
Shape front neck Keep pattern correct.
Pattern 33 sts, turn.
1ST ROW p2 tog, pattern to last st, k1 tbl.
2ND ROW pattern to last 2 sts, k2 tog.
3RD ROW as row 1 (30 sts).
Now work in pattern without further dec until front measures same as back to shoulder.
Shape shoulder Keep pattern correct.
Cast off 10 sts at beg of next row, work 1 row. Rep these 2 rows once more. Cast off remaining sts.
Slip centre 23 sts on to a pin, then work remaining 33 sts to match 1st side (shaping at neck edge).

Sleeves

Using 3.25-mm needles cast on 76 sts and work 4 rows in st st.
NEXT ROW sl 1, *k2 tog, wrn. Rep from * to last st, k1 tbl.
NEXT ROW p.
Work 4 rows in st st.
Change to pattern as follows:
1ST ROW sl 1, k4, *p3, k6. Rep from * to last 8 sts, p3, k4, k1 tbl.
2ND ROW sl 1, p4, k3, *p6, k3. Rep from * to last 5 sts, p4, k1 tbl.
Rep these 2 rows inc 1 st at each end of 2nd and every following 4th row until there are 90 sts. Work extra sts into pattern as you go. At 90 sts pattern row 1 will read — sl 1, k2, p3 *k6, p3. Rep from * to last 3 sts, k2, k1 tbl.
After 90 sts cont in pattern until sleeve measures 11.5 cm (4½ in) from cast on edge.

Shape top Keep pattern correct.
Cast off 5 sts at beg of next 2 rows, then dec 1 st at each end of every alt row until 52 sts remain.
At 52 sts change to 6 row cable pattern as on body yoke for rest of sleeve top.
At 52 sts next 6 rows should read:
1ST ROW k2 tog, *p3, k6. Rep from * to last 5 sts, p3, k2 tog.
2ND ROW sl 1, *k3, p6. Rep from * to last 4 sts, k3, k1 tbl.
3RD ROW k2 tog, pattern to last 2 sts, k2 tog.
4TH ROW sl 1, pattern to last st, k1 tbl.
5TH ROW k2 tog, pattern to last 2 sts (cable row), k2 tog.
6TH ROW as row 4.
Cont in this way decreasing 1 st at each end of every alt row (keeping pattern correct) until there are 24 sts.
NEXT ROW k4 tog, all along row. Cast off remaining sts.

Neckband

Join right shoulder seam.
Using 3.25-mm needles and with right side facing, pick up 24 sts down left front, 23 sts across centre front, 24 sts up right front, and 29 sts across back (100 sts). Work 4 rows in st st.
NEXT ROW sl 1, *k2 tog, wrn. Rep from * to last st, k1 tbl.
NEXT ROW p.
Work 4 rows in st st. Cast off VERY LOOSELY.

Making up

Leave neck open 7.5 cm (3 in), join remainder of shoulder seam. Set sleeves into place and sew in (matching cable pattern with cable yoke on body). Turn picot edge over at sleeve edges and sew edge down WITHOUT gathering edge. Turn picot neck edge over and sew into place. Sew sleeve and side seams. Make 3 buttonhole loops on neck opening, sew buttons into place.

Short sleeved sweater in knot stitch

Measurements Small, medium and large.
Materials 8 × 25 gm balls of 4-ply yarn.
3 buttons.
Needles One pair each 2.5-mm and
3.25-mm (Nos. 12 and 10) needles.
Tension See page 10.
Abbreviations See page 12.
TO MAKE KNOT p3 tog. Leaving sts on left
hand needle, wrn, then p tog again the
same 3 sts (you still have 3 sts).

Back

Using 2.5-mm needles cast on
106[114/122] sts and work in single rib
for 7.5 cm (3 in). Change to 3.25-mm
needles and pattern as follows.
1ST ROW sl 1, k to last st, k1 tbl.
2ND ROW sl 1, p to last st, k1 tbl.
3RD ROW sl 1, *k5, knot 3. Rep from * to
last st, k1 tbl.
4TH ROW as 2nd row.
5TH ROW as 1st row.
6TH ROW as 2nd row.
7TH ROW sl 1, *k1, knot 3, k4. Rep from
* to last st, k1 tbl.
8TH ROW as 2nd row.
These 8 rows form the pattern. Rep until
work measures 33 cm (13 in) from beg.
Shape armholes Cast off 5 sts at the beg
of the next 2 rows, then k2 tog at each
end of next row and following 3[4/4] alt
rows (88[94/102] sts). Keep pattern
correct and knots in line and cont until
work measures 51 cm (20 in).
Shape shoulders Cast off 15 (16/17] sts
at beg of next 4 rows. Leave remaining
sts on a safety pin to pick up for
neckband.

Front

Work as for back until work measures
47 cm (18½ in) from the beg.
Shape for neck NEXT ROW pattern

33[35/37] sts, sl next 22[24/28] sts on to a safety pin to pick up for neckband, pattern remaining 33[35/37] sts. Keeping pattern correct work on this side of front, working 2 sts tog at neck edge on next 3 rows.

Then work without shaping until armhole measures same as back ending at armhole edge.

Shape shoulders Cast off 15[16/17] sts at beg of next and following alt row. Rejoin yarn to remaining 33[35/37] sts and work to match first side reversing all shapings.

Sleeves

Using 3.25-mm needles cast on 90 sts and work 4 rows in st st.

NEXT ROW sl 1, *k2 tog, wlfwd. Rep from * all along row (to form picot edge). Work 3 more rows in st st.

Change to 3.25-mm needles and work in pattern until sleeve measures 9 cm (3½ in) from the start.

Shape top Keeping pattern correct cast off 5 sts at the beg of the next 2 rows, then dec at each end of every alt row until 24 sts remain finishing with right side facing. K4 sts tog all along next row. Cast off. Join right shoulder seam.

Neckband

Using 3.25-mm needles, with right side facing and starting at front left shoulder pick up 24 sts down left front, sts from centre front, 24 sts up right side of front and sts from centre back. Work 3 rows in st st, starting with a p row (wrong side facing).

NEXT ROW (Make holes for picot edge) sl 1, k1, *wlfwd, k2 tog. Rep from * all along row. Work 3 more rows in st st. Cast off.

Fold back at row of holes and carefully stitch down on wrong side to start of hem. Do same on sleeve edges. Join all seams leaving left shoulder seam open for 7.5 cm (3 in). Make 3 buttonholes (either crochet, blanket st or chain st) on front of opening, sewing 3 buttons to correspond on back of shoulder.

Multistitch and multicoloured cardigan

Measurements Small, medium and large.

Materials For long sleeved cardigan using 4-ply yarn 6 × 25 gm balls in cream, 3 balls in blue, 2 balls in pink, 1 ball in each of mauve, peach and yellow. For short sleeved version 4 balls in cream, 2 balls in each of blue and pink and 1 ball in each of mauve, peach and yellow. 3 buttons to match band colours up to armhole.

Needles One pair each 2.5-mm and 3.25-mm (Nos. 12 and 10) needles.

Tension See page 10.

Abbreviations See page 12.

Back

Using 2.5-mm needles and cream yarn cast on 106[114/122] sts and work in single rib for 9 cm (3½ in). Change to 3.25-mm needles and blue yarn and work in 4 × 4 basket st pattern as follows:

1ST ROW sl 1, *k4, p4. Rep from * to last st, k1 tbl.

2ND, 3RD AND 4TH ROWS as 1st row.

5TH ROW sl 1, *p4, k4. Rep from * to last st, k1 tbl.

6TH, 7TH AND 8TH ROWS as 5th row.

These 8 rows form the pattern. Rep pattern once more.

Break off blue yarn, join in cream yarn and work 4 rows in st st.

Break off cream yarn, join in pink yarn

and work in slanting 2 × 2 rib as follows:
1ST ROW sl 1, *k2, p2. Rep from * to last st, k1 tbl.
2ND ROW as 1st row.
3RD ROW sl 1, p1, *k2, p2. Rep from * to last 4 sts, k2, p1, k1 tbl.
4TH ROW Sl1, k1, *p2, k2. Rep from * to last 2 sts, k1, k1 tbl.
5TH ROW sl 1, *p2, k2. Rep from * to last st, k1 tbl.
6TH ROW as 5th row.
7TH ROW sl 1, k1, *p2, k2. Rep from * to last 4 sts, p2, k1, k1 tbl.
8TH ROW sl1, p1, *k2, p2. Rep from * to last 2 sts, p1, k1 tbl. By now the left slope to the rib will be quite apparent. Work another 8 rows. Break off pink yarn. Join in cream yarn and work 4 rows in st st. Break off cream. Join in mauve. In mauve work 16 rows in moss st. Break off mauve and join in cream, working another 4 rows in st st. Break off cream and join in peach.
In peach work in a 2 × 2 slanting rib, this time slanting to the RIGHT instead of to the left as in pink band, as follows:
1ST ROW sl 1, *k2, p2. Rep from * to last st, k1 tbl.
2ND ROW as 1st row.
3RD ROW sl 1, k1, *p2, k2. Rep from * to last 4 sts, p2, k1, k1 tbl.
4TH ROW as 3rd row. Cont this way moving the slant to the right on every other row until 16 rows have been worked. Break off peach yarn, join in cream and work 4 rows of st st. Break off cream and join in blue.
Work 16 rows in 4 × 4 basket st in blue as before, then 4 rows in st st in cream, then the 16 rows of left slanting 2 × 2 rib in pink as before. Break off pink and join in cream.
Shape armholes In cream sl 1, k2 tog tbl, k to last 5 sts, k2 tog, k2, k1 tbl.
NEXT ROW sl 1, p to last st, k1 tbl.
Rep last 2 rows once more. Break off cream and join in mauve.
NEXT ROW sl 1, k2, k2 tog tbl, work in moss st to last 5 sts, k2 tog, k2, k1 tbl.
NEXT ROW sl 1, p3, moss st to last 4 sts, p3, k1 tbl.

Rep last 2 rows, 7 times more. Break off mauve and join in cream.
Work 4 rows in cream as at start of armhole shaping. This completes armhole shaping. Break off cream and join in yellow, now used for rest of yoke. Work in broken rib as follows.
1ST ROW sl 1, *k1, p1. Rep from * to last st, k1 tbl.
2ND ROW sl 1, p to last st, k1 tbl.
Rep these 2 rows until armhole measures 18[18/19]cm (7[7/7½]in) measured on the straight edge. Cast off 13[14/15] sts at beg of next 4 rows. Cast off.

Fronts
Using 2.5-mm needles and cream yarn cast on 64[68/72] sts and work in single rib for 4 rows.
NEXT ROW (Make a buttonhole) rib 3, wlfwd, work 2 tog, rib to end. Cont in rib for 9 cm (3½ in) as on back making a second buttonhole halfway up the rib and another one on last but one row of the rib. On last row of rib, rib to last 8 sts, turn and leave these 8 sts on a safety pin for frontband.
Now work as for back to end of the peach stripe finishing at front edge.
Start shaping front slope Using cream yarn work 2 sts tog at beg of next row (front edge), work to end. Now cont to work 2 sts tog at front edge on every 4th row until the end of the 2nd pink stripe is reached.
Armhole shaping Pattern to last 5 sts, k2 tog, k2, k1 tbl on every alt row, still continuing front slope. Work in this way until the end of the cream stripe (start of yellow yoke) is reached. This finishes the armhole shaping but front slope shaping continues until 26 sts remain. Then work without shaping in broken rib until armhole measures same as back finishing at armhole end. Shape shoulders by casting off 13 sts at beg of next and following alt row.
Work second front the same as right front keeping rib band at other end of work and reversing all shapings (and omitting buttonholes).

Short sleeves

Using 2.5-mm needles and cream yarn cast on 88 sts and work 4 cm (1½ in) in single rib increasing 1 st at each end of last row (90 sts). Change to 3.25-mm needles and work blue band, cream band and pink band as on back.

Start armhole shaping as follows:
1ST ROW sl 1, k2, k2 tog tbl, k to last 5 sts, k2 tog, k2, k1 tbl.
2ND ROW sl 1, p to end.
Rep these 2 rows once more. Break off cream and join in mauve.
NEXT ROW sl 1, k2, k2 tog tbl, moss st to last 5 sts, k2 tog, k2, k1 tbl.
NEXT ROW sl 1, p3, moss st to last 4 sts, p3, k1 tbl.
Rep these last 2 rows 7 times more then rep the 4 cream rows again. Break off cream, join in yellow and working in broken moss st work without shaping for about 4 cm (1½ in). Shape top by decreasing at each end of every alt row until 48 sts remain, finishing at end of a rib row.
NEXT ROW p4 tog 12 times. Cast off.
This cardigan could just as easily be made with long sleeves.

Long sleeves

Using 2.5-mm needles and cream yarn cast on 50 sts and work in single rib for 10 cm (4 in) increasing 10 sts evenly along last row. Change to 3.25-mm needles and work in stripe pattern as on back, starting with a blue pattern. (It is a good idea to measure the stripes on body and then work out the colour stripe to start on to give right sleeve length.) Inc 1 st at each end of the 11th and every following 6th row until there are 88 sts on the needle. Cont in stripe pattern until end of blue stripe as on short sleeve. Finish as for short sleeve.
Using 2.5-mm needles rejoin yarn to 8 sts on pin for front buttonhole band and work in rib as before, making buttonholes evenly up front until start of slope. Cont until band fits up front to centre of back neck, very slightly stretched to keep garment in shape. Work

a second band to match (omitting buttonholes).
Join all seams being careful to keep stripes in line and preferably sewing each stripe in its own colour. Sew on bands using base colour. Attach buttons to correspond to buttonholes.
The colours chosen were for a spring garment. Other colours could of course be used either tone on tone colours or brights on neutral colours. Or the cardigan could be made to match other garments in your wardrobe.

Matching short sleeved sweater

Measurements Small, medium and large.
Materials See materials for short sleeved cardigan. 3 buttons for shoulder opening. opening.
Needles One pair each 2.5-mm and 3.25-mm (Nos 12 and 10) needles.
Tension See page 10.
Abbreviations See page 12.
Back and sleeves as for cardigan.

Front

Work as for back until armhole measures 11.5 cm (4½ in) on the straight edge ending with right side facing.
Shape neck Work 30[32/34] sts, turn and work on this side only, leaving remaining sts on spare needle or pin. Dec at neck edge on the following 4 rows (26[28/30] sts). Work without shaping until armhole measures same as back ending at armhole edge.
Shape shoulders Cast off 13[14/15] sts at the beg of next and following alt row. Return to remaining sts, sl 22[26/30] sts on to a safety pin (centre front to pick up for neck). Rejoin yarn to remaining 30[32/34] sts and work to match 1st side reversing all shapings.
Join right shoulder.

Neckband

With 2.5-mm needles, with right side of

work facing and starting at left front shoulder, pick up 24 sts down left side of neck, 22[26/30] from centre front, 24 sts up right side of neck and the sts from centre back. Work in single rib for 6 rows. Cast off in rib.

Making up
Join all seams being careful to keep stripes in line — preferably sewing each stripe in its own colour. Leave left shoulder seam open for 7.5 cm (3 in) and make 3 buttonholes (either crochet, blanket or chain st) on front of opening and put 3 buttons on back to correspond.

MOHAIR SWEATER

Men's Wear

Heavy moss stitch sweater with collar

Measurements Small, medium and large.
Materials 19 × 50 gm balls of double double weight yarn or double-knitting weight used double.
Needles One pair each 4.5-mm and 6-mm (Nos. 7 and 4) needles.
Tension and Abbreviations See pages 10 and 12.

Front
Using 4.5-mm needles cast on 70[78/86] sts and work in single rib for 9 cm (3½ in). Change to 6-mm needles and work as follows:
Moss st 13[15/17], turn.
Cast on 17[19/21] sts for pocket lining and then moss st back along these 30[34/38] sts. Cont to work in moss st on these sts until 40 rows have been worked from cast on edge, ending at the inside edge. Cast off 17[19/21] sts and leave the remaining 13[15/17] sts on a length of yarn. With right side facing rejoin yarn to remaining rib sts and using 6-mm needles work 44[48/52] sts in moss st continuing to work on these sts until 40 rows have been worked. Leave these sts on a length of yarn. With right side facing rejoin to remaining 13[15/17] sts. Cast on 17[19/21] sts for pocket lining and again work in moss st for 40 rows, finishing at the inside edge. Cast off 17[19/21] sts and break off yarn. Place the centre 44[48/52] sts on to the needle, then the first group of 13[15/17] sts and work in moss st across all sts: 13[15/17], 44[48/52] centre sts and next 13[15/17] sts (70[78/86] sts). Cont in moss st until work measures 45.5[45.5/48.5]cm (18[18/19]in) from

start ending with a wrong side row. Mark
this row with a piece of coloured thread
at each end to show end of side seam.
Cont in moss st and work 35[39/43] sts.
Turn and cont on these sts as follows.
Cont without shaping for 19 cm (7½ in)
after row marked with coloured thread,
finishing at NECK edge.
Shape neck Cast off 7 sts, work to end.
NEXT ROW Work to last 2 sts, k2 tog tbl.
NEXT ROW Work in moss st.
Rep these last 2 rows 3 times
(24[28/32] sts).
Shape shoulder Cast off 9 sts at beg of
next 2 alt rows. Work 1 row. Cast off
remaining sts.
Rejoin yarn to other group of sts and
work to correspond with first side,
reversing all shapings.

Pocket edges (make two)
Using 4-mm needles and front side
facing, pick up 35 sts along edge of
pocket and work in single rib for 4 cm
(1½ in). Cast off.

Back
Using 3.5-mm needles cast on 70[78/86]
sts and work in single rib for 7.5 cm
(3 in).
Change to 6-mm needles and work in
moss st until work measures
46[46/48]cm (18[18/19]in) from start
marking this row as on front. Cont in
moss st until work measures
67.5[67.5/70]cm (26½[26½/27½]in)
from beg.
Shape shoulder Cast off 9 sts at beg of
next 6 rows. Cast off remaining sts.

Sleeves
Using 3.5-mm needles cast on 46 sts and
work 11.5 cm (4½ in) in single rib
increasing evenly along last row to 56 sts.
Change to 6-mm needles and work in
moss st until sleeve measures
52[52.5/57]cm (20½[21½/22½]in)
from beg. Cast off.

Collar
Using 3.5-mm needles cast on 82 sts and

work 13 cm (5 in) in single rib.
NEXT ROW rib 20, cast off 42 sts, rib
to end.
Work on first group of 20 sts as follows.
Work 1 row in single rib.
NEXT ROW k2 tog on neck edge on this
and every alt row until 10 sts remain.
Work 1 more row. Cast off.
Rejoin yarn to other group of 20 sts and
work as on first group reversing all
shapings.

Making up
Join shoulder seams, set sleeves between
marked points on back and front. Sew
into position and join side and sleeve
seams. Pin cast off edge of collar to back
neck (with centre of cast off sts to centre
of back) and pin shaped decreased edge
of collar to front neck edge of sweater
bringing edge of collar to front edge of
sweater opening. Sew collar into position
(right sides together) and fold back.
Work a row of double crochet round
front opening and fix a toggle at neck
with a loop opposite.

Sleeveless slipover in diamond stitch

Measurements To fit 91[97/102/107]cm (36[38/40/42]in) chest.
Materials 15[15/16/16] × 25 gm balls of double-knitting yarn.
Needles One pair each 3.25-mm 3.5-mm and 4.5-mm (Nos. 10, 9 and 7) needles.
Tension and Abbreviations See pages 10 and 12.

Front
With 3.5-mm needles cast on 98[104/110/116] sts and work in single rib for 9 cm (3½ in). Change to 4.5-mm needles and pattern as follows:
1ST ROW sl 1, k3, *p1, k5. Rep from * to last 4 sts, p1, k2, k1 tbl.
2ND ROW sl 1, p1, *k1, p1, k1, p3. Rep from * to last 6 sts, k1, p1, k1, p2, k1 tbl.
3RD ROW sl 1, *k1, p1, k3, p1. Rep. from * to last st, k1 tbl.
4TH ROW sl 1, *p5, k1. Rep from * to last st, k1 tbl.
5TH ROW as 3rd row.
6TH ROW as 2nd row.
7TH ROW as 1st row.
8TH ROW as 2nd row.
9TH ROW as 3rd row.
10TH ROW as 4th row.
11TH ROW as 3rd row.
12TH ROW as 2nd row.
These 12 rows form the pattern which is used for the whole garment other than the welts, armbands and neckband. Cont working in pattern without shaping until work measures 37[38/39.5/39.5]cm (14½[15/15½/15½]in) from beg.
Shape armhole Cast off 6 sts at the beg of the next 2 rows and then work straight until work measures 40.5[42/43/43]cm (16[16½/17/17]in) from start. Start working 'V' neck:
NEXT ROW work 43[46/49/52] sts, turn.
NEXT ROW sl 1, k2 tog and being very careful to keep the pattern correct work to the end knitting into back of last st. Work 3 rows without shaping. Rep these 4 rows until 33[36/36/39] sts remain, then cont straight until work measures

63.5[65/66/67.5]cm (25[25½/26/26½]in) from start ending at armhole edge.
Shape shoulders Cast off 11[12/12/13] sts at beg of next and following 2 alt rows. Complete other side of front in the same way, reversing all shapings.

Back
Work as for front up to armhole shaping.
Shape armholes Cast off 6 sts at the beg of the next 2 rows then cont to work without shaping until work measures same as front to shoulder.
Shape shoulders Cast off 11[12/12/13] sts at the beg of the next 6 rows. Leave remaining sts on a spare needle to be picked up for the neckband.
Join right shoulder seam.

Neckband
Using 4-mm needles and right side facing pick up 66 sts down the left of the front 'V', 1 st from the centre (mark this stitch with a piece of coloured thread), 66 sts up the right front of the 'V' and then the sts from centre back. Work 7 rows in single rib working 2 sts tog on each side of the centre (marked) st on EVERY row. Cast off loosely in rib (the best way is to hold a larger needle, say a 5-mm needle, in your right hand when casting off). Join left shoulder seam.

Armbands
Using a 3.25-mm needle, with right side facing and starting from the straight part of the armhole (the 6 cast off sts will be sewn to the depth of the rib band you are working) pick up 144 sts evenly round the armhole. Work 6 rows in single rib. Cast off in rib.

Making up
Sew depth of armband rib to 6 cast off sts for armhole. Sew up sides of garment. I would not advise pressing this diamond stitch as it flattens the attractive texture.

Shetland sweater

Measurements Small and medium.
Materials Of Shetland yarn 15 × 25 gm
balls or 8 × 50 gm balls.
Needles One pair each 4.5-mm and
5.5-mm (Nos. 9 and 5) needles.
Tension and Abbreviations See pages 10
and 12.
This sweater is made in 3 pattern bands.
Pattern 1: 4 st × 4 st basket stitch (8 row
pattern).
Pattern 2: 1st row: *k1, sl 1. Rep from *
to end. 2nd row: (2 row pattern) p.
Pattern 3: 13 rows st st then 3 rows
garter st. (16 row pattern.)
Each band is separated by 4 rows of
garter st.

Back
Using 4-mm needles cast on 80[88] sts
and work 9.5 cm (3¾ in) in single rib
increasing 1 st at each end of last row
(82[90] sts). Change to 5.5-mm needles
and patterns —
Pattern 1:
1ST TO 4TH ROWS sl 1, *k4, p4. Rep from
* to last st, k1 tbl.
5TH TO 8TH ROWS sl 1, *p4, k4. Rep from
* to last st, k1 tbl.
Rep these 8 rows until work measures
28 cm (11 in) from start.
Work 4 rows in garter st.
Pattern 2:
1ST ROW sl 1, p1, *k1, sl 1. Rep from * to
last st, k1 tbl.
2ND ROW p.
Rep these 2 rows until work measures
48.5 cm (19 in) from start.
Work 4 rows in garter st.
Pattern 3: Work 13 rows in st st, then 3
rows in garter st.
Rep until work measures 68.5 cm (27 in)
from start, ending with a right side row.
Cast off.

Front
Work as for back until the beg of the
3rd pattern.
Working in pattern 3 cont as follows:
Shape 'V' sl 1, k34[38], k2 tog, k8, k2

tog, k34[38], k1 tbl.
NEXT ROW sl 1, p33[37], k2 tog, k3, k1
tbl, turn.
NEXT ROW k.
NEXT ROW sl 1, p to last 4 sts, k4.
Work on this first group of sts decreasing
1 st inside the 4 st garter st border, on
every following 3rd row until 29[33] sts
remain. Work until front is same length
as back. Cast off.
Rejoin yarn to the other group of sts and
work to correspond with the first side
reversing all shapings, but when the
shoulder is reached do not cast off the 4
garter st border sts. Cont to work on these
4 sts in garter stitch until the band fits
neatly across the centre back (about
16.5 cm [6½ in]).
Sew up shoulder seams and stitch the
neck band into place.

Sleeves
Using 3.5-mm needles cast on 40 sts and
work in single rib for 7.5 cm (3 in)
increasing evenly along the last row to
60 sts.
Change to 5.5-mm needles and work in
3rd pattern, (13 rows st st followed by 3
rows garter st) increasing 1 st at each end
of the 9th and every following 8th row
until there are 76 sts on the needle. Then
work without shaping until sleeve
measures 47[49.5]cm (18½[19½]in)
from cast on edge ending with a right
side row. Cast off.

Making up
Pin the centre of the sleeve cast off edge
to the shoulder seam, sewing neatly into
place with no pulling or gathering at all.
The sleeve seam should be quite flat. Join
side and sleeve seams. Sew in all ends.

Matching cardigan

Measurements Small and medium.
Materials Of Shetland yarn 15 × 25 gm
balls or 8 × 50 gm balls. 7 buttons.
Needles, Tension and Abbreviations as
for Sweater.

Back and sleeves are worked exactly as for the sweater

Right front

Using 3.5-mm needles cast on 40[48] sts and work as follows.
1ST ROW sl 1, k6, work in single rib to end.
2ND ROW work in single rib to last 7 sts, k7. Rep these 2 rows until work measures 9.5 cm (3¾ in). Change to 5.5-mm needles and keeping the 7 st border in garter st work in pattern as for back to the end of the 2nd pattern, finishing at front edge (garter st border). Start shaping the 'V' front slope:
1ST ROW k7, k2 tog tbl, k to end.
2ND ROW p to last 7 sts, k7.
Cont in 3rd pattern at the same time decreasing as above on every following 4th row until 27 sts remain. Then cont straight until work measures same as back to shoulders. Cast off.

Left front

Work as for right front reversing all shapings and putting the 7 st garter st border at the end of the 1st row, beg of 2nd, and so on. Work 4 rows and then work a buttonhole as follows.
5TH ROW rib to last 7 sts, k2, k2 tog, wlfwd, k to end.
Work buttonholes at 6.5 cm (2½ in) intervals up to start (or just below start) of front 'V' sloping. When shoulder level is reached do not cast off the 7 st border sts but cont to work them so band fits nicely across centre back, as for sweater.

Making up

See sweater. Attach buttons to correspond with buttonholes.

Socks

Leg length 29 cm (11½ in).
Foot length 28 cm (11 in) but quite adjustable.
Materials 8 × 25 gm balls of 4-ply yarn
Needles A pair of 2.25-mm (No. 13)

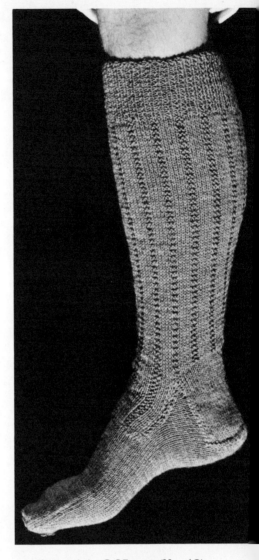

needles and 4 × 2.25-mm (No. 13) needles with points at both ends for working rounds on foot.
Tension See page 10.
Abbreviations See page 12.

With 2 2.25-mm needles cast on 96 sts and work in single rib for 6.5 cm (2½ in) increasing 1 st at end of last row (97 sts). Change to rib pattern as follows.
1ST ROW sl 1, *k4, p2. Rep from * to end.
2ND ROW sl 1, p to last st, k1 tbl.

These 2 rows form the broken rib pattern. Cont without shaping for 20 rows.

Leg
Cont in pattern and dec 1 st at each end of next row and every following 6th row until 67 sts remain. Work straight until work measures 29 cm (11½ in) from start ending with a p row.

Heel and instep
Work 50 sts, turn.
NEXT ROW work 33 sts, turn. Cont on these 33 sts for 7.5 cm (3 in) ending with a p row. Leave these sts on a length of thread. With right side facing slip 17 sts from each side of instep on to one needle and work without shaping for 36 rows.

Heel
1ST ROW k20, k2 tog, turn.
2ND ROW p7, p2 tog, turn.
3RD ROW k8, k2 tog, turn.
4TH ROW p9, p2 tog, turn.
5TH ROW k10, k2 tog, turn.
6TH ROW p11, p2 tog, turn.
7TH ROW k12, k2 tog, turn.
8TH ROW p13, p2 tog, turn.
9TH ROW k13, k2 tog, turn.
10TH ROW p13, p2 tog, turn.
Rep these last 2 rows until all side sts have been worked off. 14 sts remain.
NEXT ROW k to end then k up 18 sts along side of heel.
NEXT ROW p to end and pick up and p 18 sts along other side of heel.
Shape instep NEXT ROW sl 1, sl 1, k1, psso, k to last 3 sts, k2 tog, k1.
NEXT ROW p.
Rep these last 2 rows 7 times more (34 sts).
Cont in st st until work measures same as instep ending with a p row.
Now complete the sock using a set of 4 needles.
1ST ROUND
NEEDLE 1 k22.
NEEDLE 2 k12 from heel needle, 10 from instep.
NEEDLE 3 k23 remaining sts from instep

needle (67 sts).
Now cont in rounds until sock measures 18 cm (7 in) (or any length required) from the picked up heel sts finishing at end of 3rd needle.

Toe
1ST ROUND
NEEDLE 1 k1, sl 1, k1, psso, k to last 3 sts, k2 tog, k1. Work the 2nd and 3rd needles as the 1st then work 2 rounds without shaping. Rep last 3 rounds 5 times.
NEXT ROUND as 1st round.
NEXT ROUND k.
Rep these 2 rounds once more.
NEXT ROUND
NEEDLE 1 k1, k2 tog, k1.
NEEDLE 2 as 1st needle.
NEEDLE 3 k1, k2 tog, k2.
Break off wool and thread it through the remaining sts. Draw up and fasten off securely.

Making up
Join leg and instep seams.
This is a basic 4-ply sock pattern which is quite easy to adapt.
1. The socks could be made in st st or any other simple stitch, i.e. should they be needed to match a garment.
2. The socks could be made with a stripe down the leg — one deep band, an occasional band of stripes, a couple of rows of another colour or totally striped. It is a very good way of using up odds and ends of yarn.
3. A simple Fair Isle pattern could be worked.

Saddle shoulder sweater

Measurements Small, medium and large.
Materials 20[21/21] × 25 gm balls of double-knitting yarn, 3 buttons.
Needles One pair each 2.5-mm, 3.25-mm and 4.5-mm (Nos 12, 10 and 7) needles.
Tension and Abbreviations See pages 10 and 12.
Back
Using 2.5-mm needles cast on 95[99/103] sts and work in single rib for 9 cm (3½ in) increasing 1 st at each end of last row. Change to 4.5-mm needles and work in broken rib pattern as follows.
ROW 1 sl 1, work in single rib as set to end.
ROW 2 sl 1, p to end.
These 2 rows form the broken rib pattern which is used for the whole garment except welts and neckband. Cont without shaping until work measures 38[38/40.5]cm (15[15/16]in).
Shape armhole
ROW 1 sl 1, p1, k1, p1, k2 tog tbl, rib to last 6 sts, k2 tog, p1, k1, p1, k1 tbl.
ROW 2 p. Rep these 2 rows until 79 sts remain then cont without further shaping until work measures 54.5[54.5/58.5]cm (21½[21½/23]in) from beg. Cast off.

Front
Work as for back until work measures 51[51/54.5]cm (20[20/21½]in).
Divide for neck as follows.
Rib 25 as set, turn.
NEXT ROW p2 tog, p to end.
NEXT ROW rib as set. Rep these 2 rows until 22 sts remain. Cast off in rib. Return to other side. Slip middle 29 sts on to a safety pin to pick up for neckband and work remaining 25 sts to match first side.

Sleeves
Using 2.5-mm needles cast on 53 sts and work in single rib for 9 cm (3½ in).
1ST ROW *k1, p1, rep from * to end. Inc 1 st at each end of last row of rib (55

sts). Change to 4.5-mm needles and work in broken rib as for body increasing 1 st at each end of 13th and every following 12th row until there are 69 sts on needle. Then cont without shaping until work measures 47[48.5/49.5]cm (18½[19/19½]in) from beg.
Shape armhole
1ST ROW sl 1, p1, k1, p1, k2 tog tbl, rib to last 6 sts, k2 tog, p1, k1, p1, k1 tbl.
2ND ROW p.
Rep these 2 rows until 31 sts remain and then work without shaping for 10 cm (4 in) ending with right side facing for 1st sleeve (wrong side facing for 2nd sleeve).
NEXT ROW Rib 13 sts, turn, leaving 18 sts on a safety pin to pick up for neck.
Cont on the 13 sts for 10 cm (4 in) more (this is the extension of the saddle shoulder that goes half way across back of neck). Cast off purlwise on a p row.
Work second sleeve in the same way, remembering that saddle shoulder extension is on other side.

Making up
When making up join sleeve seam and side seams to 1.3 cm (½ in) below start of armhole shaping. Attach lower end of front part of saddle shoulder to finish of neckband and then sew into sleeve seam and across front shoulder, easing neatly round corner. Don't sew up saddle shoulder to back until neckband is done, so neckband can be joined at centre back.

Neck rib
Using 3.25-mm needles, starting at centre back, right side facing, pick up 20 sts from half back, 18 sts from end of saddle front, 8 sts down side of front neck, 29 sts from centre front, 8 sts up other side of front, 18 sts across front saddle and 20 sts from back. Work 16 rows in single rib. Cast off loosely in rib. Fold rib over, attach carefully to base of rib on wrong side.
   To set in sleeves and saddle shoulder, pin inside end of elongated bit of back shoulder to centre back of body

then stitch sleeve seam and across shoulder to this centre back point. Leave centre back seam open. Make 3 loop buttonholes (either crochet, blanket stitch or chain stitch) and attach 3 buttons to correspond.

Matching scarf

Length 183 cm (72 in) plus fringe.
Materials 12 × 25 gm balls of double-knitting yarn.
Needles One pair 7-mm (No. 2) needles.
USE YARN DOUBLE THROUGHOUT.
Using 7-mm needles and 2 strands of yarn cast on 28 sts and work as follows.
Work 6 rows in garter st (every row k).
NEXT ROW sl 1, k2, *k1, p1. Rep from * to last 3 sts, k2, k1 tbl.
NEXT ROW sl 1, k2, p to last 3 sts, k2, k1 tbl.
These 2 rows form the pattern. Work in pattern until scarf measures 180.5 cm (71 in). Work 6 rows in garter st. Cast off.

Fringe
Cut 35.5 cm (14 in) lengths and fringe with 5 lengths at a time 10 times along each end of scarf.

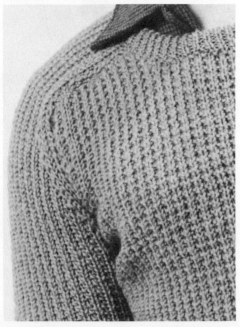

Classic 'V' neck sweater

Measurements 96.5-102[107-112]cm (38-40[42-44]in), length 66[68.5]cm (26[27]in).
Materials 24[26] × 25 gm balls of double-knitting yarn.
Needles One pair each 3.25-mm and 4-mm (Nos. 10 and 8) needles.
Tension See page 10.
Abbreviations See page 12.

Back
Using 3.25-mm needles cast on 124[132] sts and work in single rib for 9 cm (3½ in) increasing 1 st at end of last row. Change to 4-mm needles and work in st st until work measures 40.5[42]cm (16[16½]in) from beg.
Shape armholes Cast off 4[5] sts at beg of the next 2 rows.
NEXT ROW p.
NEXT ROW sl 1, k1, k2 tog tbl, k to last 4 sts, k2 tog, k1, k1 tbl.
NEXT ROW sl 1, p to last st, k1 tbl.
Rep these last 2 rows until 35[37] sts remain ending on wrong side. Leave sts on a safety pin to pick up for neck.

Front
Work as for back until 107[113] sts are on the needle ending on wrong side.

Shape neck
sl 1, k1, k2 tog tbl, k49[52], turn.
Cont on these 52[55] sts.
NEXT ROW p.
NEXT ROW sl 1, k1, k2 tog tbl, k to last 3 sts, k2 tog, k1 tbl.
NEXT ROW p.
NEXT ROW sl 1, k1, k2 tog tbl, k to end.
NEXT ROW p. Cont in st st decreasing 1 st at armhole edge on every alt row and AT THE SAME TIME decreasing at neck edge on next and every following 4th row until 8 sts remain. Cont decreasing on armhole edge until 1 st remains. Fasten off.
Leaving 1 st on a safety pin for centre of 'V' rejoin yarn to the remaining 53[56]

sts and work to match first side reversing all shapings.

Sleeves

Using 3.25-mm needles cast on 66[70] sts and work in single rib for 10 cm (4 in). Change to 4-mm needles, work in st st and inc 1 st at each end of the 8th and every following 6th row until there are 102[108] sts. Cont without further shaping until work measures 45.5[47]cm (18[18½]in) ending on wrong side.
Shape raglan As for back until 12 sts remain. Cast off. Sew in sleeves leaving left back armhole open.

Neckband

Using 3.25-mm needles with right side of work facing pick up and k 12 sts from top of sleeve, 65[67] sts down left front, the centre st from thread, 65[67] sts up right front, 12 sts across second sleeve and 35[37] sts across back (190[196]sts). Work in single rib decreasing 1 st on each side of central st on every row for 2.5 cm (1 in). Cast off in rib.

Making up

Sew up left back armhole. Sew up side and sleeve seams.

Crew neck sweater

The only difference from the 'V' neck sweater is in the front and neckband.
Front
Work as for the back until 55[57] sts are on the needle.
Shape for neck Sl 1, k1, k2 tog tbl, k15[16], cast off 17 sts, k15[16], k2 tog, k1, k1 tbl.
Work on this side of front only. Cont the raglan shaping at the armhole edge and dec at neck edge on the next and following 4 alt rows, then keep neck edge straight and just cont raglan shaping until 1 st remains. Fasten off. Rejoin yarn to other side and work to match reversing

all shapings.

Neck
Using 3.25-mm needles and with right side facing pick up 25 sts down left side of front, 15 sts from cast off sts in centre front, 25 sts up right side of front and 35[37] from centre back. Work 7 rows in single rib. Cast off ribwise.

Mohair sweater

Measurements Small and medium.
Materials 17 × 25 gm balls of mohair or similar yarn.
Needles One pair each 4-mm and 6.5-mm (Nos. 8 and 3) needles.
Tension 7 sts to a 5 cm (2 in) square using 6.5-mm needles.
Abbreviations See page 12.

Back
Using 4-mm needles cast on 63[73] sts and work in single rib for 7.5 cm (3 in). Change to 6.5-mm needles and work in st st until back measures 45.5[48.5]cm (18[19]in) from cast on edge. Mark this row with a piece of coloured thread as a guide to start of armhole. Then cont in st st until work measures 70[72.5]cm (27½[28½]in) from cast on edge, finish with a k row. Cast off knitwise.

Front
Using 4-mm needles cast on 64[74] sts and work in single rib for 7.5 cm (3 in). Change to 6.5-mm needles and work in cable pattern as follows:
1ST ROW k26[31], p2, k8, p2, k26[31].
2ND ROW p26[31], k2, p8, k2, p26[31].
3RD ROW as row 1.
4TH ROW as row 2.
5TH ROW k26[31], p2, slip next 4 sts on to a cable needle and leave at back of work, k4, then knit 4 sts from cable needle, p2, k26[31].
6TH ROW as row 2.
7TH ROW as row 1.
8TH ROW as row 2.
These 8 rows form the pattern. Cont in

pattern until front measures
45.5[48.5]cm (18[19]in) from cast on
edge. Mark each end of row with a
coloured thread.
Shape 'V' Work cable sts in pattern as far
as possible up 'V'.
NEXT ROW k31[36], turn, leave remaining
sts on a spare needle.
NEXT ROW k2 tog tbl, p to end.
Work 3 rows in st st.
Rep these 4 rows until 22[26] sts remain.
Cont without shaping until front
measures same as back. Cast off knitwise
on wrong side. Rejoin yarn to remaining
sts, k2 tog (leave this st on a pin for
centre front). Work across remaining sts
and work to correspond with first half.

Sleeves
Using 3.25-mm needles cast on 42[48]
sts and work in single rib for 10 cm
(4 in). Inc along last row of rib evenly to
63[69] sts. Change to 6.5-mm needles
and work in st st until sleeve measures
45.5[48.5]cm (18[19]in) from cast on
edge. Cast off loosely.

Neckband
Join right shoulder seam.
With right side of work facing and
3.25-mm needles pick up and k65[68]
sts down left front, the centre st, 65[68]
sts up right front and 20[30] sts across
back of neck. Work 8 rows of single rib
decreasing 1 st either side of centre st on
EVERY row. Cast off evenly in rib.

Making up
Sew up left shoulder seam and
neckband. Pin centre of sleeve to
shoulder seam, pin rest of sleeve into
place WITHOUT GATHERING SEAM. Sew in
sleeves then sew side and sleeve seams.
Sew all seams neatly.

Double-breasted waistcoat

Measurements Small and medium.
Materials 9 × 25 gm balls of 4-ply yarn.
2 buttons.
Needles One pair each of 2.5-mm and
4-mm (Nos 12 and 8) needles.
Tension See page 10.
Abbreviations See page 12.

Back
Using 2.5-mm needles cast on 106[114]
sts. Work in single rib for 32 rows,
increasing 1 st at beg of the last row
(107[115] sts).
Change to 4-mm needles.
1ST PATTERN ROW (right side) *k1, p1. Rep
from * ending k1.
2ND ROW p.
These 2 rows form the pattern. Keeping
continuity of pattern correct, inc 1 st at
each end of every following 4th row 6
times, and then cont without shaping
until work measures 28 cm (11 in)
ending with a wrong side row.
Start armholes Rib 12, k2 tog tbl, work
in pattern to last 14 sts, k2 tog. Work in
single rib to end of row.
NEXT ROW rib 12, p2 tog, p to last 14 sts,
p2 tog, rib 12. Rep last 2 rows 4 times
more (99[107] sts). Cont without further
shaping until work measures 48.5 cm
(19 in).
Shape shoulders Cast off 11[12] sts at the
beg of the next 6 rows. Cast off
remaining sts.

Left front
Using 2.25-mm needles cast on 96[100]
sts and work in single rib for 6 rows.
1ST BUTTONHOLE ROW (side edge) rib 18,
cast off 4, rib 64[68] counting sts on
needle, cast off 4, rib to end.
2ND BUTTONHOLE ROW (front edge) rib 6,
cast on 4, rib 64[68], cast on 4, rib 18.
Work 22 rows in rib then rep the 2
buttonhole rows.
Change to 4-mm needles.

Continue in pattern and work 2 rows keeping 11 sts at the front edge in ribbing for the border.

Keeping continuity of pattern and ribbed border, inc 1 st at side edge of every following 4th row 6 times, and AT THE SAME TIME dec 1 st INSIDE border of rib at front edge of next and every following 3rd row 28 times. End at armhole edge.

Start armhole Work 12 sts in single rib, k2 tog tbl, pattern to end, still decreasing 1 st at front edge inside 11 rib sts. AT THE SAME TIME dec 1 st inside armhole, rib on every row 9 times more. Now work armhole edge straight continuing to decrease 1 st at front edge only on every 3rd row until 44[47] sts remain. Cont without shaping until work measures 48.5 cm (19 in), ending at armhole edge.

Shape shoulder Cast off 11[12] sts at the beg of the next and every following alt row 3 times (11 sts). Work 26 rows in rib. Cast off in rib.

Right front

Work as for left front omitting buttonholes and reversing shapings and front border.

Making up

Sew up side seams. Sew ribbing across back of neck and sew up seam. Sew on buttons to correspond with buttonholes.

Cable and broken moss stitch sweater

Measurements One size garment, fits most sizes.

Materials 40 × 25 gm balls of double-knitting yarn (yarn used double).

Needles One pair each 3.5-mm and 6.5-mm (Nos 9 and 3) needles.

Tension See page 10.

Abbreviations See page 12. (c10 = slip next 5 sts on to a cable needle, leave at back of work, k5, k5 from cable needle.)

Front

Using 3.5-mm needles cast on 82 sts and work in single rib for 10 cm (4 in). Change to 6.5-mm needles.

1ST ROW (k1, p1) 5 times, p2, k10, p2, (k1, p1) 5 times, p2, k10, p2, (k1, p1) 5 times, p2, k10, p2, (k1, p1) 5 times.
2ND ROW (p10, k2) 6 times, p10.
3RD ROW (p1, k1) 5 times, p2, k10, p2, (p1, k1) 5 times, p2, k10, p2, (p1, k1) 5 times, p2, k10, p2, (p1, k1) 5 times.
4TH ROW as row 2.
5TH ROW (k1, p1) 5 times, p2, c10, p2, (k1, p1) 5 times, p2, c10, p2, (k1, p1) 5 times, p2, c10, p2, (k1, p1) 5 times.
6TH ROW as row 2.
7TH ROW as row 3.
8TH ROW as row 2.
9TH ROW as row 1.
10TH ROW as row 2.
11TH ROW as row 3.
12TH ROW as row 2.

These 12 rows form 1 complete pattern. Cont in pattern until work measures 48.5 cm (19 in).

Armhole shaping Keeping pattern correct cast off 4 sts at beg of next 2 rows. Dec 1 st at each end of next row. Work 3 rows. Dec 1 st each end of next row. Work 3 rows. Then dec at each end of every alt row until 48 sts remain.

Neck shaping Dec 1 st, pattern 28 sts (29 sts on needle). Slip the last 12 sts just worked on to a stitch-holder.

Pattern to last 2 sts, dec 1 st.
Cont to dec at armhole edge as before
and at the same time dec 1 st at neck
edge on next 5 rows.
Cont to dec at armhole edge as before
until 2 sts remain, p2 tog. Fasten off.
Rejoin yarn at neck edge. Work to
correspond with other side, reversing all
shapings.

Back

Using 4-mm needles cast on 70 sts. Work
in single rib for 10 cm (4 in). Change to
6.5-mm needles.
1ST ROW *k1, p1. Rep from * to end.
2ND ROW p.
3RD ROW *p1, k2. Rep from * to end.
4TH ROW p.
This is 1 complete pattern.
Work in pattern until back measures
48.5 cm (19 in).
Armhole shaping Cast off 4 sts at beg of
next 2 rows. (Dec 1 st at each end of
next row, work 3 rows) twice. Dec 1 st at
each end of every alt row until 24 sts
remain. Place these on stitch-holder.

Sleeves

Using 3.5-mm needles cast on 39 sts.
Work in single rib for 10 cm (4 in). Work
last row of rib as follows: rib 10, work
twice in next 19 sts, rib 10 (58 sts).
Change to 6.5-mm needles.
1ST ROW (k1, p1) 11 times, p2, k10, p2,
(k1, p1) 11 times.
2ND ROW p22, k2, p10, k2, p22.
3RD ROW (p1, k1) 11 times, p2, k10, p2,
(p1, k1) 11 times.
4TH ROW as row 2.
5TH ROW (k1, p1) 11 times, p2, c10, p2,
(k1, p1) 11 times.
6TH ROW as row 2.
7TH ROW as row 3.
8TH ROW as row 2.
9TH ROW as row 1.
10TH ROW as row 2.
11TH ROW as row 3.
12TH ROW as row 2.
These 12 rows form 1 complete pattern.
Cont in pattern. Inc 1 st at each end of
next row, then on the foll 6th and 12th

rows (62 sts).
Cont until work measures 49.5 cm
(19½ in).
Sleeve shaping Cast off 4 sts at beg of
next 2 rows. Keeping pattern correct dec
1 st at each end of next and every alt
row until 6 sts remain. Leave these sts on
a spare needle for neck.

Making up

Leave left raglan seam open for neck.
Sew up side seams, sleeve seams and
raglans using a flat seam.

Neck

With right side of work facing and using
4.5-mm needles k6 sts from left sleeve
top, pick up and k17 sts down left side
of neck, (k2 tog, k2) 3 times from neck
front, pick up and k16 sts up right side of
neck, k6 sts from top of right sleeve and
k24 sts from back neck (78 sts). Work
15 cm (6 in) in single rib. Cast off loosely
in rib. Join left raglan seam.

Basket stitch cardigan

Measurements Small, medium and large.
Materials 25[26/27] × 25 gm balls of
double-knitting yarn. 6 buttons.
Needles One pair each 3.5-mm, 4.5-mm
and 5-mm (Nos. 9, 7 and 6) needles.
Tension Using 5-mm needles and in
basket st, 15 sts and 20 rows to a 7.5 cm
(3 in) square.
Abbreviations See page 12.

Back

Using 3.5-mm needles cast on
88[96/104] sts and work 10 cm (4 in) in
single rib. On last row of rib inc evenly to
90[98/106] sts. Change to 5-mm needles
and basket st as follows:
1ST TO 4TH ROWS sl 1, *k4, p4. Rep from
* to last st, k1 tbl.
5TH TO 8TH ROWS sl 1, *p4, k4. Rep from
* to last st, k1 tbl.
These 8 rows form the pattern. Cont in

pattern until work measures 38[39.5/40.5]cm (15[15½/16]in) from beg.

Shape armhole Keep pattern correct throughout.
Cast off 4 sts at beg of next 2 rows.
Dec 1 st at beg of next and following alt rows until 66[74/82] sts remain. Cont in basket st until work measures 58.5[59.5/61]cm (23[23½/24]in) from beg.

Shape shoulder Cast off 9[9/10] sts at beg of next 4 rows. Cast off remaining sts.

Left front

Using 3.5-mm needles cast on 40[44/46] sts and work 10 cm (4 in) in single rib. On last row of rib inc to 42[46/48] sts. Change to 5-mm needles and work in basket st pattern to same length as back to armhole.

Shape armhole Cast off 4 sts at beg of next row, then dec 1 st at armhole edge on next 5[6/7] alt rows. At the same time shape front by decreasing 1 st at front edge on next and every following 3rd row until 18[18/20] sts remain. Cont until work is same length as back to shoulder, ending at armhole edge.

Shape shoulder Cast off 9[9/10] sts at beg of next and following alt row.

Right front

Work as for left front reversing all shapings.

Sleeves

Using 3.5-mm needles cast on 46[50/50] sts and work 9 cm (3½ in) in single rib. On last rib row inc evenly across row to 66[74/74] sts.
Change to 5-mm needles and work in basket st pattern until sleeve measures 45.5[47/48.5]cm (18[18½/19]in) from beg.

Shape top Cast off 5 sts at beg of next 2 rows. Keeping pattern correct, k2 tog at beg of every row until 24[26/28] sts remain. Cast off 2 sts at beg of every row until 16 sts remain. Cast off remaining sts.

Frontbands and shawl collar

Using 4.5-mm needles cast on 10 sts and work in garter st throughout. Always slip first st and k into back of last st.
Work 4 rows in garter st.
5TH ROW sl 1, k3, cast off 2 sts, k3, k1 tbl.
6TH ROW sl 1, k3, cast on 2 sts, k3, k1 tbl.
Work another 5 buttonholes 6.5 cm (2½ in) apart (the last should be on a level with armhole shaping).
NEXT ROW sl 1, k to last st, wlfwd, k1 tbl.
K 5 rows. Rep these 6 rows until 18 sts are on needle.
Work 40 rows without shaping.
Shape collar NEXT 2 ROWS k to last 3 sts, turn, k to end.
Work 2 rows over all sts.
NEXT 2 ROWS k to last 6 sts, turn, k to end.
Work 2 rows over all sts.
Rep these 8 rows 6 times more, then the first 2 rows once more. Work 45 rows without shaping.
NEXT ROW sl 1, k to last 3 sts, k2 tog, k1 tbl.
Work 5 rows. Rep these 6 rows until 10 sts remain. Work without shaping until work is same length as buttonhole band. Cast off.

Making up

Join shoulder seams, pin and stitch sleeves in place, pin collar into place, (the full part at the centre of the collar is the outside edge). Sew collar into place, sew sleeve and side seams, put buttons on, neaten ends.

Matching scarf

Measures 183 cm (72 in) plus fringe.
Materials 10 × 25 gm balls double-knitting yarn
Needles One pair 5.5-mm (No. 5) needles.
Cast on 36 sts
1ST ROW sl 1, k3, *p4, k4. Rep from * to end of row making sure to k into back of last st.
2ND ROW sl 1, p3, *k4, p4. Rep from * to

last st, k1 tbl.
3RD ROW as 1st row
4TH ROW as 2nd row
5TH ROW as 2nd row
6TH ROW as 1st row
7TH ROW as 2nd row
8TH ROW as 1st row
These 8 rows form the pattern. Rep the pattern until scarf measures 183 cm (72 in). Cast off.

Fringe
Using 35.5 cm (14 in) lengths of yarn fringe 4 strands 18 times along each end of scarf.

Multicoloured waistcoat

Measurements Medium — use smaller needles for small and double-knitting yarn with 4.5-mm needles for large
Materials 14 × 25 gm balls of 4-ply yarn in main colour plus 1 ball each in 7 additional colours. 5 buttons.
Should double-knitting yarn be used for large sizes, 18 balls of main colour are required. (Charts and photograph — pages 204-7)
Needles One pair each 3.25-mm and 4-mm (Nos. 10 and 8) needles.
Tension See page 10.
Abbreviations See page 12.

Colour suggestions			
Natural	= M	= Navy
Grey	= A	= Cream
Chocolate	= B	= Pale blue
Rust	= C	= Rust
Mid blue	= D	= Grey
Mink	= E	= Pale blue
Mid green	= F	= Grey
Gold	= G	= Gold

Pockets (make two)
Using 4-mm needles, cast on 26 sts and work in st st for 10 cm (4 in). Leave sts on a strand of yarn or pin.

Back and Fronts (worked in one piece to armhole)

Using 3.25-mm needles and main colour cast on 208[224] sts and work 9 cm (3½ in) in single rib.
Change to 4-mm needles and multicoloured pattern.
Work 5 rows in st st in main colour.
6TH TO 14TH ROWS INC work pattern no 1 (9 rows).
Work 4 rows in st st in main colour.
19TH TO 28TH ROWS INC work pattern no 2 (16 rows).
29TH ROW in main colour, k 10, sl next 26 sts on to a pin for pocket top, k sts from pocket lining, k to last 36 sts, sl next 26 sts on to a pin for second pocket top, k sts from second pocket lining, k10.
Work 3 rows in st st.
33RD TO 42ND ROWS INC work pattern no 3 (10 rows).
Work 6 rows in st st.
49TH TO 60TH ROWS INC work in pattern no 4 (12 rows).
Now divide work into two fronts and back, starting armhole garter st bands and front 'V' shaping.
Working in main colour in st st, k48[52], cast off 8, k96[104] (including st left over from cast off), cast off 8, k48[52].
NEXT ROW (working 2nd front) sl 1, p to last 6 sts, k5, k1 tbl.
NEXT ROW sl 1, k to last 2 sts, k2 tog.
Work 3 more rows in st st, keeping garter st armhole band all the way up armhole.
67TH TO 76TH ROWS INC work pattern no 5 (10 rows), decreasing at front edge on next and every 4th row, and keep garter st band at armhole edge IN MAIN COLOUR.
Work 6 rows in st st still decreasing at front edge every 4th row.
83RD TO 92ND ROWS INC work pattern no 6 (10 rows), still decreasing at garter st band and front.
Work 6 rows in st st, decreasing at front edge every 4th row.
99TH TO 104TH ROWS INC work pattern no 7 (6 rows), still decreasing at front edge.
Finish front decreasing here, and work another 6 rows in st st in main colour.
Shape shoulder Cast off 18[20] sts at the beg of the next and following alt rows (armhole end).

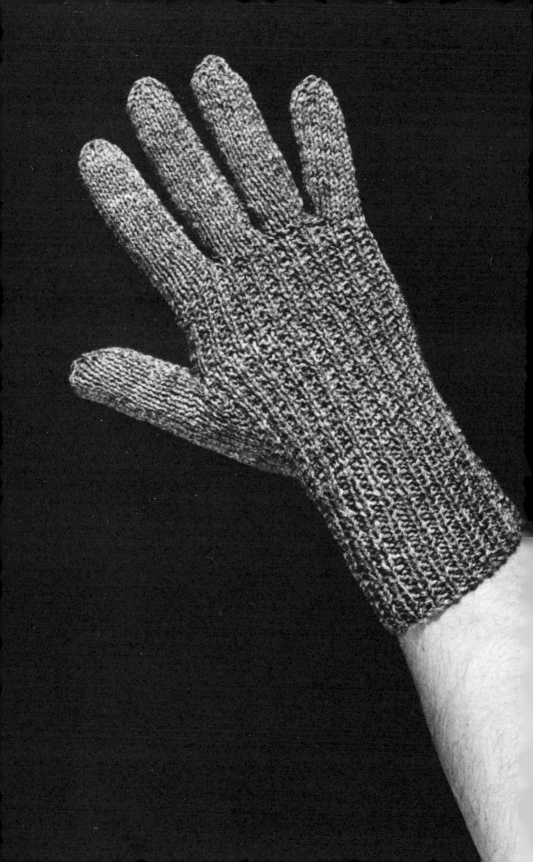

Rejoin yarn to sts left for back, and work in bands of st st and Fair Isle patterns as on front, working 6 sts AT EACH END OF EVERY ROW in garter st in main colour. Work to shoulder and then shape shoulders by casting off 18[20] sts at the beg of the next 4 rows. Cast off remaining sts.
Rejoin yarn to first front and work to match second front reversing all shapings.

Pocket tops (make two)
Using 3.25-mm needles pick up first 26 sts left on pin and work 5 rows in garter st. Cast off. Work other pocket top to match.

Frontband
Using 3.25-mm needles and main colour cast on 12 sts and work in garter st until the band fits nicely around the front edge, very slightly stretched to ensure the garment is kept in good shape.
Work a buttonhole on the 3rd and 4th rows by casting off 2 sts in the centre of the band and casting on 2 sts over the 2 cast off sts on the next row. Make 4 more buttonholes about 6.5 cm (2½ in) apart, then work in garter st until the band fits well around the front.

Making up
Sew up carefully, sewing all multicoloured ends in neatly and firmly. Sew on buttons — men's buttoning.

Gloves

Size 7½-8.
Materials 3 × 25 gm balls of 4-ply yarn.
Needles One pair 3-mm (No. 11) needles.
Tension See page 10.
Abbreviations See page 12.
Cast on 45 sts and work in single rib for 7.5 cm (3 in).
Thumb
1ST ROW (right side of work) k21, inc in each of the next 2 sts, k to end.
2ND ROW rib 22, p3, rib to end.

Rep these 2 rows once more.
5TH ROW k21, inc in next st, k2, inc in next st, k to end.
6TH ROW rib 22, p5, rib to end.
Cont in this way increasing twice in every 4th row until there are 61 sts, always making the 1st inc in the 22nd st and the 2nd inc 2 sts further on. Work 3 rows after the last inc.
NEXT ROW k39, turn, cast on 3 sts, p20 and work 20 rows of st st on these 20 sts.
NEXT ROW (k2, k2 tog) all along row.
P 1 row.
K2 tog all along the next row, break the yarn, draw the sts up together and sew the thumb seam.
The hand
Pick up and k 4 sts along cast on edge of thumb, k to end (48 sts). K 15 rows in pattern.
1ST FINGER k 32, turn, cast on 2, p 18. Work 30 rows of st st on the 18 sts and finish top as for thumb.
2ND FINGER pick up and k 4 sts along cast on edge of 1st finger, k5, turn. Cast on 4 sts, p18 and work 34 rows of st st, finishing as before.
3RD FINGER work as for 2nd finger working 32 rows straight, instead of 34.
4TH FINGER pick up and k 4 sts along cast on edge of 3rd finger, k6, turn and p16. Work 22 rows of st st and finish as before.
Sew up the side seam and make the other glove in the same way.

PATTERN 1
M — plain square
A — A

2 repeats

Row	Pattern
9	A A A A
8	A A A A A A A A
7	A A A A A A A A A A A A
6	A A A A A A A A
5	A A A A
4	A A A A A A A A
3	A A A A A A A A A A A A
2	A A A A A A A A
1	A A A A

PATTERN 3
M — plain square
E — E
C — C

2 repeats

Row	Pattern
10	
9	E E E E E E E E
8	E E E E E E E E
7	E E E E E E E E E E
6	C C C C C C C C
5	C C C C C C C C C C
4	C C C C C C C C
3	E E E E E E E E E E
2	E E E E E E E E
1	E E E E E E E E

PATTERN 4
M — plain square
G — G
A — A

2 repeats

Row	Pattern
10	G G G G G G G G
9	G G G G G G G G
8	
7	
6	A A A A A A A A A A A A
5	A A A A A A A A A A A A
4	
3	
2	G G G G G G G G
1	G G G G G G G G

PATTERN 5
M — plain square
F — F
G — G

2 repeats

12												
11	F				F		F				F	
10		F		F		F		F		F		F
9	F		F		F	F	F		F		F	F
8	F	F		F	F	F	F	F		F	F	F
7	F	F	F	F	F	G	F	F	F	F	F	G
6	G	F	F	F	G	G	G	F	F	F	G	G
5	F	F	F	F	F	G	F	F	F	F	F	G
4	F	F		F	F	F	F	F		F	F	F
3	F		F		F	F	F		F		F	F
2		F		F		F		F		F		F
1	F				F		F				F	

PATTERN 6
M — plain square
E — E
D — D
2 repeats

10											
9	E	E		E	E	E	E	E		E	E
8	E				E	E	E			E	E
7					E						E
6		D			E			D			E
5		D	D		E		D		D		E
4		D			E			D			E
3					E						E
2	E				E	E	E			E	E
1	E	E		E	E	E	E	E		E	E

PATTERN 7
M — plain square
A — A
G — G

3 repeats

```
10 |
 9 |    A A A       A A A       A A A
 8 |    A A A       A A A       A A A
 7 |    A A A       A A A       A A A
 6 |  G G G       G G G       G G G
 5 |  G G G       G G G       G G G
 4 |  G G G       G G G       G G G
 3 |    A A A       A A A       A A A
 2 |    A A A       A A A       A A A
 1 |    A A A       A A A       A A A
```

PATTERN 8
M — plain square
D — D

2 repeats

```
10 |     D D D       D       D D D       D
 9 |   D D     D D         D D     D D
 8 | D     D     D     D     D     D     D     D
 7 | D D           D D     D D           D D
 6 | D       D       D D D       D       D D
 5 | D       D       D D D       D       D D
 4 | D D           D D     D D           D D
 3 | D     D     D     D     D     D     D     D
 2 |   D D     D D         D D     D D
 1 |     D D D       D       D D D       D
```

PATTERN 9
M — plain square
E — E

3 repeats

```
6 |              E                 E                 E
5 | E             E E E         E E E             E E
4 | E E       E E E E E       E E E E E       E E E
3 | E E       E E E E E       E E E E E       E E E
2 | E           E E E           E E E           E E
1 |              E                 E                 E
```

Jackets

Heavy-weight jacket with stripe and an optional Jacquard band

Colour suggestions and yarn quantities (25 gm balls)			1	2	3
Main Colour	= M uses	40 balls	M = Chocolate	Navy	Grey
1st contrast	= C uses	8 balls	C = Cream	Cream	Cream
2nd contrast	= Y uses	2 balls	Y = Rust (brick)	Rust	Rust
3rd contrast	= B uses	6 balls	B = Mink	Grey	Camel
4th contrast	= O uses	2 balls	O = Blue	Wine	Gold
5th contrast	= X uses	4 balls	X = Rust (brick)	Rust	Rust

Should you make the wool and mohair jacket you will need half the amount in each type yarn.

The original jackets were designed using double-knitting wool, worked DOUBLE throughout. To make a really luxurious jacket, use one strand of mohair and one strand of double-knitting wool. However, any double-double weight yarn could be used AS LONG AS THE TENSION RULE IS FOLLOWED.

Measurements Lady's medium and large. For small do 1st size using 5-mm needles. This jacket is meant to be large and loose so it fits over layers of clothes.

Materials See charts following.

Needles One pair each 4-mm and 5.5-mm (Nos. 8 and 5) (5-mm for small size) needles.

Tension 9 sts to a 5 cm (2 in) square using 5.5-mm needles.

Abbreviations See page 12.

Back
Using yarn double, 5.5-mm needles and main colour cast on 84[94] sts and work in single rib for 8 rows.
Join in first contrast (from now on called C)
NEXT ROW using C k2, *sl 1, k1. Rep from * to end.

NEXT ROW using C p.
NEXT ROW using main (now called M), k.
NEXT ROW using M p.
Rep these last 4 rows 5 times more.
Break off C and work in M in st st until work measures 30.5[33]cm (12[13]in) from beg (ending on a p row).
Join in Y and work 4 rows in st st.
Join in C and work 4 rows in st st.
Join in B and work 22 rows in st st.
Join in C and work 4 rows in st st.
Join in Y and work 4 rows in st st.
These colours can be carried up the side if you prefer.

Shape raglan Using M cast off 2 sts at the beg of the next 2 rows.
NEXT ROW sl 1, k2 tog tbl, k to last 3 sts, k2 tog, k1.
NEXT ROW sl 1, p to last st, k1.
Rep the last 2 rows 3 times more (10 rows in M from armhole).
Then STILL WORKING IN SAME 2 ROWS OF RAGLAN SHAPING, join in C and work in the stripes of C and M exactly as 4 rows worked immediately after the rib until 9[11] sets of stripes, 42[44] rows have been worked. Work 2 more rows in C

(still doing raglan decrease). Using M cast off remaining sts.

Fronts

First work 2 pockets as follows:
In M, using double yarn and 5.5-mm needles cast on 26 sts and work in st st for 16.5 cm (6½ in). Leave sts on spare needle.

Right front

Using yarn double, M and 5.5-mm needles cast on 43[48] sts and work 8 rows in single rib. Join in contrast and work the 6 bands of stripes as on back and then cont in st st in M until work measures 20.5[23]cm (8[9]in) from beg, finishing at end of a p row.
Now work pocket as follows:
NEXT ROW k9[12], leave 26 sts on spare needle, k26 sts from first pocket, k8[10]. Cont in M in st st until work measures same as back to point where colour Y is joined in. Then work 4 rows of Y, 4 rows of C, 22 rows of B, 4 rows of C and 4 rows of Y, just as on back.
K 1 row in M.
Shape raglan Cast off 2 sts, p to end.
NEXT ROW sl 1, k to last 3 sts, k2 tog, k1 tbl.
NEXT ROW sl 1, p to last st, k1 tbl.
Rep these last 2 rows 3 times more. Still working raglan shaping, work in stripes of M and C as immediately after rib until 4[5] sets of stripes have been worked, finishing at the front edge.
NEXT ROW cast off 5[10] sts, work to last 3 sts, k2 tog, k1 tbl. Cont in the stripes and with raglan shaping until 18 sts remain.
NEXT ROW sl 1, k2 tog tbl, k to last 3 sts, k2 tog, k1.
NEXT ROW p. Cont in this way until 4 sts remain.
NEXT ROW k1, k3 tog tbl. Draw yarn through remaining sts.

Left front

Work as for right front, reversing all shapings.

Sleeves

In M, double yarn and using 6.5-mm needles cast on 56 sts and work in single rib for 4 rows. Change to st st and work in stripes as follows: 2 rows Y, 2 rows C, 10 rows B, 2 rows C, 2 rows C and 2 rows Y.
Change to M and 5.5-mm needles and p 1 row, decreasing 6 sts evenly along this row (NOTE: This row is purled because cuff is going to turn back and right side of work must therefore go on to other side of work to allow for this.)
Using the 5.5-mm needles and M work in st st until 9 cm (7½ in) of st st has been worked AFTER THE STRIPED CUFF.
NEXT ROW inc 1 st at each end of next and every following 6th row until 60 sts are on the needle then work without shaping until sleeve measures 81 cm (20 in) from beg.
Shape raglan Cast off 2 sts at the beg of the next 2 rows and then dec 1 st at each end of every alt row as on back. Then start M and C stripe pattern as on back. Cont to dec at each end of every alt row as on back until 2 sts remain. Cast off.

Frontbands

Using M, double yarn and 4-mm needles cast on 12 sts and work in single rib until band measures 63.5 cm (25 in) (this should fit nicely up the front of the jacket to the point where the 5[10] sts are cast off). Finish at the inside edge.
NEXT ROW cast on 5[10] sts (k into the back of these sts on the first row), rib 12. Rib 17[22] sts for another 4.5 cm (1¾ in).
Cast off ribwise.
Work another band reversing 5[10] cast on sts and MAKE SURE BOTH BANDS ARE EXACTLY THE SAME LENGTH.

Collar

Using M, double yarn and 4-mm needles cast on 151 sts and work as follows.
ROW 1 sl 1, k1, *p1, k1. Rep from * to last st, k1 tbl.
ROW 2 sl 1, *p1, k1. Rep from * to end.
Start shaping:

ROW 3 sl 1, k1, p1, k2 tog tbl, rib to last 5 sts, k2 tog, p1, k2.

ROW 4 sl 1, p1, k1, p2 tog tbl, rib to last 5 sts, p2 tog, k1, p1, k1 tbl.

Rep these last 2 rows until 77 sts remain (collar depth should now be about 15 cm (6 in)). Cast off ribwise.

Pocket tops (make two)

Using 5.5-mm needles pick up 26 sts and work 4 rows in single rib.

Cast off ribwise.

Belt

Using 5.5-mm needles cast on 9 sts and work in single rib for 127 cm (50 in).

Making up

With a heavy jacket like this making up needs to be very strong and all fastening off made really secure. Use one strand of yarn, carefully matching stripes.

Alterations to basic heavy-weight jacket with stripe interest for including multicolour on centre band

USE DOUBLE-KNITTING YARN DOUBLE

Fronts and Back

Work as pattern until 2 rows before the first 4 row stripe in Y (on back INCREASING 3[1] sts at end of last row and on fronts DECREASING 0[1] st at end of last row making sts divisible by a multiple of [4 + 3] (95 and 47 sts).

NEXT ROW k*3M, 1Y. Rep from * to last 3 sts, k3M.

NEXT ROW p 1Y, *1M, 3Y. Rep from * to last 2 sts, 1M, 1Y.

Then work the 4 rows in Y and 4 rows in C as pattern and then work 4 rows of the 22 row stripe in B.

5TH ROW k 3B *1O, 3B. Rep from * to end.

6TH ROW p 1O, *1B, 1O. Rep from * to end.

7TH ROW k 1X, 1O, *3X, 1O. Rep from * to last st, 1X.

8TH ROW p 3X, *1B, 3X. Rep from * to end.

9TH ROW k 1B, 1X, *3B, 1X. Rep from * to last st, 1B.

10TH ROW as row 8.

11TH ROW as row 7.

12TH ROW as row 6.

13TH ROW as row 5.

14TH ROW p in B.

15TH ROW k 3B, *1C, 3B. Rep from * to end.

16TH ROW p 1C, *1B, 1C. Rep from * to end.

17TH ROW as row 15.

18TH ROW p 1B, *1O, 3B. Rep from * to last 2 sts, 1O, 1B.

19TH ROW k *3O, 1B. Rep from * to last 3 sts, 3O.

20TH ROW p in O.

21ST ROW as row 19.

22ND ROW as row 18.

Now work 2 more rows in B (it is now a 24 row band).

Work 4 rows in C, 4 rows in Y.

NEXT ROW k 1Y, *1M, 3Y. Rep from * to last 2 sts, 1M, 1Y.

NEXT ROW *p 3M, 1Y. Rep from * to last 3 sts, 3M.

Then cont rest of front and back of pattern decreasing or increasing the 1 st on next row as at start of Fair Isle band.

On the sleeves

After the 4 rows of rib, work the 2 rows in Y and 2 rows in C decreasing 1 st for Fair Isle on last row.

Work rows 5 to 14 as on back and fronts instead of 10 rows in plain B (increasing the odd st at end of these 10 rows). Then cont as pattern.

Striped bomber jacket

Measurements Flat measurement 96.5-102[102-107/107-112]cm (38-40 [40-42/42-44]in) To be worn loose.

Materials Of 25 gm balls double-knitting yarn used double throughout 16 balls in main colour (A), 6 balls in B, 2 balls in C, 4 balls in D, 4 balls in E, 6 balls in F and 2 balls in G. 7 buttons.

Needles One pair each 3.25-mm, 4-mm and 6.5-mm (Nos. 10, 8 and 3) needles.

Tension 7½ sts to a 5 cm (2 in) square using 6.5-mm needles.

Abbreviations See page 12.

Colour suggestions

	A	= Black
	B	= Camel
	C	= Cream
	D	= Rust
	E	= Mocha (mid brown)
	F	= Chocolate
	G	= Cream
Claret red =	A	= Navy
Burgundy =	B	= Bright denim blue
Natural =	C	= Royal blue
Burgundy =	D	= Bottle green
Grey =	E	= Grey
Black =	F	= Mid green
Natural =	G	= Royal blue

STRIPE ORDER FOR THIS PATTERN AS FOLLOWS
6 rows B, 4 rows C, 8 rows D, 4 rows A, 4 rows E, 6 rows F, 2 rows G, 6 rows B, 6 rows A.

Back

Using yarn double, A and 3.25-mm needles cast on 70[78/86] sts and work in single rib for 10 cm (4 in).
Change to 6.5-mm needles and work in stripes as above in st st until back measures 60[61/62]cm (23½[24/24½] in) from beg.
Shape shoulders Cast off 11 sts at beg of the next 4 rows. Cast off remaining sts.

Front

Using yarn double, A and 3.25-mm needles cast on 42[46/50] sts and work 10 cm (4 in) in single rib. Put first 10 sts of last row on to a spare needle for frontband.
Change to 6.5-mm needles and work in stripes until front measures 51.5[53/54] cm (20¼[20¾/21¼]in) from beg, ending at neck edge.
Shape neck Cast off 2 sts, work to end.
NEXT ROW Work to last 2 sts, k2 tog tbl.
NEXT ROW k2 tog, work to end.
Rep these 2 rows until 29 sts remain.
NEXT ROW k2 tog, work to end.
NEXT ROW Work in st st, no dec.
Rep these 2 rows until 22 sts remain, finishing at side edge.
Shape shoulders Cast off 11 sts at beg of next and following alt row.
Work right front to match reversing all shapings and working a buttonhole on 5/6 rib rows and last 2 rib rows.
Buttonhole rows:
ROW 1 sl 1, rib 3, cast off 3, rib to end.
ROW 2 sl 1, rib 3, cast on 3, rib to end.

Sleeves

Using yarn double, A and 3.25-mm needles, cast on 46 sts and work in single rib for 10 cm (4 in) inc evenly on last row to 56 sts.
Change to 6.5-mm needles and work in stripes and st st until sleeve measures 46[48/49.5]cm (18[19/19½]in) from beg. Cast off.

Frontbands

Using yarn double, A and 3.25-mm needles, pick up sts from holder of left front, and work in single rib to fit nicely up front, slightly stretched.

Buttonhole band

Knit as frontband, working buttonholes evenly up front 7.5 cm (3 in) apart, the last coming as near the end of the band as possible.

Collar

Using yarn double, A and 4-mm needles

cast on 36 sts and work in rib throughout. Work 1 row, then cast on 3 sts at beg of every row until 84 sts remain. Work 2 rows with no inc, then cast off 3 sts at beg of every row until 36 sts remain. Work 1 row. Cast off LOOSELY.

Making up

Join shoulder seams, pin sleeves into place and sew neatly. Join side and sleeve seams neatly in correct colours. Sew bands into place and buttons. Place right side of collar to right side of garment, sew the middle point of the 10 straight rows to front edge, sew right round easing in to fit, fold over and stitch down to inside of garment.

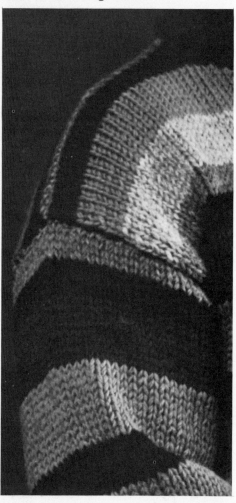

Aran-weight, three-band jacket

Measurements Lady's medium, man's medium.

Materials Of 50 gm balls Aran weight yarn 9 balls A, 5 balls B, 4 balls C. 6 buttons.

Needles For lady's one pair each 4-mm and 5.5-mm (Nos. 8 and 5) and for man's one pair each 4.5-mm and 6-mm (Nos. 7 and 4) needles.

Tension Using 5.5-mm needles 9½ sts to a 5 cm (2 in) square.

Abbreviations See page 12.

Colour suggestions		
Brown = A =		Navy
Natural = B =		Grey
Dull green = C =		Rust
Burgundy = A =		Brown
Grey = B =		Camel
Pilot blue = C =		Gold

Back

Using 4-[4.5-]mm needles and A cast on 88 sts and work 6.5 cm (2½ in) in double rib (k2, p2).

Change to 5.5-[6-]mm needles and B and work as follows:

ROW 1 sl 1, *k1, p1. Rep from * to last st, k1 tbl.

ROW 2 as row 1.

ROW 3 sl 1, *p1, k1. Rep from * to last st, k1 tbl.

ROW 4 as row 2.

Rep these 4 rows until work measures 22[23.5]cm (8¾[9¼]in) from cast on edge.

Change to A and work 8 rows in garter st.

Change to C and basket st pattern as follows:

1ST ROW sl 1, *k4, p4. Rep from * to last 7 sts, k4, p2, k1 tbl.

2ND ROW sl 1, k2, p4, *k4, p4. Rep from * to last st, k1 tbl.

3RD ROW as row 1.

4TH ROW as row 2.

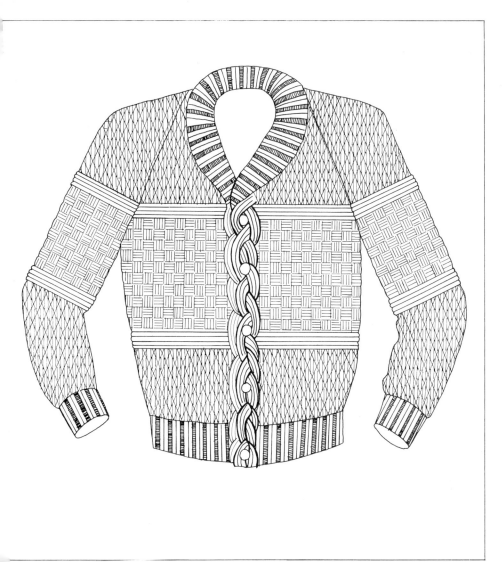

TH ROW sl 1, *p4, k4. Rep from * to last
sts, p4, k2, k1 tbl.

TH ROW sl 1, p2, k4, *p4, k4. Rep from
to last st, k1 tbl.

TH ROW as row 5.

TH ROW as row 6.

ep these 8 rows until work measures
9.5[43]cm (15½[17]in) from cast on
dge.

hange to A and work 6 rows in garter
. Cont in A for rest of back.

hape raglan Cast off 6 sts at the beg of
e next 2 garter st rows, work in pattern
hile dec raglan shaping.

Now work in broken moss st as follows:

ROW 1 sl 1, k2 tog tbl, *k1, p1. Rep from
* to last 3 sts, k2 tog, k1 tbl.

ROW 2 sl 1; p to last st, k1 tbl.

ROW 3 sl 1, k1, *p1, k1. Rep from * to
last 2 sts, k1, k1 tbl.

ROW 4 sl 1, p to last st, k1 tbl.

Rep these 4 rows until 72 sts remain.
Then dec 1 st at each end (as row 1
decreasing) of every alt row (keep the
broken moss st pattern correct) until 30
sts remain. Work any rows needed to
bring overall length to 66[70]cm
(26[27½]in). Cast off.

Frontband (a cable strip)

This is worked in A from cast on edge, going up front to start of 'V' slope. Twist yarn A round colour in use for body (blue) to prevent any holes. The frontband cable consists of the following 28 rows. Rep these rows until beg of 6 rows in garter st after band C.

Frontband will be referred to as BAND 13.

1ST ROW sl 1, sl 4 sts on to cable needle, leave at front of work, k4, k4 from cable needle, k4.

2ND ROW p to last st, k1 tbl.

3RD ROW k.

4TH ROW as row 2.

5TH ROW k.

6TH ROW as row 2.

7TH ROW sl 1, k4, sl 4 sts on to cable needle, leave at back of work, k4, k4 from cable needle.

8TH ROW as row 2.

9TH ROW k.

10TH ROW as row 2.

11TH ROW k.

12TH ROW as row 2.

13TH ROW as row 1.

14TH ROW as row 2.

15TH ROW k.

16TH ROW as row 2.

17TH ROW k.

18TH ROW as row 2.

19TH ROW as row 7.

20TH ROW as row 2.

21ST ROW k.

22ND ROW as row 2.

23RD ROW k.

24TH ROW as row 2.

25TH ROW as row 7.

26TH ROW as row 2.

27TH ROW k.

28TH ROW as row 2.

Right front

Using 4-[4.5-]mm needles and A cast on 51 sts. Work first 13 sts as band 13, work rest of row in double rib (p2, k2). Work in double rib and band 13 (at correct end of row) until work measures 6.5 cm (2½ in).

Change to 5.5-[6-]mm needles, keeping 13 st frontband in A, twisting yarns to prevent holes, working remaining 38 sts in B and pattern for this colour as on back.

Work until front measures 22[23.5]cm (8¾[9¼]in) from cast on edge.

Change to A, work band 13 sts and remaining sts in garter st.

Work 8 rows in all.

Keeping band 13 sts correct in A and twisting yarns to prevent holes work remaining 38 sts in C and pattern for this colour as on back.

Cont until work measures 39.5[43]cm (15½[17]in) from cast on edge.

Work in A for rest of front (frontband cable has now finished).

Cast off 8 sts at beg of next row, k to end. Work 3 more rows in garter st.

NEXT ROW k2 tog, k to end.

Work 2 more rows in garter st.

Shape raglan and front Cast off 6 sts at beg of next row, k to last 2 sts, k2 tog.

NEXT ROW sl 1, work in pattern as on raglan shaping for back to last 3 sts, k2 tog, k1 tbl.

Work in pattern as on back for rows 2, 3 and 4.

Dec on raglan edge in this way AND AT THE SAME TIME dec 1 st at front edge on every 4th row. When you have 28 sts dec at raglan edge on every alt row, keeping front edge dec on every 4th row. Work until 4 sts remain, dec on raglan edge only until 2 sts remain. Should be same length as back raglan, k2 tog. Fasten off.

Left front

Work as for right front, reversing all shapings (raglan dec = k2 tog tbl, k1 tbl) and reversing the position of frontband, i.e. — work in double rib ending p2 to last 13 sts, work these 13 sts for frontband working rows in reverse, i.e.

ROW 1 k4, sl next 4 sts on to cable needle leave at back of work, k4, k4 from cable needle, k1 tbl.

ROW 7 sl 4 sts on to cable needle, leave at front of work, k4, k4 from cable needle, k4, k1 tbl.

Pockets (make two)

Using 5.5-[6-]mm needles and B on one front and with WRONG side facing, ignore frontband, pick up and k 41 sts on first row of colour B band. Work in pattern as on front for this colour until pocket measures same as band B — 15[18]cm (6[7]in). Cast off in pattern.

Work pocket on other front in exactly the same way.

Sleeves

Using 4-[4.5-]mm needles and A cast on 50 sts and work 11.5 cm (4½ in) in double rib, inc along last rib row to 58 sts.

Change to 5.5-[6-]mm needles and B and work pattern as on back AT THE SAME TIME inc 1 st at each end of every following 8th row (work extra sts into pattern) until 72 sts are on needle. This pattern then measures same length as body.

Then work 8 rows garter st in A, change to C and pattern as on back. When 72 sts are on needle cont without shaping until this pattern is same length as on body. Change to A and work 6 rows in garter st.

Shape raglan Cont in A for rest of sleeve. Cast off 6 sts at beg of next 2 rows, working in garter st.

Work in broken moss st as on back raglan band for rest of sleeve.

Dec 1 st at each end of every alt row until 16 sts remain. Work any rows needed to bring raglan to same length as back. Cast off in pattern.

Making up

Join raglan seams, join sleeve seams. Join side seams as far as pocket, sew 1.3 cm (½ in) of both pocket lining and side seams, then sew just pocket lining and back side seam to 1.3 cm (½ in) from beg of rib. Sew all 3 thicknesses tog, sew rib. Sew seams in correct colours. Sew pocket lining at top and front edge.

Collar (in colour A)

Using 5.5-[6-]mm needles cast on 54 sts and work 2 rows in double rib. Now

work as follows:

Working extra sts in double rib, cast on 45 sts at beg of every row until there are 122 sts then cast on 2 sts at beg of every row until there are 142 sts. Work 8 rows in double rib, cast off in double rib using a 7-mm needle. Sew 54 cast on sts of collar to raglan and back cast off sts. Sew inc sts down raglan fronts. Sew 8 rows of double rib to frontband cast off sts. Sew buttons into place, buttonholes are cables.

Heavy-weight moss stitch jacket

Measurements Men's small, medium and large (worn loose by ladies).
Materials 46 × 25 gm balls double-knitting yarn. 6 buttons (7 for large size).
Needles One pair each 4-mm and 6-mm (Nos. 8 and 4) needles.
Tension 7½ sts to a 5 cm (2 in) square on 6.5-mm needles.
Abbreviations See page 12.
NOTE: Use yarn SINGLE FOR ALL RIBBED PARTS (welts, bands and collar). Use yarn DOUBLE for main body and sleeves

Back

Using yarn single and 4-mm needles cast on 70[78/86]sts and work in single rib for 10 cm (4 in).
Change to 6-mm needles, join in a 2nd strand of yarn and, using yarn double, work in moss st as follows:
1ST ROW sl 1, *k1, p1. Rep from * to last st, k1 tbl.
2ND ROW sl 1, *p1, k1. Rep from * to last st, k1 tbl.
Rep these 2 rows (moss stitch) until work measures 40.5[43/48.5]cm (16[17/19]in). Mark this row at each end with a piece of coloured thread to indicate the end of the side seam and beginning of the sleeve seam. Then cont in moss st until back measures 62[65/68.5]cm (24½[25½/27]in) finishing at the end of a 2nd row.
Shape shoulders Cast off 11 sts at the edge of the next 4 rows. Cast off.

Fronts

Using yarn single and with 4-mm needles cast on 32[36/40] sts and work in single rib for 10 cm (4 in). Change to 6-mm needles, join in 2nd strand of yarn, work in moss st across 8 sts, turn. Cast on 17[19/21] sts for pocket lining and moss st back across these 25[27/29] sts. Then cont to work in moss st on these sts until 40 rows have been worked, ending at

inside edge.
Cast off 17[19/21] sts and leave the remaining 8 sts on a safety pin.
With right side facing rejoin yarn to remaining rib sts. Using double yarn and 6-mm needles moss st across these sts for 40 rows. On the next row moss st across all sts including the 8 sts left on pin and now cont to work in moss st until work measures 40.5[43/48.5]cm (16[17/19]in) finishing at side edge.
Mark this row at both ends as for back to indicate end of side seam, then cont until work measures 54.5[56.5/61]cm (21½[22¼/24]in) ending at neck edge.
Shape neck as follows. Cast off 2 sts, work to end.
NEXT ROW moss st, to last 2 sts, k2 tog tbl.
NEXT ROW k2 tog, moss st to end.
NEXT ROW moss st, to last 2 sts, k2 tog tbl.
Rep the last 2 rows until 27[29/29] sts remain.
NEXT ROW k2 tog, moss st to end.
NEXT ROW work in moss st.
Rep these 2 rows until 22 sts remain working 1 more row if needed to finish at side edge.
Shape shoulder Cast off 11 sts at the beg of next and following alt row.
Work 2nd front to match, reversing all shapings. NOTE You will have to work 1 row of moss st before starting the row to turn after 8 sts.

Sleeves

Using yarn single and 3.25-mm needles cast on 46 sts and work in single rib for 10 cm (4 in) increasing evenly along the last row to 66 sts. Change to 6-mm needles and join in a 2nd strand of yarn. Work in moss st until sleeve measures 49.5 cm (19½ in). Cast off. When casting off hold a larger needle (7-mm) in right hand so casting off is loose to make sure armhole is deep enough to lie flat and fit easily into armhole length allowed on body.

Frontband

Using 3.25-mm needles and single yarn cast on 18 sts and work in single rib for 4 rows.

NEXT ROW (buttonhole row) sl 1, (k1, p1) 3 times, cast off 3 sts, rib to end.
NEXT ROW sl 1, rib to cast off sts, cast on 3, rib to end.
Cont in single rib working a buttonhole every 9.5 cm (3¾ in) until 5 more have been worked (6 in all). On large size work an extra buttonhole. Cont in rib until band measures 51.5[54/58.5]cm (20¼[21¼/23]in). Cast off ribwise. This band should now fit up the front, very slightly stretched. Work another plain band same length.

Collar
Using 3.25-mm needles and single yarn cast on 76 sts.
NEXT ROW sl 1, *k1, p1. Rep from * to last st, k1 tbl.
NEXT ROW cast on 6 sts, rib to end (collar is in single rib).
Rep this last row until there are 148 sts on the needle. Then cast on 2 sts at the beg of the next 6 rows (160 sts).
Work 10 rows without shaping.
Cast off 2 sts at beg of next 6 rows, then cast off 6 sts at the beg of every row until 76 sts remain. Work 1 row.
Cast off ribwise.

Pocket edges (make two)
Using 4-mm needles and front side facing pick up 35 sts along edge of pocket and work in single rib for 4 cm (1½ in). Cast off ribwise. Sew down each end of pocket to body.

Making up
Join shoulder seams on back and front using overstitch or flatstitch. Sew sleeves into place evenly between points marked with coloured thread making sure not to pull tightly or gather at all. Join sleeve and side seams. Sew frontbands on carefully. Attach buttons to correspond with buttonholes. Place right side of collar to right side of garment, sew the middle of the 10 straight rows to the front edge of jacket, sew all round easing in to fit nicely, fold over in half and stitch down to inside of garment.

Coat/cardigan with stripe

Measurements One size — meant to be loose and wrap-around. For a smaller size use 5.5-mm (No. 5) needles for main body.
Materials Of 25 gm balls double-knitting yarn 34 balls colour A, 6 balls of colour B and 4 balls each of colours C and D.
NOTE The double-knitting wool is to be used DOUBLE, if you wish you can use double double weight yarn instead.
Needles One pair each 3.25-mm, 4-mm and 6-mm (Nos. 10, 8 and 4) needles.
Tension See page 10.
Abbreviations See page 12.

Colour suggestions		
	1	2
Pilot blue =	A =	Aubergine (dull mauve)
Burgundy =	B =	Mid blue
Cream =	C =	Silver grey
Soft blue =	D =	Black
	3	4
Navy =	A =	Camel
Rust =	B =	Chocolate
Cream =	C =	Cream
Grey =	D =	Rust
	5	6
Black =	A =	Cream
Camel =	B =	Mid brown
Cream =	C =	Grey
Rust =	D =	Gold

First front
Using 6-mm needles, A, and yarn double cast on 60 sts.
1ST ROW sl 1, *k1, p1. Rep from * to last st, k1 tbl.
Rep this row 5 times more.
7TH ROW sl 1, *k1, p1. Rep from * 5 times, k1, p to last 13 sts, *k1, p1. Rep from * 6 times, k1 tbl.
8TH ROW sl 1, *k1, p1. Rep from * 6 times, k to last 12 sts, *p1, k1. Rep from * 6 times.
Rep these 2 rows 4 times.

NEXT ROW sl 1, *k1, p1. Rep from * 5 times, k1, p2 tog, p to last 15 sts, p2 tog, *k1, p1. Rep from * 6 times, k1 tbl.
NEXT ROW as row 8.

Rep these last 12 rows from row 7, 3 more times and then rep rows 7 and 8 only until work measures 11.5 cm (4½ in) ending with an 8th row). Still repeating rows (rib at sides and reverse st st in centre) work in coloured stripes as follows:

3 rows in colour B, 2 in A, 2 in C, 2 in D, 2 in C, 2 in A, 2 in D, 2 in A, 2 in C, 2 in D, 2 in C, 2 in A, 8 in B. Then cont as before just in A until 20.5 cm (8 in) have been worked from the end of the stripe band finishing with the right side facing (reverse st st in the centre is the right side).

NEXT ROW work to the last 13 sts, turn leave these 13 sts (rib) on a spare needle (or neckband).
NEXT ROW k2 tog tbl, work to end in pattern.
NEXT ROW work to last 2 sts, p2 tog.
Rep these last 2 rows twice more.
NEXT ROW k2 tog tbl, work to end.
NEXT ROW pattern to end.
Rep these last 2 rows until 31 sts remain and then cont without shaping until work measures 29 cm (11½ in) from end of coloured stripe finishing with wrong side facing.
Cast off for shoulder knitwise knitting every 4th and 5th st tog across the st st part. Cast off rib part ribwise.

Second front
Work other front to match starting stripe and at the end of a 7th row instead of 8th (to ensure that the loose end of colours of wool come at the side) and reverse all shapings.

Back
Using 6-mm needles, A and yarn double cast on 96 sts and work exactly as for the first front (leaving out neck shaping of course), working without shaping until back measures 29 cm (11½ in) after end of stripe. Cast off for shoulders as on front

casting off the first 31 sts, work to end. Cast off next 31 sts for second shoulder and then leave remaining sts on a needle or stitch-holder for the neck.

Sleeves
Using 3.25-mm needles, A and single yarn cast on 45 sts and work in single rib for 13 cm (5 in) increasing on every 3rd st on the last row (60 sts).
Change to 6-mm needles and join in 2nd strand of yarn as for body and, using yarn double, work in reverse st st (starting with a p row) increasing 1 st at each end of every 6th row until there are 70 sts on the needle. Work without shaping until work measures 30.5 cm (12 in) from the beg, then work band of coloured stripes as on fronts and back (38 rows). Cast off loosely on the 8th row in B (last stripe band) casting off knitwise.

Neckband
Using 4-mm needles, A and yarn double pick up 83 sts round neck including front rib sts. Work in single rib (keeping continuity off rib on front ribs) for 6.5 cm (2½ in). Cast off loosely ribwise.

Tie belt
Using 6-mm needles, A and yarn double cast on 10 sts and work in single rib for 127 cm (50 in). Cast off.

Making up
Sew up neatly and firmly.

Multicoloured jacket in wool and mohair

Measurements To fit 86.5-91.5 cm (34-36 in) chest. For a larger size use 6-mm needles for the body.

Materials 26 balls of both double-knitting wool and mohair, as follows:
Colour M 14 balls DK, 14 balls mohair
Colour O 5 balls DK, 5 balls mohair
Colour X 5 balls DK, 5 balls mohair
Colour Y 2 balls DK, 2 balls mohair
8 buttons.

Needles One pair each 4-mm, 5.5-mm and 6.5-mm (Nos. 8, 5 and 3) needles.

Tension 13 sts to a 7.5 cm (3 in) square over multicoloured body pattern on 5.5-mm needles.

Abbreviations See page 12.

Colour suggestions			
Red	= **M**	=	Beige
Black	= **O**	=	Black
Beige	= **X**	=	Mid brown
Grey blue	= **Y**	=	Mid blue
Mink	= **M**	=	Mid blue
Black	= **O**	=	Navy
Beige	= **X**	=	Soft blue
Blue	= **Y**	=	Burgundy

First front

Using 4-mm needles, AND ONE STRAND OF EACH YARN, colour M, cast on 53 sts and work 9 cm (3½ in) in single rib. On last row leave first 12 sts on a spare needle for the frontband. Change to 5.5-mm needles and work rows 1-62 on multicoloured chart in st st.

Shape raglan Cont in multicolour starting at row 1 again. Cast off 3 sts at the beg of the next row (armhole edge).
Work 1 row.
NEXT ROW k2 tog, work multicolour pattern to end.
NEXT ROW Work in multicolour pattern (p row). Rep these 2 rows until 2 sts remain (this should have completed row 38).

Shape neck Work 1 row (still working raglan shaping). Cast off 4 sts (at neck edge) work to end.
Carry on from chart keeping raglan decreasing as before, and AT THE SAME TIME decreasing 1 st at neck edge on next 4 rows. Cont in multicolour pattern decreasing only at raglan edge until row 46 has been worked (8 sts), and now finish last few rows in main colour. K2 tog all along next row. Work 1 row. K2 tog, twice. Cast off.

Second front

Cast on 53 sts as for 1st front, working a buttonhole on 5th row as follows:
rib 5, cast off 2 sts, rib to end. On next row, cast ON 2 sts over 2 cast off sts. Work this front as 1st, reversing all shapings.

Back

Using 4-mm needles and M (one strand of each yarn) cast on 77 sts and work in single rib for 9 cm (3½ in). Change to 5.5-mm needles and follow the multicolour chart, rows 1-62.

Shape raglan Starting at row 1 of the chart, cast off 3 sts at the beg of the next 2 rows.
NEXT ROW k2 tog, pattern to last 2 sts, k2 tog.
NEXT ROW p in pattern.
Rep these 2 rows until row 46 has been worked (24 sts).
NEXT ROW in M *k1, k2 tog. Rep from * to end (18 sts). Cast off.

Sleeves

Using 6.5-mm needles and M (one strand of each yarn) cast on 57 sts and work 4 rows in single rib. Change to multicolour chart and work rows 5-23 inclusive. Change to 5.5-mm needles and M. P 1 row decreasing 6 sts evenly along the row (51 sts).

Colour chart

Row

Row							Row					
62	M	M	M	M	M		15	X	X	X	X	X
61	Y	Y	Y	Y	Y		14	M	X	X	X	M
60	Y	Y	Y	Y	Y		13	X	M	X	M	X
59	M	M	M	M	M		12	M	X	M	X	M
58	M	M	M	M	M		11	X	M	M	M	X
57	X	X	O	X	X		10	M	M	M	M	M
56	O	X	X	X	O		9	O	M	M	M	O
55	X	X	O	X	X		8	M	O	M	O	M
54	Y	X	X	X	Y		7	O	M	O	M	O
53	Y	Y	X	Y	Y		6	M	O	O	O	M
52	Y	Y	X	Y	Y		5	O	O	O	O	O
51	Y	X	X	X	Y		4	X	X	X	X	X
50	X	X	O	X	X		3	X	X	X	X	X
49	O	X	X	X	O		2	O	O	O	O	O
48	X	X	O	X	X		1	O	O	O	O	O
47	O	X	X	X	O							
46	M	M	M	M	M							
45	M	M	M	M	M							
44	Y	Y	Y	Y	Y							
43	Y	Y	Y	Y	Y							
42	M	M	M	M	M							
41	M	M	M	M	M							
40	X	X	O	O	X							
39	O	X	X	O	O							
38	O	O	X	X	O							
37	X	O	O	X	X							
36	X	X	O	O	X							
35	O	X	X	O	O							
34	M	M	M	M	M							
33	Y	M	M	M	Y							
32	M	Y	M	Y	M							
31	X	X	Y	X	X							
30	M	X	X	X	M							
29	M	M	X	M	M							
28	M	X	X	X	M							
27	X	X	Y	X	X							
26	M	Y	M	Y	M							
25	Y	M	M	M	Y							
24	M	M	M	M	M							
23	M	M	M	M	M							
22	X	X	X	X	X							
21	X	X	X	X	X							
20	O	O	O	O	O							
19	X	O	O	O	X							
18	O	X	O	X	O							
17	X	O	X	O	X							
16	O	X	X	X	O							

4 ST. REPEAT

Starting with a p row work 21.5 cm (8½ in) in st st in M (after the multicolour band). Cont in st st inc 1 st at each end of next and every following 6th row until there are 61 sts on the needle. Work without further shaping until the sleeve measures 47.5 cm (18¾ in) from the end of the Fair Isle.

Shape raglan (and from here on top of sleeve is in multicolour pattern):

Starting at row 1 from the multicolour chart work raglan as for back to row 40. Rows 41- 46 inclusive, dec 1 st at each end of EVERY row (5 sts).
NEXT ROW k1, (k2 tog) twice.
NEXT ROW k1, p2 tog. Cast off.

Frontband (button band)

Using 4-mm needles and M pick up sts from the left front and work band in single rib to fit up front of jacket slightly stretched. Cast off ribwise.

Buttonhole band
Using 4-mm needles and M (one strand of each yarn) pick up sts from right front, work a buttonhole as before on the next 2 rows. Work a further 6 buttonholes evenly up this band. (It is best to pin positions on the button band to get even spacing and work buttonholes to correspond. The last button should be 4 rows from the top of the band). After last buttonhole work 4 rows in rib.

Collar
Using 4-mm needles and M (one strand of each yarn) cast on 141 sts and work 2 rows in single rib.
Shaping ROW 1 sl 1, k1, p1, k2 tog tbl, rib to last 5 sts, k2 tog, p1, k1, k1 tbl.
ROW 2 sl 1, p1, k1, p2 tog tbl, rib to last 5 sts, p2 tog, k1, p1, k1 tbl.
Rep these 2 rows until 75 sts remain. Work 1 row without decreasing. Cast off ribwise.

Making up
Sew raglan seams (in correct colour threads). Sew side seams, and sleeve seams as far as cuff. Turn sleeve to right side and sew up cuff, and fold back on to sleeve. Sew frontbands into place and buttons on other band to correspond. Pin collar into position so that it meets at front when jacket is buttoned, sew into place easing neck where needed. Sew in all ends.

Glossary

Buttonholes

For a horizontal buttonhole, cast off number of stitches required according to size of button (normally 2 or 3) and on the return row cast on the same number as you cast off (diagram 1).
For vertical buttonholes, the work is divided at the required place and both sides are worked separately for required depth of the buttonhole (diagram 2).

There are various ways of tidying up the edges of buttonholes, i.e. working into the backs of cast on stitches, casting on one stitch less than those cast off, picking up an extra stitch in the corner of the buttonhole in the cast on row, or double crocheting or blanket stitching round each buttonhole after it is made.

Casting on

Thumb method
This is certainly the best method in that it produces a really neat, firm, yet elastic edge. Use left hand thumb and one needle in the right hand. Estimate a length of yarn sufficient to cover the number of stitches to be cast on (about a metre is right for a normal lady's sweater). Make a slip loop, slipping the loop on to the needle held in right hand. Holding the needle and the wool from the ball in the right hand, and the length of wool in the left hand close to the needle (diagram 3), wind yarn over and round thumb of left hand and put needle into the loop round thumb (holding the rest of the length of yarn firmly between left hand fingers). Using yarn from the ball pass it over the point of the needle, through thumb loop. Gently tighten left hand thread, and let yarn fall off thumb. Continue in this way

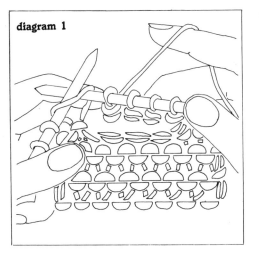

diagram 1

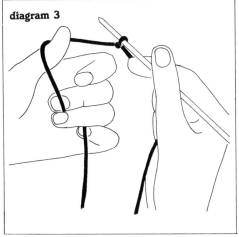

diagram 3

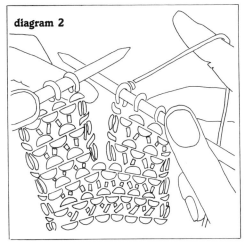

diagram 2

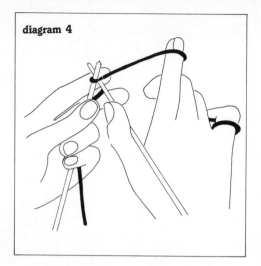

diagram 4

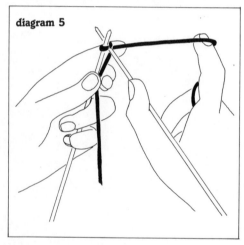

diagram 5

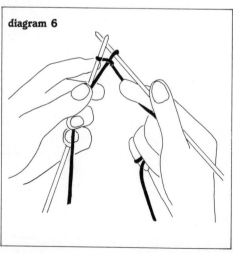

diagram 6

until you have the required number of stitches.

Two needle method
This method produces a loopy untidy edge and one must knit into the back of each stitch on the first row in order to neaten the loops. However, use this method when casting on extra stitches at any point in a pattern. Make a loop at the end of the yarn and put it on a needle. Hold this needle in the left hand and the second needle and ball of yarn in the right hand. Put the point of this right hand needle from left to right through the front of the loop (diagram 4), take yarn from the ball round the point of the right hand needle, pass it between the points of the two needles (diagram 5). Using the right hand needle draw yarn through the loop around the two needles so there is now a loop on each needle (diagram 6). Slip loop of yarn on right hand needle on to the left hand needle thus making a new stitch. Repeat for as many stitches as are required.

Corded method
This method is sometimes used for particularly heavy garments or those likely to be subjected to very heavy wear. Work as for the two needle method until two sts are on left hand needle. Make third and every following stitch by inserting point of right hand needle between the TWO loops on the left hand needle (instead of into only the first loop) (diagram 7).

Casting off

Knit the first two stitches then with the left hand needle slip the first stitch over the second. Continue in this way for the specified number of stitches and if the whole row is cast off, break yarn and pull through last loop. It is always best to cast off in the stitch being used, i.e. knitwise on the knit side, purlwise on the purl side, ribwise when ribbing and so on. If working a pattern that includes any form of increasing avoid casting off on an increase row, or if you cannot avoid it work as many sts as are necessary together while casting off. If extra elasticity is needed at the cast off edge, i.e. when garments have to be pulled over heads, it is a good idea to cast off holding a needle two sizes larger in the right hand as doing so. Extra elasticity can also be given by double casting off, which means casting off the loop between stitches as well as the stitches. However, this method is not so neat.

diagram 7

Casting off two needles together
This can be used for sock toes, backs of hoods, gussets, shoulders etc. Divide stitches equally on to two needles and with wrong side facing work one stitch from each needle together, work another two stitches in the same way, slipping first stitch over second as above and so on.

Decreasing

This is simply done by knitting or purling two stitches together, by slipping a stitch, knitting the next stitch and passing the slipped stitch over the knitted stitch. Or by purling a stitch, putting it back on left hand needle and slipping the next stitch over it. Alternatively one can knit or purl two stitches together into the back of the loops instead of into the front. These different ways give different slants to the resultant stitch which are important when the decreases show.

The method of increasing and decreasing to be used will be specified in the patterns.

Fair Isle knitting or Multicoloured

This is considerably simpler than many knitters realize. This form of knitting in

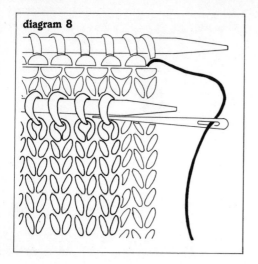

diagram 8

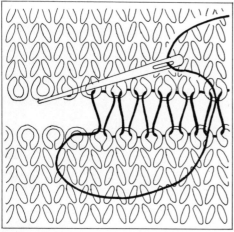

diagram 9

traditional patterns with many colours is derived from the Fair Isles in Scotland. When beginning a new colour leave an adequate length when starting it, and when you come to knit the new colour just pass the first colour to the left hand, knitting the new colour in the natural way, and so on. Make sure that the wool being stranded across is not too taut. The whole success of this type of knitting depends on even stranding — THE LOOSE THREAD MUST STRETCH EASILY BEHIND THE OTHER STITCHES — without altering the tension of the stitches.

The other way to deal with Fair Isle knitting is WEAVING, and when the wool has to be taken across a fairly large number of stitches this weaving method should be used. Hold the colour to be woven in the left hand while knitting with the main colour. On every alternate stitch pass the point of the right hand needle through the stitch, then under the colour that is being woven, pass the main colour over the point of the needle and draw a loop through, thus allowing the second colour to drop. To purl, work in a similar way, first under and then over the wool that is being woven.

The Fair Isle designs in this book are very simple in that I have not used more than two colours in a single row.

Grafting

This is the best way of joining stitches from two separate needles without a ridge. Again, the stitches should be divided equally on two needles with wrong sides facing each other and a length of yarn, preferably left when breaking off wool. Thread this length of wool through a needle and pass the needle purlwise through the first stitch on the front needle, leaving stitch on needle. Then pass the needle knitwise through first stitch on back needle, again leaving stitch on needle. *Pass wool knitwise through first stitch on front needle, slipping the stitch off the needle, pass wool purlwise through second stitch on front needle without slipping off; pass wool purlwise through first stitch on back needle and slip off, pass wool knitwise through 2nd stitch on back needle without slipping off. Repeat from * until all stitches are worked off (diagram 8). Sew in end of yarn thoroughly when finished.

A quicker easier method of grafting is to slip all stitches off the needles before grafting (diagram 9).

Increasing

Probably the most popular method is to work first into the front, and then into the back of the same stitch, either knitwise or purlwise according to the pattern. This does show certain irregularity in the texture and is best used only at the edges of a garment.

Knit or purl into the loop between two stitches of the previous row. Pick up the loop and knit or purl into the back of it as this makes the finish much tidier.

If you have to increase in the middle of a row, or somewhere where the increase must be almost invisible then knit or purl into a stitch on the previous row rather than into the loop between the two stitches.

Necklines

'V' necks
Should be approx 13 cm (5 in) from side to side before a border is added. The best place for the base of the V is either level with the start of the armhole shaping, or slightly below, although, of course, this can be adjusted according to personal taste. Bearing in mind that the widest part of the V, across the neck, is 13 cm (5 in) it is fairly simple to work out from

your tension how many stitches this represents, and by halving this number to work out how many stitches needed to decrease from base of V to shoulder. In this way too, it is relatively easy to estimate length of V from base to shoulder, and how many rows this represents. Now you can work out how far apart each decrease should be. For example, if the garment you are altering has a tension of 15 sts and 20 rows equalling a 7.5 cm (3 in) square, you would need to allow about 25 sts for the top width of the V, thus having to decrease 12 sts each side from base, and if you wanted a V depth of say 23 cm (9 in), thus representing 60 rows, you would need to decrease up each side of the V on 1st and every following 5th row at neck edge.

Thus, to work a 'V' neck decide where you want the base point, work to the middle of this row, turn. Working on one side at a time decrease at beginning of next and every following 5th row at neck edge 11 times (12 decreases in all). Then continue without shaping until work is the right length to shoulder. Work other side to match. The best way to finish a 'V' neck is to pick up stitches all round neck edge. Join the left hand shoulder leaving other shoulder open and with right side facing, starting at open shoulder pick up as many stitches down the V slope as there are rows (approximately), one stitch from centre V, same number of stitches up other side of V and the stitches left after shoulders have been shaped at back of neck (its best if these back of neck stitches have been left on a spare needle or safety pin ready to pick up). Using the size of needle used for the welts of the garment work about seven rows in single rib DECREASING 1 STITCH ON EACH SIDE OF CENTRE V STITCH ON EVERY ROW (it is a good idea to mark this centre stitch with a piece of coloured thread). Always cast off ribwise still working 2 sts together each side of centre stitch on the cast off row.

Round necks

The basic width is about the same as for
a V neck. The depth is about 6.5 cm
(2½ in) for smaller sizes, 7.5 cm (3 in)
for larger sizes. This is for a neat fitting
neck. Allow extra width and depth if you
want a lower neck. When you reach the
point below shoulder where you want
your round neck to start, work to centre
15 stitches (based on same tension as
above), slip these stitches on to a spare
needle or safety pin, and then work on
one side of neck at a time decreasing at
neck edge on the following five rows,
then working without shaping until right
length to shoulder (this gives the same 25
stitches from side to side of round neck).
When both sides have been worked join
one shoulder as for 'V' neck and pick up
stitches as for V — about 80 sts all round
on 3.25-mm needles for a double-knitting
weight garment, and 125 all round on
2.5-mm needles for a 4-ply garment.
These are, of course, only approximate
guidelines. Again work about seven rows
in single rib, although number of rows is
personal choice. No shaping is needed for
a round neck. Cast off ribwise.

Square necks

The depth and width are much the same
as for a round neck. In the case of a
square neck it is just a question of casting
off the number of stitches for required
width from the middle of the row at
required depth from shoulder, leaving an
equal number of stitches each side. Then
work straight on these side stitches for
required depth. It is best to cast off the
neck stitches in this case as leaving them
on a spare needle may make the neck
become too wide with wear. A row or
two of neat double crochet is a good
finish for a square neck.

Crew necks

A crew neck is a rather wide and shallow
round neck, finished with several rows of
fine rib as for the V and round necks. A
crew neck should be about 2.5 cm (1 in)
wider and 13 mm (½ in) shallower than

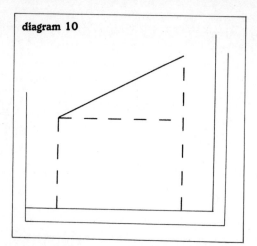

diagram 10

the normal round neck. As with a square neck it is advisable to cast off the centre back and front stitches rather than leaving them on a spare needle or safety pin.

Polo necks

These are excellent for outdoor wear. An ordinary round neck shaping can be used, but instead of working a few rows of rib, the depth should be 15 cm or 18 cm (6 in or 7 in) or even longer, and the second half of the collar should be worked on a size larger needles as it has to fold over the first half.

Boat (straight) necks

The very easiest neckline to work and a very flattering one too. Work straight up to the shoulder line on both back and front and cast off straight across. The shoulder seams are joined leaving a centre opening of approximately 30.5 cm (12 in). With a boat neck it is a good idea to work the last few rows of back and front in a stitch that lies flat such as garter stitch or moss stitch. Then the edge will not curl over and it saves making a border.

Pockets

Patch pockets

These are the very simplest form of pocket. They are made quite separately and sewn on to the garment when finished. They can vary in shape, size and colour, go in any suitable position, and either be merely functional or be a prominent fashion feature.

Inset pockets (diagram 10)

These are knitted into the garment and are therefore stronger and more practical. To make straight inset pockets the linings are knitted first — just cast on number of stitches to give required width of pocket, knit (normally in stocking stitch) as many rows as are needed to give required depth and leave these stitches on a spare

needle or safety pin to pick up later.
When the required position for the pocket
is reached in the garment slip the same
number of stitches as on pocket on to a
safety pin and leave these stitches at the
front of the work. Now knit across pocket
stitches and carry on with the main body
of the garment. At a suitable stage the
stitches left on pin are picked up and a
few rows of any chosen stitch knitted to
give a border to top of pocket.

A slanted inset pocket is a little more
difficult, but is an attractive feature. The
pocket linings are made as for straight
inset pockets. The garment is then knitted
to the lowest point of required slant, and
stitches are divided at this point. Working
on the pocket side of the slant first,
decrease one stitch at slant edge on either
every row, or every other row, according
to angle of slant required and work
in this way until the horizontal
measurement of this decreased line is
equal to the width of the pocket lining
i.e. until the number of stitches decreased
equals number cast on for lining. Leave
these stitches on a spare needle and
return to the other side then working the
pocket lining stitches on to the same
needle to take the place of the decreaed
stitches. Work until the number of rows
equals the number of decreased rows on
the slant edge — then put the stitches of
both sides on to one needle again and
proceed with the garment. A curved, or
any other shaped pocket can be made in
like way just changing the pattern of
decreases.

Sleeves

It is very easy to change a short sleeve
into a long sleeve and vice versa. No
alteration should be made above the
armhole shaping or it may not fit
armhole of body correctly. To work out
widths, for a fitted sleeve, if you measure
the required width for the wrist, and
subtract this from the widest part of the
sleeve, it will give you the approximate

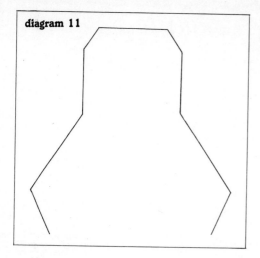

diagram 11

number of stitches that need to be increased up the sleeve. If you then work out the approximate number of rows needed to give the additional length, and divide these by the number of increases to be made, this guides you to the number of rows between each set of increases. Allowances must be made, of course, for differing lengths of welts. A wrist welt is normally about 9 cm (3½ in) long, whereas a welt on a short sleeve is often as short as 2.5 cm (1 in). If a full sleeve is required the full number of stitches should be increased on the last row of the welt — worked out evenly.

Fitted sleeves

If a sleeve is a fitted one and you wish to alter it to a puff sleeve (diagram 11), bear in mind that you need extra length at the top to allow for the extra fullness. The easiest way to achieve this is to work as for a normal fitted sleeve for about 7.5 cm (3 in) then work straight for as many cms as will cover the extra fullness required.

Continue with the normal fitted sleeve, shaping and gathering sleeve in at the top as you sew it in, or cast off knitting 3 stitches together all along row before cast off. This gives a built in fullness at top of sleeve.

TO SHAPE AN ARMHOLE FOR A FITTED SLEEVE

The measurement from sleeve seam to sleeve seam across body is normally about 7.5-10 cm (3-4 in) less than full chest measurement of garment. With an example tension of say six stitches to 2.5 cm (1 in), this would mean decreasing about 20 stitches for the armhole (ten stitches each side). This can be done in two ways:

a) By casting off say five stitches at the beginning of the first two armhole rows and then decreasing at each end of every alternate row five times, or

b) For a fully fashioned effect decrease one stitch at each end of every alternate row ten times working these increases two or three stitches from the edge with these two or three edge stitches kept in stocking stitch, i.e.

1ST ROW sl 1, k2, k2 tog tbl, pattern to last 5 sts, k2 tog, k2, k1 tbl.

2ND ROW sl 1, p3, pattern to last 4 sts, p3, k1 tbl.

The k2 tog tbl on right side and plain k2 tog on left side gives the right slant to the decreases. After repeating these two rows nine times more (or however many rows are necessary) work straight and take pattern from edge to edge.

The same armhole shaping should be done on the sleeves (diagram 12).

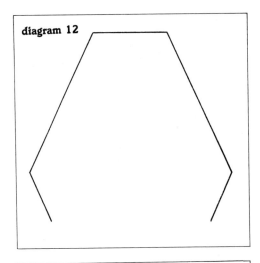

diagram 12

Raglan sleeves

A raglan sleeve shaping slopes regularly from start of armhole to neck edge (see diagram 13).

It is very simply worked by decreasing at each end of every alternate row from start of armhole shaping until you are down to the number of stitches required for back of neck. Cast off. In the case of the fronts of a cardigan, or front of a sweater the decreasing will take you down to one stitch, which pulls through loop. Raglan sleeves are worked with exactly the same number of decreases as on body, normally leaving a few stitches (say six or eight); for sleeve centre top. Cast off.

The raglan sleeve is extremely popular. There is no problem with shoulder fit and normally the armhole is deeper giving a free and easy fit to the garment.

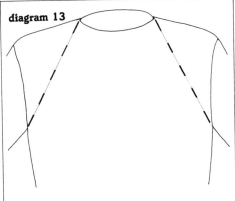

diagram 13

Saddle shoulder (diagram 14)

The armhole is shaped as for a fitted sleeve, preferably the fully fashioned style and then worked straight until the armhole measures 4-5 cm (1½-2 in) short of shoulder level. All stitches are then cast off — this applies to both front and back, except that mid-centre front stitches are usually left on a spare needle or safety pin to pick up for the neck. (Were the neck to be lower, or 'V' the front would have been already divided.) The sleeve seam is worked to match body armhole until it is the same length and at

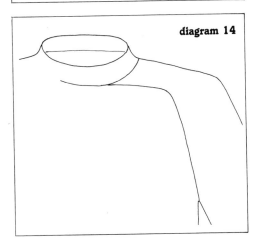

diagram 14

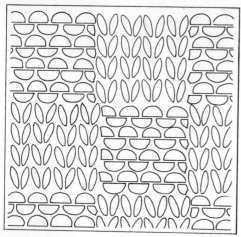

diagram 15

this point the remaining stitches represent the width of the shoulder. Work straight for desired length of shoulder to start of neck. The stitches are then divided, the back sts worked straight to halfway across centre back and cast off, front sts worked straight for a couple of inches and then graduated down according to required neckline. (For an example of the saddle shoulder see pattern on page 189.)

Stitches

Basket stitch (diagram 15):
Normally 4 × 4 stitches requiring the number of stitches to be divisible by 8 + 4.
1ST ROW k4, *p4, k4. Rep from * to end.
2ND ROW p4, *k4, p4. Rep from * to end.
Rep these 2 rows once more.
5TH ROW as 2nd.
6TH ROW as 1st.
Rep these 2 rows once more. Cont to rep these 8 rows.
　　Basket stitch can be varied very easily with a 2 × 4 stitch, 3 × 3 stitch and so on.

Blackberry stitch
A very attractive stitch giving a bobble texture. Cast on a number of sts divisible by 4 + 2.
1ST ROW (right side) p.
2ND ROW sl 1, *p 3 tog, (k1, p1, k1 into next st). Rep from * to last st, k1 tbl.
3RD ROW p.
4TH ROW sl 1, *(k1, p1, k1 into next st,) p3 tog. Rep from * to last st, k1 tbl (diagram 16).
These 4 rows form the pattern. Rep for length required.
There are of course a large number of patterns which include some of the aforementioned when instructions will be clearly given in the individual patterns.

Bobbles
These can also be made to shape various patterns.

To make a bobble (MB): (p1, k1, p1, k1, p1) into next st, thus making 5 sts out of this 1 st, turn, k5, turn, p5, then slipping 2nd, 3rd, 4th and 5th sts over 1st st, push the bobble to the front of the work. A smaller bobble can be made, making only 3 sts instead of 5 from the one stitch, only then having to pass 2nd and 3rd sts over 1st st to make bobble.

Broad basket stitch (diagram 16):
Cast on a number of stitches divisible by 10 + 3.
1ST ROW *k3, p7. Rep from * to last 3 sts, k3.
2ND ROW *p3, k7. Rep from * to last 3 sts, p3.
3RD ROW as 1st row.
4TH ROW p.
5TH ROW p5, *k3, p7. Rep from * to last 8 sts, k3, p5.
6TH ROW k5, *p3, k7. Rep from * to last 8 sts, p3, k5.
7TH ROW as 5th row.
8TH ROW p. These 8 rows form the pattern. Rep for length required.

Broken rib stitch
This is a variation of rib used on the body of a garment, often between cables. The first row is worked as for single rib and the second row is purled.

Cable stitch
Cable patterns are very easy to work, although they look complicated. Cable is an ideal stitch for sportswear and heavy garments and is very attractive in general. The number of stitches in a cable pattern can vary and the pattern necessitates twisting a number of stitches by altering the order in which they are knitted. A six stitch cable is worked as follows. Slip first three sts on to a cable needle and leave either at the back or front of the work according to instructions and the direction of twist needed. Knit the next three stitches in the usual way and then knit the three stitches from the cable needle (diagram 17). A cable needle is short with points at both ends, but if

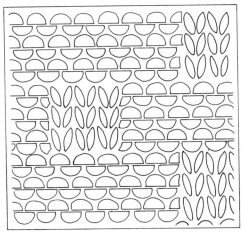

diagram 16

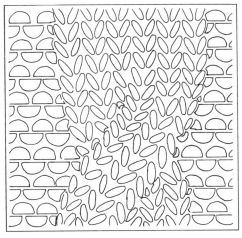

diagram 17

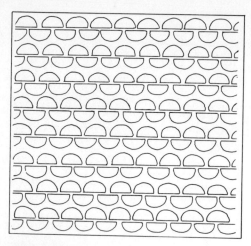

diagram 18

you are without one just use a broken needle as long as it has a point at one end. For delicate work a four stitch cable can be used and for very heavy garments a ten or twelve stitch cable looks very effective. Cable patterns are inclined to hold the work very firmly and draw it in a little so it is a good idea to have a few extra stitches if ever cables are included in a garment not designed for them.

Diamond stitch

Cast on a number of sts divisible by 6 + 2.

1ST ROW sl 1, k3, *p1, k5. Rep from * to last 4 sts, p1, k2, k1 tbl.
2ND ROW sl 1, p1, *k1, p1, k1, p3. Rep from * to last 6 sts, k1, p1, k1, p2, k1 tbl.
3RD ROW sl 1, *k1, p1, k3, p1. Rep from * to last st, k1 tbl.
4TH ROW sl 1, *p5, k1. Rep from * to last st, k1 tbl.
5TH ROW as 3rd.
6TH ROW as 2nd.
7TH ROW as 1st.
8TH ROW as 2nd.
9TH ROW as 3rd.
10TH ROW as 4th.
11TH ROW as 3rd.
12TH ROW as 2nd.

These 12 rows complete the pattern. Rep for length required.

Garter stitch (diagram 18):

Every row is knitted producing a ridged texture.

Knot stitch pattern

The number of stitches between knots can vary. For the following example cast on a number of stitches divisible by 8 + 2. To make the knot (MK): p3 tog, leaving stitches on left hand needle, wrn then p tog again the same 3 sts on left hand needle (still 3 sts). This forms a very attractive knot (diagram 15).

1ST ROW k.

2ND ROW p.

3RD ROW k.

4TH ROW p.

5TH ROW sl 1, *k5, knot 3. Rep from * to last st, k1 tbl.

6TH ROW p.

7TH ROW k.

8TH ROW p.

9TH ROW sl 1, *k1, knot 3, k4. Rep from * to last st, k1 tbl.

10TH ROW p. Rows 3-10 inclusive form the pattern.

Cont to rep for the required length (8 row pattern).

Lacy patterns

The majority of lacy patterns are formed by making holes, giving varying shapes and patterns. There are several ways of making holes:

(1) To make a hole between two knit stitches, bring yarn forward and then knit in the usual way.

(2) For a hole between two purl stitches the wool is passed from the front of the work over the right hand needle and between the needle points (wrn) then purl in the usual way.

(3) When a hole has to be made between a purl and a knit stitch the wool, which is at the front, in the purl position, is passed over the right hand needle (won) thus making an extra stitch, bringing the wool into position for knitting the next stitch. To make it perhaps simpler to understand, just leave the yarn forward after a purl stitch and knit in the usual way. Otherwise, after wlfwd, wrn or won, just work the next two stitches together.

diagram 19

Moss stitch (diagram 19): Cast on an odd number of stitches and work every row in k1, p1. This produces a totally reversible texture with alternate purl and knit stitches, both horizontally and vertically. If there is an even number of stitches on the needle start the first row k1, p1 and the second row p1, k1.

Reverse stocking stitch

Worked as ordinary stocking stitch but the ridged side is on the right side of work. Very good for use with bouclé and fancy yarns.

Ribbing

Nearly always used for welts, cuffs, neckbands etc, due to its elasticity and close fit. With this stitch the purl and plain stitches form vertical lines. Single rib is the most elastic and this is simply worked on an even number of stitches, k1, p1 all along every row. Double rib is produced by working k2, p2.

Shell pattern

Cast on a number of stitches divisible by 7 + 2.

1ST ROW sl 1, *k4, k2 tog, k1, wlfwd. Rep from * to last st, k1 tbl.

2ND ROW sl 1, p2, *p2 tog, p3, wrn, p2. Rep from * to last 6 sts, p2 tog, p3, wlfwd, k1 tbl.

3RD ROW sl 1, k1 * wlfwd, k2, k2 tog, k3. Rep from * to end of row.

4TH ROW sl 1, p2, *p2 tog, p1, wrn, p4, Rep from * to last 6 sts, p2 tog, p1, wrn, p2, k1 tbl.

5TH ROW sl 1, k3, k2 tog, *wlfwd, k5, k2 tog. Rep from * to last 3 sts, wlfwd, k3.

6TH ROW sl 1, p2, wrn, p1, *p2 tog, p4, wrn, p1. Rep from * to last 5 sts, p2 tog, p2, k1 tbl.

7TH ROW sl 1, k1, *k2 tog, k2, wlfwd, k3. Rep from * to end of row.

8TH ROW sl 1, *p2, wrn, p3, p2 tog. Rep from * to last st, k1 tbl.

9TH ROW *k2 tog, k4, wlfwd, k1. Rep from * to last 2 sts, k1, k1 tbl.

10TH ROW sl 1, p2, *p5, wrn, p2 tog. Rep from * to last 6 sts, p5, k1. (diagram 20).

These 10 rows form the pattern. Repeat for length required.

Simple lacy stitch

This is a one 1 pattern as follows:
sl 1, *k1, wlfwd, k2 tog. Rep from * to last st, k1 tbl.
This necessitates casting on a number of stitches divisible by 3 + 2 and this single pattern row is repeated throughout.

Stocking stitch (diagram 21)

Knit one row, purl one row. This brings all ridges to the reverse side and a plain smooth finish on the right side. This is the most basic knitting stitch and is economical with regard to yarn and time.

    In the case of perfectly straightforward stocking stitch or rib stitches there are many knitters who prefer to work into the back of the knit stitches. This gives a slightly different slant to the resultant texture, and is really a question of personal choice.

diagram 20

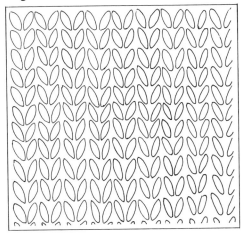

diagram 21